THE POWER OF

OF

⊘ YES

[TAKING STEPS IN SURRENDER TO JESUS]

BRAD BLAKELEY

THE POWER OF YES

The Power of Yes:
Taking Steps in Surrender to Jesus

Cover design by Janessa Holway
Illustrations by Michelle Kamrath
Formating by Melissa Renteria
Revised: April 2021

Special Thanks:

I'd like to thank my editors: Greg Ambrose, Dr. John Dunne, Victoria Nay, Allison O'Donnell, Dave Synder, Kim Tassi, and Madison Tassi. They all worked hard to help this project become a reality. The fact three of these editors are former students of mine was a special treasure for me. I'd like to thank my longtime friend Shari Delgado for her expert help with the typeset and overall formatting of this book. Thanks Shari! Michelle Kamrath's illustrations are beautiful and far exceeded what I had hoped for this book. Michelle, you embody humility, grace and servant-hood. Thank you! I'd like to thank my wife Michelle Blakeley, for putting up with the long hours I spent evenings and weekends working on this. Babe, thank you for your constant support and encouragement. I'd like to thank my three girls Taryn, Carson and Mackenzie. They've had to miss many nightly stories because I was writing! Finally, I'd like to thank my mom, Eddie and Mike for your encouragement as I worked on this project. I love being a part of this leadership team! I pray that this book helps to build up Christ's body in our small part of his great Kingdom.

I

This workbook is designed to help you develop as a Jesus follower. As you get started, here are a few things that will help you get the most out of this study. First, consider reading through the New Testament as you work through this book. I suggest reading a couple of chapters a day (or reading for about 10 minutes). If you do this daily and complete one lesson a week from this book, you will be finishing up the New Testament and The Power of Yes at about the same time.

Second, this workbook is best studied in community. There are a range of topics covered, and it's important for you to be able to ask questions. This workbook could be read as a textbook for a class, in a small life group setting or in a one-on-one mentoring relationship.

Next, there are a lot of opportunities in this book to look up "additional" information. This is optional. Each of us are at a different place in our spiritual walk. Some readers might be new to Christianity or out of the habit of reading books. So for them, just getting through one lesson is a major win! Others might be ready for more. For those readers, I encourage you to look up the biblical references, read the footnotes and do the optional work. "True transformation as a Jesus follower only begins when you put your faith into action."

Finally, the Christian life isn't just about learning. It's about doing. It's about saying "Yes!" (See: Matthew 7:21-27). True transformation as a Jesus follower begins when you give God your strong "Yes!". It all begins when you start putting your faith into action. So, I want to strongly encourage you to begin taking concrete action with your faith as you read through this workbook. This may look like volunteering at church, attending a life group or simply looking for people to love as Jesus loved. You could start your day with this simple prayer: "God, I'm totally yours today. Make these hands your hands, these feet your feet, my voice your voice. Use me today in whatever way that will bring you glory! Let me overflow with your love today. I'm ready to say yes!" Prayers like this set us up for an incredible life with Jesus.

As you begin, just know you've been prayed for. The entire team that helped with this book is praying that you experience God's amazing transformation. We believe glorious growth awaits you in your walk with Jesus.

- Pastor Brad

TABLE OF CONTENTS

THE POWER OF YES!

WELCOME TO THE FAMILY

The decision to become a Jesus follower is the single most important choice a person can make in this life. Whether you know it or not, when you said "Yes" to Jesus you joined a family—a spiritual family of believers united in faith from every nation, language, race and ethnicity. God is forming a beautiful mosaic of diverse people all united around a commitment to Jesus of Nazareth.

Jesus' command to, "Love one another, just as I have loved you" (John 13:34) has mobilized generations of Jesus followers to bring hope and healing to the brokenness of this world. Jesus followers founded the world's first hospitals, orphanages, relief agencies, schools and universities. Christians led the world's first slave-abolition movements.[1] As Christianity spread in ancient Rome, protections for the weak and vulnerable were established. In the West, Jesus followers have worked to establish rights for women, children and other minorities.[2] Prior to Jesus, most of human civilization had made very little progress in establishing human rights for all people. But as the spread of Christianity grew, so too grew the spread of God's love for everyone and as a result—the world has gradually transformed. There's still much work to do, but the change Jesus and his followers have made upon this world is undeniable.

Following Jesus means that your life has been given over to his authority. It means he has your "yes." King Jesus is leading his Church to continue its mission of seeing the Kingdom of God advance, "on Earth as it is in Heaven" (See: Matthew 6:10). His kingdom is advancing. God's desire is to set people free from all forms of oppression: spiritual, social, and physical (See Luke 4:18-19). This workbook is an introduction to this new life. We pray working through this material will help you establish a lifelong practice of deepening your discipleship to Jesus Christ.

LESSON #1: "Follow Me"

Jesus changed the world. Have you ever really thought about how wonderful (and unlikely) that is? Jesus didn't command an army. He didn't live anywhere important. He spent his entire life in poverty. Yet somehow, Jesus started the greatest social revolution in human history. Because of this, even for the non-believer, Jesus is intriguing. Whether we think about his insights into the human condition, or the way he impartially loved everyone, or his powerful authority over the forces of darkness, without question, Jesus was the most incredible human to have ever lived!

Though he performed miracles, preached sermons to crowds of thousands, and even defeated death by resurrecting on the third day, the simple way Jesus invited common people to follow him was perhaps the most remarkable and overlooked thing he did here on earth. For example, after borrowing Simon Peter's boat to address a crowd, he turned to the fisherman and said, "Come, follow me, and I will show you how to fish for people!" (Matthew 4:19 NLT). Later, as he was passing by a toll booth, he met a toll-collector named Levi. Again, he boldly said, "Follow me."

1. Stark, R. For the Glory of God. (Princeton, NJ: Princeton University Press) 2015. p 327-360
2. Schmidt, Alan. How Christianity Changed the World. (Grand Rapids: Zondervan) 2004 p. 97-121

6

And just like Peter, Levi got up and followed him (See: Mark 2:14). It was like that everywhere he went. Jesus would quietly call people to leave what they were doing and just follow him. Jesus seemed to ignore the fact that this call would completely disrupt their lives. He presumed he was more important than anything else they were doing. And he was![1] So, without reservation or apology, Jesus invited men and women to, "Follow."[2]

Liar, Lunatic or Lord?

I grew up going to church and must have heard the stories of Jesus dozens of times. But it wasn't until my early career as a high school teacher when I was going through the writings of C.S. Lewis that I realized just how truly strange some of Jesus' actions and sayings are. Keep in mind that the people in the Bible were real people and that their decisions to follow Jesus would have been very difficult. His teachings require major life changes for his followers. Here is what Lewis wrote about Jesus' remarkable claim to be able to forgive sin:

> In the mouth of any speaker who is not God, these words would imply what I can only regard as a silliness and conceit unrivaled by any other character in history. Yet (and this is the strange, significant thing) even His enemies, when they read the Gospels, do not usually get the impression of silliness and conceit. Still less do unprejudiced readers... I am trying here to prevent anyone saying the really foolish thing that people often say about Him: 'I'm ready to accept Jesus as a great moral teacher, but I don't accept His claim to be God.' That is the one thing we must not say.[4]

Based on the historical New Testament records, Lewis states only three logical possibilities for this man who claimed to be God—none of them being a "great moral teacher." He writes:

> [Jesus] would either be a lunatic — on a level with the man who says he is a poached egg — or else he would be the Devil of Hell. You must make your choice. Either this man was, and is, the Son of God or else a madman or something worse. You can shut Him up for a fool, you can spit at Him and kill Him as a demon; or you can fall at His feet and call Him Lord and God. But let us not come with any patronizing nonsense about His being a great human teacher. He has not left that open to us. He did not intend to.[5]

If you believe in the historical Jesus as presented in the gospels, then he has only left us these three options. Jesus is either a Liar, a Lunatic, or Lord. Because you are reading this book, you've probably already made your decision about who Jesus is and have started your new life as a disciple of Christ. You've joined this social revolution we call the Church. Jesus is our king and his kingdom is advancing!

---

3. For an example of the shocking way Jesus spoke about himself and following him see: Luke 14:25-33; John 6:52-71.

4. Not everyone Jesus called followed him. The most notable example is the "rich young ruler". (see: Matthew 19:22; Mark 10:22; Luke 18:23). For other examples see: Matthew 8:18-22; Luke 9:59-62.

5. Lewis, C. S. Mere Christianity. (New York, Harper Collins), 1952. p.55

6. ibid.

What to Expect

This workbook is divided up into three sections. First, we'll begin with a crash course on basic Christian beliefs. As a Jesus follower, you need to have a solid grasp of the fundamentals of Christian faith. Next, we'll discuss some important practical steps on how to follow Jesus in your daily life. Finally, we'll talk about the role other believers need to play in your life. Consider these last recorded words of Jesus in Matthew's gospel.

> Go therefore and make disciples of all nations, baptizing them in the name of the Father and of the Son and of the Holy Spirit, teaching them to observe all that I have commanded you. And behold, I am with you always, to the end of the age.
>
> -Matthew 28:19-20 (ESV)

For two thousand years, disciples have been making disciples. We've been teaching others what Jesus commanded and showing them what it means to follow him. You're among the latest generation of Jesus followers. God knows your spiritual ancestry, and he can trace the origin of your faith all the way back to the original disciples whom Jesus first taught. What a legacy we get to be a part of!

So here you are, stepping out in faith, surrendering your life and habits to learn the teachings of Jesus for yourself. And as you commit to living the life of a Jesus follower, God will lead you in incredible ways. Before long, you will be helping someone else in their Christian discipleship, as you experience the power of "Yes!" in your life. May God bless you as you start this amazing life!

THE INVITATION:

The invitation to follow Jesus changed everything for the disciples who left all and followed him. Just as it was then, we must also answer when Jesus calls. He will have no rivals for our allegiance; his call is absolute. And so the call of Jesus always creates conflict—a conflict within ourselves, and perhaps with those we love (See: Luke 12:51). Jesus has come, and he is Lord. His invitation is paradoxical. It's an offer to "find life" by "losing it" (See: Mark 8:34-35). It's the promise of abundant life filled with joy and purpose, found in absolute surrender. It's a call to serve the "least" of all (See: Matthew 25:39) but also to rule with Jesus in his eternal kingdom (See: I Corinthians 6:3; II Timothy 2:12; Revelation 20:6).

Welcome to the upside-down Kingdom of God; there's nothing like it! In this kingdom, our Resurrected King rules over all, death has been defeated, and the victory has been secured. We've been invited to share in his victory and anticipate his soon and glorious return! This is the life of a Jesus follower. This is the life lived in the power of "Yes!"

BIBLE STUDY [Answer the following questions to enhance your learning.]

What stood out to you in the "Welcome to the Family" section?

Do a word study in the four gospels: Note each time Jesus says the words, "Follow me" to someone. Look up each of the references below and think through the significance of Jesus' call.

1.) Matthew 4:19; 8:22; 9:9; 10:38; 16:24; 19:21. List your observations or impressions.

2.) Mark 1:17; 2:14; 8:34; 10:21. List your observations or impressions

3.) Luke 5:27; 9:23, 59, 61; 14:27; 18: 22. List your observations or impressions.

4.) John 1:43; 8.12; 10:27; 12:26; 13:36; 18:36; 21.19-22. List your observations or impressions.

Did you find any surprises in the way Jesus called people to follow him? If so, please write about what was surprising. What was the most significant thing you learned in this exercise on following Jesus?

Write your story:

How did you come to start following Jesus? What was your life like before meeting Jesus? How have things changed since? What do you hope to get from this study? Discuss these answers with someone this week.

MEMORY VERSE:

"And calling the crowd to him with his disciples, he said to them, "If anyone would come after me, let him deny himself and take up his cross and follow me. For whoever would save his life will lose it, but whoever loses his life for my sake and the gospel's will save it."

-Mark 8:34-35 (ESV)

FOR FURTHER RESOURCES ON THIS TOPIC:

Matthew W. Bates. Salvation by Allegiance Alone: Rethinking Faith, Works, and the Gospel of Jesus the King. Grand Rapids, MI: Baker Academic, a Division of Baker Publishing Group, 2017.

C.S. Lewis. Mere Christianity. New York, Harper Collins, 1952

Scot McKnight. The King Jesus Gospel: The Original Good News Revisited. Grand Rapids, MI: Zondervan, 2011.

John Stott. Basic Christianity. Grand Rapids Michigan: Wm. B. Eerdmans Publishing, 2008.

In this first section, we'll survey the major teachings of theChristian faith. In every faith, there are essential and non-essential beliefs. Christianity is no different. So, there are some things that all Christians must believe in order to be considered "Christian" in the historic sense. And yet, there are other, non-essential beliefs that Jesus followers have differed on throughout the ages.[7] These differences are important and should be studied but, in this book, we'll mostly stick with the essential truths that all Christian churches agree on.[8]

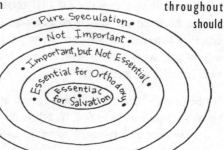

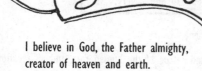

I believe in God, the Father almighty,
creator of heaven and earth.

I believe in Jesus Christ, God's only Son, our Lord,
who was conceived by the Holy Spirit,
born of the Virgin Mary,
suffered under Pontius Pilate,
was crucified, died, and was buried;
he descended to the dead.
On the third day he rose again;
he ascended into heaven,
he is seated at the right hand of the Father,
and he will come to judge the living and the dead.

I believe in the Holy Spirit,
the holy universal Church,
the communion of saints,
the forgiveness of sins,
the resurrection of the body,
and the life everlasting. Amen.

-The Apostles Creed, c. A.D. 250

---

7. Navigating the differences between Christians can be difficult at times but German theologian Rupertus Meldenius' wisdom is timely. "In essentials unity, in non-essentials liberty, in all things charity."

8. The major branches of Christianity include the Roman Catholic Church, the Orthodox churches, and the Protestant churches. All branches of Christianity agree on the essentials as outlined in the Apostles' creed.

LESSON #2: The Bible

As a pastor, I am often asked how the Bible "fits" together. People want to know what the big picture is, but summarizing a book that has 1,187 chapters is daunting! I realize how easy it is to get bogged down in the details and miss the main message. I'm hoping this brief sketch will give you a view of the Bible's big picture so you won't get lost as you begin the process of deepening your faith. But I've got to warn you, there's a lot to cover and even hitting the highlights can seem like drinking from a fire hose. So buckle up, here we go!

The Bible, God's Word and the Holy Scriptures are all names that Jesus followers have for the book we believe has been inspired by God. We believe the Bible is God's revelation of himself to the human race.[9] It is a composite book containing 66 smaller books written by a number of human authors over several centuries.

> "Human history is the sad story of humans seeking to
> find freedom apart from God, only to find slavery."

The Old Testament

The Bible, as a whole, is the single story of God's love and rescue of the human race and all creation. This story is divided into two major parts. The Jewish Old Testament and the Christian New Testament. The Old Testament begins with an account of God creating all that exists with His powerful word. However, special care and attention are given when God created human beings. We are the only creature that is said to have been made in the very image of God (See: Genesis 1:26-27; 9:6). As a result, humans were given the special job to care for the earth.

Unfortunately, near the beginning of the narrative, humans rebelled against God and sought autonomy apart from His loving authority. This tragic decision introduced sin into God's creation. Sin is depicted throughout the Bible as a sort of "evil infection" that corrupts and distorts creation, including humankind. As the narrative continues, we read tragic stories of the chaos and ruin caused by human sin and rebellion from God. From the biblical perspective, human history is the sad story of humankind seeking to find freedom apart from God, only to find slavery instead.

But God is a good Father, and so the rest of the Bible is the account of His great rescue effort for His creation. The first part of God's plan to save humankind involved His special love and rescue of an ancient people known as the children of Israel. He planned to establish a unique relationship with these people. Through this relationship, He sought to bring His healing and salvation to all the people of the Earth (See: Deuteronomy 4:5-8; Isaiah 49:6). Early on God made a covenant with Abraham, the patriarch of these people. God told him that his descendants would be blessed and protected and that one day, through Abraham's descendants, all of the nations of the world would be blessed (See: Genesis 12:1-5; Acts 3:24-26). Buried in these promises was the prophecy of a Messiah, a deliverer who would usher in God's kingdom and bring Israel (and the world) back into harmony with the Creator God.

---

9. The word "Revelation" means "unveiling." Theologians believe that God has revealed Himself to the human race in two main ways: General revelation and Special Revelation. General revelation refers to the general creation of the physical universe. The entire universe reveals that there is a God. (See: Psalm 19). Special revelation refers to the Bible. It is God's special work of unveiling who he is and what he is like. Of course, the clearest revelation of who God is, is Jesus the incarnate Word. (See: John 1:1-14; John 14:8-11).

However, things ended tragically. The nation of Israel failed to remain faithful to their covenant with God. Like a microcosm of the entire human race, they rejected God's rule. In effect, they forfeited His loving protection and blessing. Eventually they were conquered by a foreign power and the wonderful promise of the Messiah went unrealized. When the Old Testament comes to a close, it appears that God's plan for our rescue was thwarted. As professor N.T. Wright observed, the Old Testament ends as a story unfinished, in search of an ending.

The New Testament

But God wasn't done! The New Testament begins with the birth of Jesus. The first four books in the New Testament are ancient biographies of the life of Jesus of Nazareth, known as "gospels."[11] The word gospel is an Old English translation of a Greek word that means "good news." These gospels announce the "good news" of God's rescue plan for humanity.

Mark's gospel begins like this, "This is the Good News about Jesus the Messiah, the Son of God" (Mark 1:1 NLT). Like a lightning bolt from a blue sky, the bold announcement declares that God was once again on the move. The long-awaited arrival of God's good rule had now begun (Mark 1:14-15). Each gospel demonstrates that Jesus was the one who would renew and fulfill the covenant God made to Israel. Jesus would be faithful where the nation of Israel had failed.

Significantly, these gospel-biographies clearly record Jesus' authority over Satan[12] and the forces of darkness. Jesus demonstrated limitless power over death and disease. It's as if every consequence of human rebellion was undone in the presence of Jesus. He had come to "set the captives free",[13] and everywhere Jesus went, that's exactly what he did (See: John 4:24-42; Also: Luke 4:40; 5:15; 6:18; 7:21)!

As the Jesus movement grew, naturally his disciples expected that Jesus would liberate the Jewish people from imperial Rome. They assumed he would immediately establish himself as Israel's king (See: Luke 19:11). However, that wasn't God's plan. Jesus would be crowned king, sure enough, but the crown would be made of thorns and his royal seat would be on a cross. Jesus hadn't come to destroy Rome but to destroy the forces of darkness that stood behind Rome (See: Mark 3:25-28; John 14:30; 1 John 3:8). In order to do this, he needed to offer the ultimate sacrifice to break the power of sin over us. To serve as our savior, Jesus took on himself the consequences of all human rebellion: death (See: Isaiah 53:4-6; 1 Peter 2:21-24).

Each gospel writer interprets Jesus' death as a sort of substitutionary sacrifice. The Innocent One, willingly died as a criminal, so we the true criminals, could be set free (See: Romans 5:8-10,18; II Corinthians 5:14-15, 21). His blood was sin's antidote. However, this isn't the end of the story. In the greatest display of power since Creation itself, God raised Jesus from the dead. His resurrection vindicated his innocence and validated his message (See: Acts 2:22-38). His resurrection proved he was God's promised Messiah, and his defeat of death demonstrated sin's power was broken. Now salvation is offered to all who surrender to Jesus and enter his eternal kingdom.

---

10. Wright, N.T,. The Day the Revolution Began: Reconsidering the Meaning of Jesus' Crucifixion. (San Fransisco Harper One), 2016. p.93

11. The word "gospel" means, "good news" these biographies were written with that in mind.

12. It may be proper to capitalize the proper noun, "satan." I just can't do it. Sorry!

13. For more on Jesus's mission to set people free see: Luke 4:18-20; John 8:31-38

The end of the gospel of John summarizes this message, "The disciples saw Jesus do many other miraculous signs in addition to the ones recorded in this book. But these are written so that you may continue to believe that Jesus is the Messiah, the Son of God, and that by believing in him you will have life by the power of his name" (John 20.30-31 NLT).[14]

The remainder of the New Testament records the history of the Jesus movement after his death and resurrection. The book of Acts recounts the incredible growth of the Church throughout the Roman empire, even in the midst of extreme persecution. Additionally, the New Testament contains over 20 ancient letters written by leaders to various churches and individuals. These letters contain the earliest teachings of the Jesus movement. They have shaped the doctrine and teaching of the church for the past 2000 years.

The Bible ends with the enigmatic book of Revelation. There we read of the victorious return of Jesus when all things will be made new. God's glorious throne will descend to Earth (See: Revelation 21:1-5), and the disciples of Jesus will be resurrected. Death and disease will be finally and forever destroyed. And as Handel's beautiful Hallelujah Chorus imagines it, we will hear the angel choir singing, "And he shall reign forever and ever. King of kings and lord of lords. King of kings and lord of lords. And he shall reign forever and ever!" (See: Revelation 11:5).

We could say that it's God's great story of love, loss, redemption and recovery. It has four major themes: God's loving creation of the world; human rebellion against God; God's rescue and redemption of the human race and creation; and finally, the future consummation of creation when Heaven and Earth are rejoined and God reigns over all forever.

Biblical Authority

Before we finish this lesson, we need to talk about the role the Bible should play in the life of a Jesus follower. First, we consider the Old Testament authoritative because Jesus frequently cited it and regarded it as the source of truth. He referred to it on topics such as worship (See: Matthew 4:4,7,10), creation and marriage (See: Matthew 19:4-7), and even his own mission and future rule (See: Matthew 26:56; Mark 14:62; Luke 22:37,67).

The New Testament is a bit different. We consider it authoritative because Jesus, in effect, pre-authorized it. He promised his disciples that after his departure, the Holy Spirit would come and "guide [them] into all the truth..." (John 16:13 ESV) (See also: John 16:12-15). He also promised that the Spirit would, "teach you all things and will remind you of everything I have said to you" (John 14:26 NIV). This is exactly what happened. After Jesus' ascension to Heaven, the Holy Spirit was poured out on his disciples. They began preaching and teaching to all who would listen (See: Acts 1:8; 2:1-41). As mentioned in the previous section, as the church grew and became more spread out, the Holy Spirit began directing some disciples to write important letters to churches and individuals (See: I Corinthians 2:10-13; I Timothy 4:1-3; I John 2:20-27).

---

14. For more on this topic see: Wright, N.T,. The Day the Revolution Began: Reconsidering the Meaning of Jesus' Crucifixion. (San Francisco: Harper One), 2016.

Finally, before the first generation of disciples began to die, they wrote biographies of Jesus' life. Each gospel-biography was written by either an eyewitness of Jesus (e.g. Matthew, John) or close associate of an eyewitness (e.g. Mark, Luke). Together, these letters and gospels make up the New Testament. By the end of the first century, these books were copied dozens of times and spread throughout the churches of Jesus. Eventually the 27 books of the New Testament that we read today were all understood by the Church as inspired by God and considered authoritative (See: II Timothy 3:16; II Peter 1:20-21; II Peter 3:15-16).

Conclusion

Following Jesus' example, we believe the Bible is inspired and authoritative over our lives. However, it's no secret that the Bible is a controversial book. Whether we think about the creation account in Genesis 1-2, the many miracles recorded throughout or even some of the things the Bible condemns as "sinful," there's plenty of material for debate and disagreement. While proper biblical interpretation can alleviate many of these controversies, some will remain.[16]

As a Jesus follower, I've had to ask myself some important questions about the Bible. Does God's word have authority over my life? Will I stand as judge over it or as a disciple under it? At the end of the day, I've had to admit there are limits to my understanding. There are things I'll simply never know. But there are some things I can be absolutely convinced of. I am absolutely sure Jesus lived. I am absolutely certain he died on a Roman cross in Jerusalem. And I'm absolutely convinced that Jesus of Nazareth rose again from the grave three days later. It's for these reasons, I trust that God has inspired His word. For me, I believe the Bible[17] because I believe in Jesus. My allegiance to Jesus grounds my allegiance to the Bible. But maybe you're not quite there yet. That's OK! Just continue learning. Lean into what God might be saying to you, and give the Bible the benefit of the doubt. Above all, continue your journey with Jesus. There's going be another lesson later in the book on how to interpret the Bible. So stick around!

THE SUMMARY:

We believe the Bible to be the only inspired, authoritative written Word of God (See: Matthew 5:18; II Timothy 3:16; II Peter 1:20-21). It's the great love story of God. It gives the account of God's creation of humankind and our rebellion against Him. It tells us of God's incredible gift of his son so that we could be saved (See: John 3:15-18; Romans 8:3). Jesus paid our debt and defeated our death. In his death, he triumphed over evil. One day, our King will return to establish an eternal kingdom of unending love and peace.

---

15. The Church eventually recognized 27 books as inspired. This process was known as "canonization." For more information on the process the church went through to determine which letters and books were inspired see: F.F. Bruce, The Canon of Scripture. Downers Grove, IL: InterVarsity Press., 1997. See also: Timothy P. Jones. How We Got the Bible. Torrance, CA: Rose Publishing, 2015.
16. Lesson 15 is devoted to learning the basics of biblical interpretation.
17. There are many reasons why people consider the Bible to be inspired by God. I have listed some of those reasons in lesson 15. For our purposes in this book, I think it's sufficient to simply follow Jesus' example regarding the Bible. If we're Jesus followers and he considered the Bible authoritative, then that seems all we need on the issue. However, some of the facts listed in lesson 15 may help a non-believer understand the utter uniqueness of the Bible and why our belief in its inspiration is rational.

BIBLE STUDY [Answer the following questions to enhance your learning.]

Read these verses: Matthew 5:17-18 (See also: Matthew 4:4,7,10; 19:3-9)
What do these verses indicate about Jesus' view of the Jewish Old Testament?

Read these verses: II Timothy 3:16 (See also: II Peter 1:20-21)
What do these verses teach about scripture?

Read these verses: John 14:25-26 (See also John 16:13-14)
What is the role the "Helper" (i.e. Holy Spirit) will have in the life of the disciples?

Reflect and pray over what you've learned in this lesson. Write out a prayer below.

MEMORY VERSE:

"All Scripture is breathed out by God and profitable for teaching, for reproof, for correction, and for training in righteousness, that the man of God may be complete, equipped for every good work."

- II Timothy 3:16-17 (ESV)

FOR FURTHER RESOURCES ON THIS TOPIC:

Craig L. Blomberg. Can We Still Believe the Bible?: An Evangelical Engagement with Contemporary Questions. Grand Rapids, MI: Brazos Press, 2014.

Francis Chan. Multiply Disciple-making for Ordinary People. Colorado Springs, Co.: David C Cook, 2012.

N.T, Wright. The Last Word. New York: HarperCollins, 2005.

N.T Wright. The Day the Revolution Began: Reconsidering the Meaning of Jesus' Crucifixion. San Fransisco Harper One, 2016.

N. T. Wright, How God Became King: The Forgotten Story of the Gospels. New York: HarperOne, 2016.

N. T. Wright, Simply Christian: Why Christianity makes sense. New York: HarperOne, 2010.

LESSON #3: God—One Being; Three Persons

Over the centuries, two Christian doctrines have been under attack more than any other doctrines. They are: the doctrine of the Trinity and the doctrine of Jesus. Since these two doctrines have been so scrutinized, a lot has been written in their defense throughout the history of the church. My intent with this lesson is to give a simple introduction to these important issues. I hope you'll do more in-depth study in the future. Necessarily, this lesson will have quite a few biblical references. In order to get the most out of this teaching, I encourage you to have your Bible handy to look them up!

I remember having a conversation with a Jehovah's Witness one day. As I was finishing up some construction work over at his house, the topic of his religious background came up. This rather friendly guy suddenly became a bit defensive. He started using vocabulary that didn't seem to be his own, as if he was repeating a well-rehearsed script that someone else had written. He asked me how I could logically explain how God could be "three and one" at the same time.

I remember having some answers to his questions, but as I tried to point him to verses in the Bible I thought would help, it became obvious that he really didn't want to listen. Sadly, he wasn't open to thinking critically or studying the Bible with me. The Witnesses had convinced him that God was "Father" but not "Son" or "Spirit." According to them, Jesus was the first creation of the Father (See: Colossians 1:15).[18] No matter what I said, I wasn't getting anywhere. He had his interpretation, and I had mine. Our conversation stalled. We parted as friends, but I walked away frustrated.

This experience highlights how important learning basic Christian doctrine is. Unfortunately, there's a lot of bad teaching in our world today and a lot of people that sincerely believe it and propagate it. That's why going through a book like this is important. Learning how to identify and address incorrect doctrine can prepare you for conversations like the one I described above.

In a future lesson, we'll look at the rules for biblical interpretation and learn how to avoid the mistakes that lead to incorrect doctrine. However, in the meantime, you'll notice a wealth of scriptural citations to support everything we study in each lesson. My hope is that you look up these references and study God's Word for yourself. The biblical support you'll see in these lessons should give you confidence in what you're learning.

So let's get into today's lesson. Why did the Church conclude nearly 2000 years ago, that God was "Three" and yet "One?"

God Is One

Among the ancient Near Eastern people, the Jewish understanding of God was utterly unique. In a sea of polytheism, the Jews believed that God was "One" (also known as monotheism).[19] "Hear, O Israel: The Lord our God, the Lord is one" (Deuteronomy 6:4 ESV). This ancient Jewish prayer known as the "Shema"

---

18. Jehovah's Witnesses have interpreted Colossians 1:15 to mean that Jesus is a created being and therefore not co-equal with God the Father. They have unfortunately misunderstood the Apostle Paul's point in Colossians. Paul isn't suggesting Jesus was created, but rather that Jesus is the "inheritor" of all creation. Ironically, the very next verse explains that Jesus is the Creator of all things, which is obviously an attribute of God.
19. There is some debate among scholars if the earliest Jewish conception was actually "monotheistic" or "henotheistic." Henotheism is the belief that there are (possibly) other gods but that there is one Supreme deity. Whereas strict monotheism believes there is only one being that is rightly called God. There are references in the Bible to other "gods" (see: Psalms 95:3; 1 Chronicles 16:25-26). It is understood that these spiritual beings are not "gods" in the sense of sharing the Divine essence of Yahweh (the one true God of Israel) but are spiritual beings created by Yahweh that may or may not be in opposition to Yahweh. (See also Daniel 10:10-21).

reflects this central belief. For thousands of years, the Jews held that God was unique in His being (there's Lord our God, the Lord is one" (Deuteronomy 6:4 ESV). This ancient Jewish prayer known as the "Shema" reflects this central belief. For thousands of years, the Jews held that God was unique in His being (there's nothing else like him anywhere) and that He had eternally existed (See also: Deuteronomy 32:36-39; Isaiah 45:5-6, 21; 46:9).[20]

The Father

The Jewish people also referred to God in fatherly terms. In fact, there are many places in both the Old and New Testaments where God is referred to as "Father" (See: Deuteronomy 32:6; 1 Chronicles 29:10; Isaiah 63:16; 64:8; Jeremiah 3:19). Jesus, of course, referred to God as his "Father" numerous times (See: Matthew 5:45; 6:4, 9, 14, 26; John 5:19-29).[21] Jesus' influence upon his disciples can be seen in the way they constantly referred to God as "the Father"[22] (See: Romans 15:6; 1 Corinthians 8:6). So, it is obvious and uncontroversial that the Scripture teaches that the Father is God.

The Son

So, what about Jesus? Once again, buried in the prophecies and promises of the Old Testament was the idea that one day God himself would come to save Israel (See: Isaiah 9:6; 49:25-26; 50:2-3; 52:1-10; Zachariah 12:1-9). In fulfillment of this promise the gospel of Matthew declares, "And she will have a son, and you are to name him Jesus, for he will save his people from their sins." All of this occurred to fulfill the Lord's message through his prophet: "Look! The virgin will conceive a child! She will give birth to a son, and they will call him Immanuel, which means 'God is with us'" (Matthew 1:21-23 NLT). As we consider the entirety of the gospels, it's clear they claim that Jesus was the answer to God's promise that He alone would "save Israel" (See: Luke 19:10; John 1:1:1-3,14, 29; 3:16-19).[23]

Further, Jesus was uniquely declared to be the "beloved Son" (See: Matthew 3:17; 17:5; Mark 9:7; Luke 1:35; John 1:34).[24] Jesus claimed to have a special and unique relationship with the Father (See: John 5:32-37; 8:18-29).[25] However, the gospel of John declared that he was "in then beginning with God" (John 1:1 ESV) and that "all things were made through him" (John 1:3 ESV). Both are characteristics unique to God. This supports the belief that Jesus was present in eternity past and participated in the creation of all things. It's important to understand that the "Son" didn't come into existence when Jesus was conceived in Mary's womb. Christian theologians explain that the Son of God has eternally existed along with the Father and the Spirit but that he assumed human flesh at a point in history. Essentially, the Son added a human nature to his divine nature when Jesus entered the world (See: John 17:4-5; Philippians 2:5-8; Hebrews 1:5-8).

Further, when Jesus ministered on earth, he did things that were considered blasphemous since he claimed an authority that belonged to God alone.[26] For example, on several occasions Jesus told people their sins were forgiven (See: Mark 2:6-11; Luke 5:17-27; 7:41-50). Perhaps overlooked but nonetheless shocking are

20. See also: Nehemiah 9:6; Mark 12:29; 1 Corinthians 8:4; James 2:19
21. See also: Matthew 7:21; Mark 14:36; John 8:14-59
22. See also: Ephesians 4:6; 1 Peter 1:2 23. See also: John 12:47; 20:30 24. See also: Luke 3:22; 9:35; John 12:8-30
25. See also: John 17:1-25 26. See also: John 5:18; 8:53; 10:33
27. The Jews were a proud nation that would rather die than yield to Greek or Roman idolatry. In fact, the great Maccabean revolution (167 BC to 160 BC) against their Seleucid oppressors all started because Mattathias a Jewish high priest refused to sacrifice to a Greek idol.

DOCTRINE OF THE TRINITY

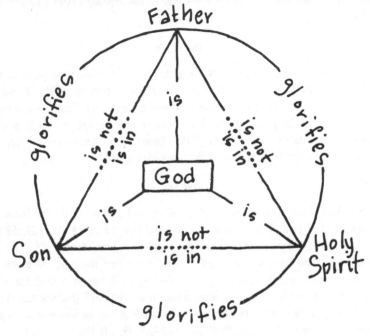

the times when people actually worshiped Jesus. In the Jewish world, giving worship to anyone beside the one true God was expressly forbidden[27] (See: Exodus 20:4-6; Deuteronomy 5:9). Yet even more incredibly, Jesus did nothing to stop it (See: Matthew 14:33; 28:9,17; John 9:38).[28]

When we read beyond the four gospels, it's clear the earliest disciples believed Jesus was God. Notice an early Christian creed that Paul cites in his letter to the Philippians,

> Have this mind among yourselves, which is yours in Christ Jesus, 6who, though he was in the for(m of God, did not count equality with God a thing to be grasped, 7but emptied himself, by taking the form of a servant, being born in the likeness of men. 8And being found in human form, he humbled himself by becoming obedient to the point of death, even death on a cross.
>
> -Philippians 2:5-9 (ESV)

Further, the author of Hebrews declared, "But of the Son he [the Father] says, 'Your throne, O God, is forever and ever..." (Hebrews 1:8). Even more bluntly Paul stated, "...Christ [Jesus] who is God over all, blessed forever. Amen" (Romans 9:5). So having considered even a small sampling of what the Bible says about Jesus, we conclude that Jesus is God.

---

28. There's a "Digging Deeper" section at the end of this lesson where I've included several more passages where Jesus acted as if he were God in the flesh.

The Holy Spirit

There are several reasons to conclude that the Bible teaches that the Holy Spirit is also God and a separate divine person. First, Jesus promised his followers that after his departure, he would send a "helper"—the Holy Spirit (See: John 16:7-11). Jesus is clearly referring to a separate person from himself or the Father. Second, the Holy Spirit is referred to as "God" in some of the earliest teachings of Chris tianity. We see this clearly in Acts chapter 5. In this passage, Peter confronted a man and his wife who had lied to the church about a gift they gave. They wanted to appear more generous and sacrificial than they actually were. (It's incredible how human nature hasn't changed much in 2000 years!) Peter told Ananias that he lied to the Holy Spirit; but when Peter repeated the charge, he effortlessly substituted "Holy Spirit" with "God." Here's the text.

> Peter said, "Ananias, why has Satan filled your heart to lie to the Holy Spirit and to keep back for yourself part of the proceeds of the land? ⁴While it remained unsold, did it not remain your own? And after it was sold, was it not at your disposal? Why is it that you have contrived this deed in your heart? You have not lied to man but to God."

> - Acts 5:3-5 (ESV)

Third, the Holy Spirit is identified as a separate divine person from both the Father and the Son at the baptism of Jesus (See: Matthew 3:16-17; Mark 1:10-11). Fourth, the apostle Paul warned believers against "grieving" and "quenching" the Holy Spirit (See: Ephesians 4:30; 1 Thessalonians 5:18). These actions only make sense if the Holy Spirit is a person with a will or a desire that can be resisted. Lastly, in the Genesis account, we see the Spirit involved in the Creation of all things (See: Genesis 1:2; Psalms 104:30). Throughout the Bible, God alone is the Creator of Heaven and Earth. Thus, the Spirit's involvement in creation indicates that the Holy Spirit is God. There will be a later lesson devoted entirely to the nature and work of the Holy Spirit, but here we're simply establishing that the Holy Spirit is God. He's a divine person separate from the Son and the Father.

Three in One

Finally, as we wrap up this lesson, there are several places in the New Testament where all three "persons" are named in the same passage (See: Matthew 28:19; 1 Corinthians 12:4; II Corinthians 13:14; 1 Peter 1:2)! These passages strongly suggest that the early church believed that each divine person was co-equal and co-eternal. As we think of all that we've covered in this lesson, we must conclude that the Bible teaches there is one God who has eternally existed in a community of three persons. Although the word "Trinity" is never used in scripture, it's the only conclusion which takes seriously all that the Bible says about the "Father", the "Son" and the "Holy Spirit." This doctrine is known officially as "Trinitarian Monotheism."

> "The Holy Spirit is a divine person separate from the Son and the Father."

THE SUMMARY:

We believe that there is one God, eternally existent in three persons, also known as "Trinitarian Monotheism": the Father, Son, and Holy Spirit (See: Genesis 1:1-2; Matthew 28:19; Ephesians 2:18 and II Corinthians 13:14).

BIBLE STUDY [Answer the following questions to enhance your learning.]

Review the verses referenced in the section "God is One." Which verse do you believe best teaches this truth?

Review the verses referenced in "The Father" section. Which best indicates the Father is God?

Review the verses referenced in "The Son" section. Which passage or verses do you believe best teach that the Son is God? (You may want to review some of the verses in the "Digging Deeper" section.)

Review the section on the Holy Spirit. Should we believe that the Holy Spirit is also a divine "person?"

Why do Christians believe that God is one eternal being existing in three divine persons?

What was the most significant thing you learned in this section?

Pray over what you've learned in this lesson. Write out a summarizing prayer below.

MEMORY VERSE:

"Go therefore and make disciples of all nations, baptizing them in the name of the Father and of the Son and of the Holy Spirit, teaching them to observe all that I have commanded you. And behold, I am with you always, to the end of the age."

-Matthew 28:19-20 (ESV)

FOR FURTHER RESOURCES ON THIS TOPIC:

Mark Driscoll. Doctrine: What Christians Should Believe. Wheaton, Ill: Crossway, 2010. (Ch. 1)

Don Thorsen. An Exploration of Christian Theology. Grand Rapids: Baker Academic, 2010. (Ch. 6)

DIGGING DEEPER:

Do a deeper study looking up each passage that teaches that Jesus was God. Some of the passages simply imply that Jesus was God while other passages explicitly state so. Knowing these passages will help you further establish your belief about who Jesus was.

Implicit claims of deity:

- Forgave sins: Matthew 9:5-8; Mark 2:6-11; Luke 5:17-27; 7:41-50.

- Received/allowed worship: Matthew 2:2,11; 8:2; 14:33; 15:25; 20:20; 28:9,17; Luke 24:52; John 9:38; Hebrews 1:6

- Claimed to be the ultimate Judge: Matthew 7:21-23; 25:31;Mark 8:38; John 5:22-24.

- Superior to all of Israel's ancestors: Matthew 22:41-46; John 5:46-47; 8:58.

- Required complete allegiance: Matthew 10:34-39; Luke 9:23-27; John 12:25.

Explicit claims of deity:

- John 1:1-3; 14,18; 8:58-59; 10:33; 20:27-29

- Romans 1:4; 9:5

- Philippians 2:5-11

- Colossians 1:15-16

- Titus 2:13-14

- Hebrews 1:1-8.

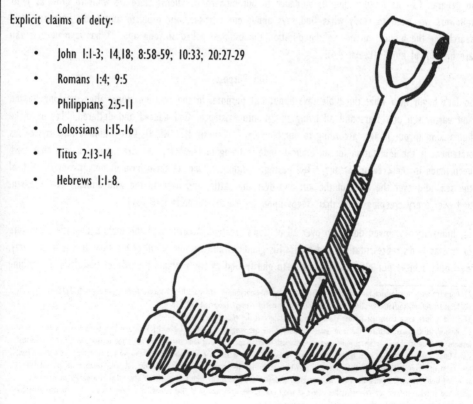

LESSON #4: Humanity

The question "What is a human being?" has been explored and debated throughout the ages. Ancient Greek philosophers had their own opinions, as do modern ethicists. Today, the question seems more relevant than ever as new technologies push the boundaries of ethics and science. For example, scientists have conducted experiments splicing human and animal DNA.[29] In other fields, computer engineers tell us we may only be a few decades away from creating an artificial intelligence that rivals or surpasses human intelligence[30] There's even speculation that we may one day be able to upload human consciousness into the cloud. The boundary between humans, animals and now machines seem more blurred than ever.

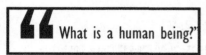
What is a human being?

This question about who we are has moral and political components as well. News stories reporting controversies surrounding gay marriage and gender identity are commonplace. As our culture moves further and further away from its historic Christian roots, we're reexamining fundamental questions that were once taken for granted. What is marriage? Is gender identity fixed or fluid? Is our humanity something we can construct or is it something determined by God, or is it a bit of both? These very specific topics deserve more time and attention than this book will allow (though there are several excellent resources on these topics if you wish to look into any of these questions farther).[31] With this lesson, I want to hone in on what the Bible says about humanity in general. Can its insights give us guidance to our modern questions? Since we want to grow as Jesus followers, we need to study what God says about our purpose, our problem and God's promise. We'll search for the biblical answer to the question the psalmist asked so long ago, "What is man that you are mindful of him?" (Psalm 8:4).

Our Purpose

So let's begin with what the Bible says about our purpose. In the creation story, after speaking heaven and earth, sun and stars and all living things into existence, God paused and declared, "Let us make humankind in our image, according to our likeness..." (Genesis 1:26 NRSV). This profound and mysterious statement is the foundation for all biblical understanding of humanity. We are created beings that have been made in the Creator's image.[32] The passage continues, "and let them have dominion over the fish of the sea, and over the birds of the air, and over the cattle, and over all the wild animals of the earth, and over every creeping thing that creeps upon the earth" (Genesis 1:26 ESV).

So, humanity was given dominion over all of God's creation. According to the biblical narrative, we were to rule as God's representatives and reflect His goodness and wisdom to all of creation. It was in this way, we would achieve our ultimate purpose——to glorify God as His servants (See: Revelation 4:11). Everything

---

29. https://news.nationalgeographic.com/2017/01/human-pig-hybrid-embryo-chimera-organs-health-science/#close (accessed 4/25/18)

30. https://futurism.com/father-artificial-intelligence-singularity-decades-away/ (accessed 4/25/18)

31. I will include some books for further reading on these topics at the end of the lesson.

32. Biblical scholars have debated the term "image of God." There are roughly three basic views: 1.) Structural view-God's image is found in who humans are. Humans have certain qualities (e.g. psychological, rational, spiritual) that indicate that we are made in God's image. 2.) Functional view- God's image is found in what humans do. We are to live in a moral and wise way; when we do this we are reflecting God's image. Also, we are to rule over creation as God's representatives. When we do not live morally or don't exhibit wise rule over creation we are not fully reflecting God's image. 3.) Relational view- Humans enjoy a degree of relate-ability with God and each other that is unparalleled in nature. Since God is relational, we are relational. Regardless of what exactly the term, "image of God means," it is unmistakable that humans were given a unique status as image bearers and vocation as rulers over creation.

that God did in forming us was designed toward that end. He's a good and wise creator who has designed us for his good purposes (See: Psalm 100:3; Proverbs 3:19; 16:4; Isaiah 43:7; Revelation 4:11).

Additionally, we read that God created humans (and other animals) with biological genders (See: Genesis 1:27; Matthew 19:4). Drilling down a bit more into the gender question, the Genesis text tells us that God saw that the man was alone and so wasn't able to fulfill the purpose God had given to him (Genesis 2:18). In response, God does something utterly unique. Let's read,

> So the Lord God caused a deep sleep to fall upon the man, and while he slept took one of his ribs and closed up its place with flesh. [22]And the rib that the Lord God had he made into a woman and brought her to the man.
>
> -Genesis 2:21-22 (ESV)

Here's a few important observations. First, and most obvious, is the special way the woman was created. Unlike every other creature (including man), the woman was created out of a preexisting creature - the man. Biblical scholar, John Walton points out that this ensures that both the man and woman are equally created in God's image. He writes, "Her identity is that she is his ally, his other half."[33]

Second, she was created to help Adam. The man and the woman are equally engaged in the task that God had given to them. Since God didn't simply create another man to help Adam, it's obvious that the woman was designed with important and unique capacities that Adam lacked. Adam was Man.[34] Adam is masculinity. Eve was different from Adam. Eve was Woman. She is femininity. These two are equally created in God's image but remain uniquely different. Notice the text once again,

> Therefore a man shall leave his father and his mother and hold fast to his wife, and they shall become one flesh. And the man and his wife were both naked and were not ashamed.
>
> -Genesis 2:24-25 (ESV)

It is only now this human pair can reproduce and begin accomplishing God's command to "fill the Earth" (See: Genesis 1:27-28; also: Genesis 2:24; 4:1; 9:1; Malachi 2:15; Matthew 19:4-6). Marriage between a male and female fulfills God's plan for the family. Sexual intercourse was designed to take place within the protection of a marriage covenant (See: 1 Corinthians 6:18, 7:2—5; Hebrews 13:4). (Think of how much pain our society could avoid if we all followed God's design here!) As we consider the rest of scripture, gender differences are mentioned and assumed throughout. Both genders are cherished and are vital to accomplish God's purposes for humanity[35] (See: Genesis 2:18; Malachi 2:13-16; 1 Corinthians 11:3; Ephesians 5:22-25; Colossians 3:18-19; 1 Timothy 5:1-2,14). However, as we are about to see, that purpose became derailed by human rebellion.

---

33. Walton, John H. The Lost World of Adam and Eve: Genesis 2-3 and the Human Origins Debate. (Downers Grove: InterVarsity Press), 2015. p. 81

34. In the original language of the Old Testament, "Adam" literally means "man."

35. While it is clear (at least to me) that the biblical narrative identifies genuine differences between male and female, I want to caution against taking this further than the text allows. There are social/cultural components in our understanding of gender. So, in some ways our concept of gender is a bit fluid. For example, what is considered "manly" or "womanly" in one culture wouldn't necessarily be identical in another. We can see that everything from clothing styles and fashions to the types of jobs or responsibilities considered appropriate for men and women can vary wildly from culture to culture. This observation forces us to ask how much of what we typically associate with gender is actually God's design or human construct? This is important because we can easily stereotype certain activities as "male" or female" when we shouldn't. As a teacher for many years, I've seen young men bullied because they weren't athletic enough and would rather perform in the arts. On the other hand, many times female athletes don't fit the "mold" of our cultural femininity. While there are good biblical reasons to disagree with those who would suggest that all gender distinctions are wrong, the national debate has helped correct gender stereotyping. This affirms the old wisdom, we can always learn from those with whom we may disagree.

THE POWER OF YES

Our Problem

Tragically, very soon after creation, Adam and Eve disobeyed God's command. Life now would be difficult and painful (See: Genesis 3:16-19). The image of God in us had been marred by our disobedience. Christian theologians refer to this tragic event as "The Fall." This disobedience ushered sin into the human race, and now sin has become part of our human nature (See: Romans 5:12-21). Notice what the early church leader, Paul wrote,

Once you were dead because of your disobedience and your many sins. You used to live in sin, just like the rest of the world, obeying the devil—the commander of the powers in the unseen world. He is the spirit at work in the hearts of those who refuse to obey God. All of us used to live that way, following the passionate desires and inclinations of our sinful nature. By our very nature we were subject to God's anger, just like everyone else.

-Ephesians 2:1-3 (NLT)

What a heartbreaking assessment of humanity! We've fallen from our original created glory. Jesus said something similar in a conversation with some of the Jewish leaders of his day. The Jews believed that their status as "God's chosen people" automatically included them into God's kingdom (See: Deuteronomy 7:6-11). Jesus pointed out that ancestry wasn't the real problem, it didn't matter who your father was. The real problem was humankind's slavery to sin.

So Jesus said to the Jews who had believed him, "If you abide in my word, you are truly my disciples, ³²and you will know the truth, and the truth will set you free." They answered him, "We are offspring of Abraham and have never been enslaved to anyone. How is it that you say, 'You will become free'?" Jesus answered them, "Truly, truly, I say to you, everyone who practices sin is a slave to sin.

-John 8:31-34 (ESV)

This gets us to the real issue. Humanity needs to be freed from sin. It is a corrupting force that has infected the totality of our being. Sin affects our thinking, our emotions, the way we interact with others, and even our physical bodies. But here's where the hope of God's promise speaks.

God's Promise

Jesus alone can break sin's enslaving power over us. He is God's promised deliverer (See: Matthew 1: 21; Luke 2:25-32). He's come to set us free. When Jesus was just beginning his preaching ministry in his hometown of Nazareth, he was invited to read from the Jewish scriptures during the Sabbath worship service. Luke tells us that he selected Isaiah 61 as his text. Notice what Luke recorded,

The scroll of Isaiah the prophet was handed to him. He unrolled the scroll and found the place where this was written: "The Spirit of the Lord is upon me, for he has anointed me to bring Good News to the poor. He has sent me to proclaim that captives will be released, that the blind will see, that the oppressed will be set free, ¹⁹and that the time of the Lord's favor has come.

- Luke 4:17-19 (NLT)

29

Jesus then did something that was highly unusual. He stopped reading mid-passage and sat down. Luke tells us that every eye was fixed on him and then like a thunderbolt from heaven Jesus said, "The Scripture you've just heard has been fulfilled this very day!" (Luke 4:21 NLT).

Not surprisingly, his hometown audience scoffed at such claims. How could this peasant son of a carpenter be the prison-breaker, oppressor-killer, they had all been waiting for?!? Yet this was exactly who Jesus of Nazareth was. As we'll study in a later lesson, Jesus broke the power of sin with his death on the cross (See: Romans 6:10, 22). His resurrection proved his victory over death and gives us the power to live our lives in victory (See: Philippians 3:7-11) As we follow Jesus, we gain the ability to overcome sin when we abide daily in his word (See: John 8:31).[36]

Engaging the Culture

Before we leave this topic, I think it's important that we circle back and think about how this lesson speaks to the issues of our day. Most importantly we need to approach our culture in a wise way that honors Jesus and demonstrates love for others. As we mentioned earlier, things are rapidly changing. As recently as 1996, a democratic president, Bill Clinton signed, The Defense of Marriage Act (DOMA) into law. This law was passed as a protection for traditional, heterosexual marriage. However less than 20 years later, it was ruled "unconstitutional."[37] The pace of our cultural change has only quickened since. As a result, today a solid majority favor recognizing homosexual marriage.[38] So, it's no surprise that many see the biblical view of marriage and gender as outdated, or worse, bigoted.

Of all the issues we may face today, this subject must be handled with a great deal of Spirit-filled love and wisdom. Thankfully, the gospel records for us how Jesus handled people who were considered "sinful" by the larger religious community. In all of his interactions, Jesus never acted in a hateful or demeaning way. In fact, he taught us to do just the opposite. He was always "full of grace and truth" (See: John 1:14). The problem is that it's easy to learn truth but forget about grace.

Being raised in a Christian home, I was taught the biblical view of sexuality from a young age. I knew the truth about God's design, but I didn't have much grace for people who struggled in these areas. In fact, it was easy for me to just judge someone in the gay and lesbian lifestyle as a "willful sinner!" (See: Romans 1:26-34). And since, I'd never personally met anyone who identified as trans-gender and knew very few people who were gay, I carried many assumptions that actually stopped me from caring about this community in   any meaningful way.

As is usually the case, things get a little messy when you become friends with someone struggling with something you don't understand. I remember the first time I really listened to someone who confided in me about their same-sex attraction. I wept as I heard how difficult it was for him to feel accepted by the Church. Of course, this experience affected his view of God as well.

But I knew God loved him. I knew this because the Bible said so. But I knew it for another reason too. I knew it because I began experiencing God transforming my own heart. It broke me. I had to repent.

36. Lesson 12 and Lesson 20 address the ways God transforms us away from our old sinful nature.
37. Obergefell v. Hodges (2015)
38. . http://www.people-press.org/2017/06/26/support-for-same-sex-marriage-grows-even-among-groups-that-had-been-skeptical/ (accessed 4/23/18)

I came to see how un-Christlike my thinking had been. If I was honest, I hadn't made the effort to understand those in the LGBTQ community. Simply, I hadn't extended genuine love to my neighbor.

After this experience, I determined to change my approach. I came to realize many of my assumptions and judgments were wrong. As I heard from more people, formed more friendships and read more on the topic, I understood that most didn't want to feel the way they felt.[39] Same-sex attraction wasn't something they had pursued. Instead, it was a painful burden that left them feeling confused and isolated from their families, peers, church and God!

Today, I'm not the same person. There's grace now, not just truth. Now when I meet people struggling with gender identity or same-sex attraction, my first move is radical acceptance and hospitality, just as Jesus did (See: Matthew 11:19; Luke 7:34;19:2-8). I see them as people to love, not "sinners" to judge.

What was so remarkable about Jesus is that he treated everyone with equal dignity and love. He cared for the prostitutes as much as the religious Pharisees (See: Mark 10:14-21; Luke 7:37-48; 8:40-56). And since Jesus was the only sinless One, for him, every time he hung out with anyone, he was hanging out with "sinners."[40] So, he didn't buy into the cultural tradition that divided people into categories of "sinners" and "saints." In fact, whenever he could, he corrected these stereotypes (See: Luke 13:3-6; John 9:1-5). Surprisingly, his strongest words were reserved for those who everyone considered righteous (See: Matthew 23:1-37). As Jesus followers, we must treat people exactly like Jesus did. We can't put people into categories. After all, we're all in the same "category"—sinners who need the Savior! Truly, the only difference between a Christian and anyone else, is that we've found the One who can forgive our sins! We're in no place to judge.

However, following Jesus doesn't mean we back away from uncomfortable or difficult subjects. We can't; Jesus never did (See: Matthew 18:8; 19:20-23; Mark 8:34; Mark 10:17-21; Luke 9:23-62; 18:23; John 8:11). Just like Jesus, we can love and accept the person but disagree with their practice. One of the biggest lies in the gay and lesbian community is that their sexuality equals their identity. We must lovingly show them that their true identity is found in Christ. Jesus came into the world to set us free and transform us into a brand new creation (See: I Corinthians 6:9-11; II Corinthians 5:17). But they'll never hear that message without radical love and acceptance. Acceptance and love open the heart to truth. This is true for anyone we're talking to. It's only after we've demonstrated we're for them and not against them that they'll listen. People can't hear us until then. Their natural defenses won't let them.

Even still, some may not agree with us. That's OK. Hopefully we've demonstrated genuine love and care and can remain friends. Living this way gives us the confidence to know that we've honored Jesus in our relationships. Jesus made it clear that our primary calling is to simply love the broken just as he did (See:

39. Notice the American Psychological Association's current statement (2017) regarding sexual orientation: "There is no consensus among scientists about the exact reasons that an individual develops a heterosexual, bisexual, gay or lesbian orientation. Although much research has examined the possible genetic, hormonal, developmental, social and cultural influences on sexual orientation, no findings have emerged that permit scientists to conclude that sexual orientation is determined by any particular factor or factors. Many think that nature and nurture both play complex roles; most people experience little or no sense of choice about their sexual orientation." http://www.apa.org/topics/lgbt/orientation.aspx (my emphasis). See also: Yarhouse, Mark A., Janet B. Dean, Stephen P. Stratton, and Michael Lastoria. Listening to Sexual Minorities: A Study of Faith and Sexual Identity on Christian College Campuses. Downers Grove, IL: InterVarsity Press, 2018. p. 146
40. I'd like to thank Tessa McQuillan for pointing out this insight.

Matthew 5:43-46; 19:19; 22:38). Thankfully, it's not our job to "fix" people. (Have you ever tried?!) We can't even fix ourselves! Instead, our job is to simply point others to the One who can.

THE SUMMARY:

We're made in the image of God; the supreme objects of God's creation. Although people have tremendous potential for good, we have been marred by an attitude of disobedience toward God called sin. Sin separates people from God. This is the reason God sent his Son Jesus to rescue us from the consequences of our sin and give eternal life to those who repent and believe (See: Genesis 1:27; Psalm 8:3-6; Isaiah 53:6; Romans 3:23; Isaiah 59:1-2).

We believe that God created humanity as gendered beings (See: Genesis 1:27; 2:18, 22). Human gender reflects the wise design of the Creator, and each gender is endowed with special roles and responsibilities in our stewardship of creation. Human marriage was instituted by God and affirmed by Jesus Christ (See: Genesis 2:18, 23-24; Matthew 19:1-9). It is the covenant-union between one man and one woman for the purpose of procreation (See: Genesis 1:27-28; Malachi 2:15). Human sexuality is designed by God to take place within the covenant-union of marriage between a man and a woman (See: I Corinthians 6:18, 7:2—5; Hebrews 13:4).

BIBLE STUDY [Answer the following questions to enhance your learning.]

Read Genesis 1:1-31. Summarize what the text says about humanity's role and responsibility?

Read Genesis 3:1-24. What does the story of the Fall of humankind tell us about the consequence of sin? How did the Fall change the relationship with each other?

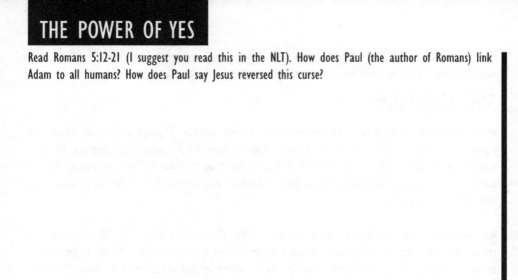

THE POWER OF YES

Read Romans 5:12-21 (I suggest you read this in the NLT). How does Paul (the author of Romans) link Adam to all humans? How does Paul say Jesus reversed this curse?

What was the most significant thing you learned in this lesson?

Pray over what you've learned in this lesson. Write out a summarizing prayer below.

MEMORY VERSE:

"So God created man in his own image, in the image of God he created him; male and female he created them."

- Genesis 1:27 (ESV)

FOR FURTHER RESOURCES ON THIS TOPIC:

Sean McDowell, and John Stonestreet. Same-sex Marriage: A Thoughtful Approach to God's Design for Marriage. Ventura, CA: Baker Books, 2014.

Mark Driscoll. Doctrine: What Christians Should Believe. Wheaton, Ill: Crossway, 2010. (Ch. 4)

Tim Keller. The Meaning of Marriage. New York: Riverhead books, 2013.

Wesley Hill. Washed and Waiting: Reflections on Christian Faithfulness and Homosexuality. Grand Rapids, MI: Zondervan, 2016.

Nancy Pearcey. Love Thy Body: Answering Hard Questions about Life and Sexuality. Grand Rapids, MI: Baker Books, 2018.

Don Thorsen. An Exploration of Christian Theology. Grand Rapids: Baker Academic, 2010. (Ch. 11-12)

Mark A. Yarhouse, Understanding Gender Dysphoria: Navigating Transgender Issues in a Changing Culture. Downers Grove, IL: IVP Academic, an Imprint of InterVarsity Press, 2015.

Watch: https://www.youtube.com/watch?v=YbipxLDtY8c

THINKING DEEPER:

The great 17th Century French mathematician Blaise Pascal observed that man is a strange animal. We're a Jekyll and Hyde creature capable of great nobility and horrible cruelty. He observed, "Man's greatness and wretchedness are so evident that the true religion must necessarily teach us that there is in man some great principle of greatness and some great principle of wretchedness."[41]

Pascal believed that other philosophies and religions either overplayed human potential and goodness or did not affirm human goodness enough. Today, we see this in modern humanists or in New Age leaders like Oprah Winfrey. They believe humanity is basically good with limitless potential. On the other extreme, pantheistic religions such as Hinduism undermine human goodness and uniqueness altogether.

Pascal believed only Christianity was able to hold both truths about humanity in tension. It gave an account of how we could be capable of such wonderful virtues and of such horrible violence. The goodness in us is owing to the divine image still retained within us. The wickedness in us was due to the evil infection of sin enslaving each of us.

He summarized the biblical view of humanity as "deposed kings." He said we had an innate sense that we were made to rule but paradoxically live in the frustration of being unable to rule our own hearts. To use Pascal's word, we know we're "wretched."

Pascal believed it was only in Jesus that we have hope. He wrote, "Jesus is a God whom we can approach without pride and before whom we can humble ourselves without despair."[42] Philosopher Douglas Grouthus summarized it nicely, "Though we are royal ruins, we can find total forgiveness, redemption and eternal life through the one who truly understands our condition" (See: John 3:16-18; 10:10; and Romans 5:1-8).[43] Or as the writer of Hebrews put it, "So then, since we have a great High Priest who has entered heaven, Jesus the Son of God, let us hold firmly to what we believe. This High Priest of ours understands our weaknesses, for he faced all of the same testings we do, yet he did not sin.16So let us come boldly to the throne of our gracious God. There we will receive his mercy, and we will find grace to help us when we need it most" (Hebrews 4:14-16 NLT).

---

41. Blaise Pascal, Pensées. Translator: A. J. Krailsheimer. (New York: Penguin Books) 1995. p.149.
42. ibid., p.69
43. https://www.bethinking.org/christian-beliefs/a-royal-ruin

LESSON #5: Salvation

> "He came to give his life for the rescue and redemption of humanity."

We've now come to the lesson that explores God's great rescue of His creation. As noted in the previous lessons, the entire Bible presents the human race in a negative light. Without God's love and rescue, we're doomed. We rightfully deserve his judgment. Our rebellion against Him has allowed hate to run unchecked, and history is full of sad tales of human evil and aggression. Not only has our rebellion caused the human race great pain, the whole of creation itself has suffered because of our sin (See: Leviticus 18:24-28; Romans 8:19-22; Revelation 21:1-5).

We see this right away in the first book of the Bible,

> The Lord observed the extent of human wickedness on the earth, and he saw that everything they thought or imagined was consistently and totally evil. So the Lord was sorry he had ever made them and put them on the earth. It broke his heart.
>
> -Genesis 6:5-6 (NLT)

And in the last book of the Bible,

> But the people who did not die in these plagues still refused to repent of their evil deeds and turn to God. They continued to worship demons and idols made of gold, silver, bronze, stone, and wood—idols that can neither see nor hear nor walk! And they did not repent of their murders or their witchcraft or their sexual immorality or their thefts.
>
> -Revelation 9:20-21 (NLT)

From beginning to end, the consensus of scripture is clear—the human race is in rebellion against God. This diagnosis is understood in judicial terms. We are "under God's wrath" or "condemnation" (See: John 3:16-18; 36; Romans 1:18-32; 3:10-23; Ephesians 2:1-3; Titus 3:3). The truth is we didn't need the Bible to tell us this. As just mentioned, human history already tells us the awful truth about our race. The news is filled with glaring examples of human depravity and selfishness. It seems with every new advance we make, new ways of hurting one another are also devised. We need to be rescued!

This is exactly why Jesus came. He came to give his life for the rescue and redemption of humanity. Listen to what Jesus said of his own mission.

> For God so loved the world, that he gave his only Son, that whoever believes in him should not perish but have eternal life. For God did not send his Son into the world to condemn the world, but in order that the world might be saved through him. Whoever believes in him is not condemned, but whoever does not believe is condemned already, because he has not believed in the name of the only Son of God.
>
> -John3:16-19 (ESV)

THE POWER OF YES

On the cross, Jesus willingly offered himself for us (See: John 10:18). He referred to himself as the good shepherd who, "lays down his life for the sheep" (John 10:11 ESV). During his time with the disciples, Jesus repeatedly told them that he would be crucified but would rise again (See: Matthew 16:21; 17:22-23; 20:18-19; Mark 8:31; 9:31; 10:32-33; Acts 2:23; 4:27-28). At his final meal with his disciples just before his death, Jesus explained what they were about to witness. He told them that his blood would be, "poured out for many for the forgiveness of sins" (Matthew 26:28 ESV). He clearly understood that his life would be offered as a sacrifice.

At this point, it's reasonable to ask, "why did Jesus believe that his death could free humanity from the consequence of rebellion and sin?" Did God simply tell him? If so, why would anyone believe that? These are important questions.

First, throughout the Old Testament there is a concept that human sin must have an "atonement." This word in English means "at-one-ness."[44] This is connected to the Hebrew concept of Shalom or peace. Human rebellion has created hostility with God and so atonement or "Shalom" was needed (See: Romans 5:10-11; II Corinthians 5:18-21; Ephesians 2:16).

Second, throughout the Old Testament there is a consistent promise of a future reconciliation between God and humanity. Hints of this promise begin immediately. Just after the Fall in the Garden of Eden, God said that one day a child would be born that would destroy the serpent and end hostilities between God and humanity. Immediately after this promise, God clothed the man and woman covering their shame and nakedness——a clear allusion to God's intention to rescue His creation from the consequence of sin.

Another example is in Genesis 22, when God asked Abraham to offer his son Isaac as a human sacrifice! This outlandish request is clearly meant as a test for Abraham (See: Genesis 22:1). However, on the way up the mountain when his unsuspecting son asked where the animal was for the sacrifice, Abraham prophetically declared, "God will provide for himself the lamb for a burnt offering, my son" (Genesis 22:8 ESV).

In a vivid picture of what would one day happen to Jesus, Abraham placed the wood on his son Isaac to carry up the mountain to the place of sacrifice. Only here, just before Abraham kills his son, the Angel of the Lord said, "'Abraham! Abraham!' 'Yes,' Abraham replied. 'Here I am!' 12'Don't lay a hand on the boy!' the angel said" (Genesis 22:10-12 NLT).

Abraham wouldn't be required to give his son, but one day God would. And, instead of Isaac, a ram was offered on the altar that day (See: Genesis 22:11-13). God had provided that day, and would again

when Jesus died as the "Lamb of God" (See: John 1:29, 36; Acts 8:32; I Corinthians 5:7; I Peter 1:19).

However, it's the prophet Isaiah's mysterious "Suffering Servant" that Jesus and the earliest disciples pointed to that most clearly predicted Jesus' atoning sacrifice (See: Matthew 8:17; 20:28; Mark 15:34; John 11:49-52; Luke 22:37; Acts 8:26-40; I Peter 1:19). This passage is so important we need to quote it at length.

---

44. Michael Bird, What Christians Ought to Believe. (Grand Rapids, Zondervan) 2016. p.128

Who has believed what he has heard from us? And to whom has the arm of the Lord been revealed? ²For he grew up before him like a young plant, and like a root out of dry ground; he had no form or majesty that we should look at him, and no beauty that we should desire him. ³He was despised and rejected by men, a man of sorrows, and acquainted with grief; and as one from whom men hide their faces he was despised, and we esteemed him not. ⁴Surely he has borne our griefs and carried our sorrows; yet we esteemed him stricken, smitten by God, and afflicted. ⁵But he was pierced for our transgressions; he was crushed for our iniquities; upon him was the chastisement that brought us peace, and with his wounds we are healed. ⁶All we like sheep have gone astray; we have turned—every one—to his own way; and the Lord has laid on him the iniquity of us all. ⁷He was oppressed, and he was afflicted, yet he opened not his mouth; like a lamb that is led to the slaughter, and like a sheep that before its shearers is silent, so he opened not his mouth. ⁸By oppression and judgment he was taken away; and as

"He came to give his life for the rescue and redemption of humanity."

for his generation, who considered that he was cut off out of the land of the living, stricken for the transgression of my people? ⁹And they made his grave with the wicked and with a rich man in his death, although he had done no violence, and there was no deceit in his mouth. ¹⁰Yet it was the will of the Lord to crush him; he has put him to grief; when his soul makes an offering for guilt, he shall see his offspring; he shall prolong his days; the will of the Lord shall prosper in his hand. ¹¹Out of the anguish of his soul he shall see and be satisfied; by his knowledge shall the righteous one, my servant, make many to be accounted righteous, and he shall bear their iniquities. ¹²Therefore I will divide him a portion with the many, and he shall divide the spoil with the strong, because he poured out his soul to death and was numbered with the transgressors; yet he bore the sin of many, and makes intercession for the transgressors.

- Isaiah 53 (ESV)

When we consider this passage was written centuries before Jesus' birth and is a part of the Jewish scriptures, it's easy to see why it is repeatedly cited in the New Testament (See Matthew 8:16; Luke 22:37; John 12:38; Romans 10:16; 15:21; I Peter 2:21; Acts 8:32-33). In addition to the places where this passage is directly cited, the concept of Jesus bearing the sin of the guilty shows up all over the New Testament. Consider what Paul wrote, "For God made Christ, who never sinned, to be the offering for our sin, so that we could be made right with God through Christ" (II Corinthians 5:21 ESV). The same point appears in I Corinthians 15:3, "I passed on to you what was most important and what had also been passed on to me. Christ died for our sins, just as the Scriptures said..." (See also: Acts 2:38; Romans 3:21-26; 8:2-4; Galatians 3:13; Ephesians 5:2; Hebrews 9:15; I Peter 1:19; 2:21-24; 3:18; Revelation 1:5).

As we've surveyed what Jesus said about his own death and what the earliest disciples wrote, the consensus is clear—Jesus' came, "to give his life as a ransom for many" (Matthew 20:28; Mark 10:45). When God (the Son) took on a human nature, he was demonstrating the greatest act of love imaginable. He lived the perfect human life. Jesus succeeded where Adam failed. He perfectly fulfilled the Jewish Torah. Jesus did what the nation of Israel couldn't. And finally, in his greatest test, Jesus surrendered fully to the Father's will (See Mark 14:26). He, the innocent One, died the guilty sinner's death. But the story doesn't end there! The Father raised Jesus from the dead, vindicating his innocence and validating his message (See: Matthew 28; Mark 16; Luke 24 John 20-21; Acts 2:22-36; I Corinthians 15). Jesus brought us peace with God (Romans 5:1; II Corinthians 5:18-20)!

The promise of the Christian good news (gospel) is that faith and allegiance to Jesus sets us free from the consequence of our sin (See: Matthew 16:24-27; Mark 8:34-38). Paul wrote,

> For I am not ashamed of this Good News about Christ. It is the power of God at work, saving everyone who believes—the Jew first and also the Gentile. [17]This Good News tells us how God makes us right in his sight. This is accomplished from start to finish by faith. As the Scriptures say "It is through faith that a righteous person has life.
>
> -Romans 1:16-17 (ESV)

As we conclude our study on God's salvation, we can't help but be overwhelmed by his great love. In our world of pain and suffering, disease and death, it's easy to conclude that God has abandoned us. While the problem of pain and suffering remains extremely difficult for us, and at times we can become paralyzed by grief, the life and death of Jesus has forever settled the question of God's love for us (See: I John 3:16). We look forward with longing and expectation to the day when every tear will be dried and all of creation will be restored to the beautiful condition God intended (See: Revelation 21:1-4). Some of the last words recorded of Jesus appear in the final book of the Bible. Here Jesus is seated on his throne, glorious and victorious, and declares, "'Behold, I am making all things new …Write this down, for these words are trustworthy and true'" (Revelation 21:5 ESV). So we look forward in faith to this great day, when every eye will see and every tongue will confess King Jesus as Lord over all (See: Philippians 2:9-11)!

THE SUMMARY: Jesus came to give eternal life to those who follow him and become his disciples (See: John 1:4; John 4:14; John 6:40; John 14:6; I John 5:20). As we've learned in our first lesson, a disciple is someone who has acknowledged Jesus' absolute authority over their lives. They've answered his call to deny themselves and follow him (See: Matthew 10:36-39; 16:24-27; Mark 8:34-37; Luke 9:23-26; John 10:27-30). This incredible call to become a disciple of Jesus is a gift of God, and it is His grace that enables us to respond with faith and allegiance (See: Romans 5:15-17; Ephesians 2:8-9). We believe that it is the blood of Christ that fully justifies us before the Father (See: John 3:16-18; 20:31; Romans 5:9; Colossians 1:14; Hebrews 9:22). Now that we've been saved by his grace, disciples of Jesus continually grow in that grace as they follow Jesus here on earth (See: II Peter 1: 3-11; II Peter 3:17-18).

BIBLE STUDY [Answer the following questions to enhance your learning.]

Why does humanity need "salvation?" Be sure to support your answer using the Bible.

Why did Jesus believe his death could free humanity from the ultimate consequences of our sin? Support your answer using the Bible.

Read Acts 2:22-38. Why should we believe that Jesus' death actually does have the power to release us from sin?

What was the most significant thing you learned in this section?

Pray over what you've learned in this lesson. Write out a summarizing prayer below.

MEMORY VERSE:

"Surely he has borne our griefs and carried our sorrows; yet we esteemed him stricken, smitten by God, and afflicted. ⁵But he was pierced for our transgressions; he was crushed for our iniquities; upon him was the chastisement that brought us peace, and with his wounds we are healed."

-Isaiah 53:4-5 (ESV)

FOR FURTHER RESOURCES ON THIS TOPIC:

Scot McKnight. The King Jesus Gospel: The Original Good News Revisited. Grand Rapids, MI: Zondervan, 2011.

Lee Strobel. The Case for Faith: A Journalist Investigates the Toughest Objections to Christianity. Grand Rapids: Zondervan, 2014. (Especially objection #1 pgs. 25-56)

N. T. Wright, Evil and the Justice of God. Grand Rapids: InterVarsity Press, 2014.

N. T. Wright, Simply Good News: Why the Gospel is News and What Makes It Good. New York: HarperOne, 2011.

N.T, Wright. The Day the Revolution Began: Reconsidering the Meaning of Jesus' Crucifixion. San Fransisco Harper One, 2016.

LESSON #6: The Resurrection (Part 1)

The entire Christian faith rests on the historical, bodily resurrection of Jesus Christ. This event is the cornerstone of the New Testament gospel (good news). It is the central message each time the apostles preached to a crowd of people or testified to specific individuals (See: Acts 2:22-24; 3:15; 4:2,33; 10:39-41; 13:30-37; 17:31). The resurrection of Jesus quite literally changed the world. This topic will be divided into two lessons: the resurrection of Jesus of Nazareth and the hope of the believer's future resurrection.

The Resurrection of Jesus of Nazareth:

It was a cold crisp day in late February 2010. I was in Reno, Nevada that weekend, watching the high school state basketball championships. While my family was checking out of the hotel, I went to grab the car and pull it up to the curb for them. It was cold, and I didn't want them to have to make the walk to the car. As I was pulling around, my cell phone rang. It was Jamie, the wife of my adopted brother, Jonathon.

As it is with family, I can't actually remember meeting Jonathon. He was just always around. I've been told it was my grandma who first started watching him when he was still in diapers. It didn't take long before he was just one of the grandkids. He was the only child of a single mom who was doing the best she could, but even at that age, Jon was a handful.

As he got older, his larger-than-life personality made it easy for him to find friends, but since his home life wasn't very structured, it didn't take him long to find trouble too. As I reminisce, I can't help but smile, thinking of all the crazy stuff he did as a teenager. He was rambunctious and so full of life.

I remember when he permanently moved into my parent's home his sophomore and junior year of high school. He had run away a few times, and it was impossible for his mom to keep him under control. He needed guidance and a lot more discipline. So he moved in with us. At one point, he and I shared a room. I'd just finished college and was back home saving some money so I could get married. We really became brothers then.

Because he was doing well, Jon's mom wanted him to move back home for his senior year. Unfortunately, the lack of structure at his mom's house left the door open for more poor choices. After that, Jon kind of dropped off the map for a few years. Then one day, he called me out of the blue. He told me that he'd found the love of his life and wanted all of us to meet her. He was young. So was she. But they were getting married. He was impetuous like that. But Jon knew he hadn't really been closely following Jesus and wanted to make some changes. He wanted Jamie to know Jesus, and his "Blakeley family." They started coming to church and soon she became a Jesus follower. At his wedding, he insisted that my parents sit in the family section and that his two older "brothers", B.J. and I, be groomsmen.

It wasn't long before Jon and Jamie had children, and, of course, my mom and dad were introduced as "Grammy and Pa Pot." Jon was sure of that. He was determined that his kids had my parents in their life.

43

So when Jamie called me that cold Sunday morning, it wasn't too abnormal. She was family. Then those words I'll never forget—"Brad, Jonny died sometime last night! I just woke up next to him, and he was gone." I later learned that two days before, Jon had minor elective surgery that placed unexpected stress on his body and resulted in his death. He was gone. Life had changed that morning in 2010.

As it happened, I was just finishing my graduate work at BIOLA university and had completed a course on the resurrection of Jesus. We had spent an entire year reading books by Christians and skeptics alike, examining evidence and counter-evidence on the resurrection. Growing up, I'd of course heard about Jesus' resurrection each Easter. But somehow, I'd never really grasped how central this was to the Christian faith. It was Jon's death that brought everything into sharp focus.

As I reflected on all that I learned that previous year, I came to see that the resurrection of Jesus needed to be at the very center of my faith. When I was younger, I thought that Christian faith rested on the Bible. If the Bible said something, it was true. Period.[45] But as I learned in that class, this wasn't how the earliest disciples saw things or why they followed Jesus. If anything, the crucifixion of Jesus seemed to undermine his claim to be Israel's long awaited Messiah (See: Acts 13:26-31;17:3). Instead, the earliest disciples continued to follow Jesus after his death for only one reason: they were utterly convinced he had risen from the dead![46] The resurrection of Jesus was the "why" behind their faith (See: I Corinthians 15:17; Philippians 3:10).[47]

Jon's sudden death made me ask hard questions but I came to believe more than ever in the hope we have as believers. In the next lesson, I'll talk about how my new confidence in Jesus made all the difference at my brother's funeral. For now, I want to share some of the evidence we have for the resurrection of Jesus. I pray this lesson will fill you with this same confidence. Jesus has defeated death—and this changes everything!

Christianity's Unique Claim

One of the things that distinguishes Christianity from other religions is that Christianity's core belief is a historical event—the resurrection of Jesus of Nazareth. Unlike most religions which are based on the prophetic teachings of a solitary leader (e.g. Mohammad; Joseph Smith), Christianity is based on the eye-witness testimony of men and women who claimed to see Jesus alive after his public crucifixion. And since most major religions are founded by prophets or leaders who claim special insight from God, those who follow their teachings must simply accept them on blind faith. However, Christianity's core belief is historical, and so we can use the same investigative tools that are used to establish other historical facts. It still requires faith to believe that Jesus defeated death, but unlike other religious systems, there are historical reasons for this belief. Therefore, Christian faith is utterly reasonable.

---

45. The Bible plays a critical role in the believer's life. It is God's inspired word and is authoritative over
46. A "crucified messiah" was so foreign to a religious Jew that believing it required an entirely different understanding of the Old Testament. Simply put: no Jew was expecting their messiah to die on a cross. (See: Luke 24:13-27; Acts 2:22-36; 6:8; 7:1-54 Galatians 1:11-24).
47. Incidentally, this caused another shift for me. I realized my goal wasn't to convince people the Bible was true (sometimes a difficult task with lots of potential rabbit trails), I simply needed to demonstrate that Jesus had, in fact, rose again from the dead!

So why should anyone really believe that Jesus rose from the dead? The 18th century Scottish philosopher David Hume scoffed at this notion. His reason: "Dead people can't rise again." In other words, it's not rational to actually believe in dead men rising again. Hume simply dismissed the possibility of a miracle altogether. While most wouldn't just outright deny the possibility of all miracles, Hume's skepticism reminds us that we shouldn't simply assume that a miracle happened. So if we're going to really believe that Jesus rose again, we must have good reasons for doing so.

Before we explore some of these facts, we need to briefly explain how historical facts are established. First, history isn't an exact science. Reconstructions of past events are pieced together using artifacts and written sources from people who lived near the events. All history works this way.

Second, historians regard all ancient sources as imperfect records of past events. So whether the modern historian is examining the writings of Tacitus or the gospel of Luke, the historian assumes that bias and some distortion exists in the written record. However, as we will see, these challenges do not stop the historian from reaching reasonable conclusions about the events in history. In the evidence that follows, we will use both secular and biblical sources to establish the historical evidence for the resurrection.

Finally, it's important to note that we're not "using the Bible to prove the Bible." We're simply using the ancient writings contained in the New Testament as ancient sources that may or may not accurately tell us what happened. In other words, in this section, we're not treating the New Testament as an inspired text. It's just an ancient text that dates to this period and records the events we're interested in. We will need to use good historical investigation to see if what was recorded is most likely true.

Let's explore just five of these facts together.

FACT #1:

Jesus of Nazareth existed and was publicly crucified in Jerusalem.

> There once was a time when it was fashionable to question if Jesus even existed.[48] However, today scholars no longer doubt this.[49] Jesus is mentioned as a historical figure by ancient Christian, Jewish, and Roman sources. It's beyond doubt that Jesus existed.

> It is also clear that Jesus was publicly crucified in Jerusalem. This event is recorded in each gospel. For example, notice the pains that John goes to "certify" the death of Jesus,

>> But when they came to Jesus, they saw that he was already dead, so they didn't break his legs. One of the soldiers, however, pierced his side with a spear, and immediately blood and water flowed out.[35] (This report is from an eyewitness giving an accurate account. He speaks the truth so that you also may continue to believe.)

>> -John 19:33-35 (NLT)

49.Russell, Bertrand. Why I Am Not A Christian. (New York: Simon and Schuster,)1957. p. 16
50. For a useful one volume book that has collected most of the relevant data from antiquity on the historicity of Jesus of Nazareth see: Habermas, Gary. The Historical Jesus: Ancient Evidence for the Life of Christ. Joplin, Mo. College Press Pub., 1996.

This is abnormal. It's almost as if John is saying, "He died, he really died! I'm not lying. I was there. I saw it, he was really dead."

Again, we're not saying you should believe John just because his book is in the Bible. We're simply saying this very ancient eyewitness has written something interesting here. However, when historians find the same event recorded in multiple sources, they tend to believe that this establishes a historical fact. In addition to biblical sources, several secular sources (Josephus and Tacitus, to name two) mention the crucifixion of Jesus.[50] For these reasons, we can confidently say, "Jesus of Nazareth lived and was publicly crucified in Jerusalem."

FACT #2:
Jesus was buried in a private tomb.

Jesus was, of course, a Jew, and Jewish cultural burial customs were very important to them. All four gospels record that some disciples of Jesus asked if they could give him an honorable burial (See also: I Corinthians 15:3-8). But what's interesting is that the two disciples mentioned are relatively unknown. The primary disciple responsible was a man named Joseph of Arimathea (See: Matthew 27:57; Mark 15:43; Luke 23:51 John 19:38). This is surprising since we would expect a lead disciple like Peter, James or John to do the brave and honorable thing and ask for their leader's body to give him a proper burial. It's when historians see these kinds of surprising details in an ancient source that high credibility is given to the recorded event. For these reasons and many others, it is historically reasonable that Jesus was buried shortly after his public death.[51]

FACT #3:
The tomb of Jesus was found empty.

This is obviously the most explosive fact regarding the case for the resurrection of Jesus. Good thing the evidence for the empty tomb is very strong. Biblical scholar Gary Habermas has put forth a helpful acronym that quickly summarizes some of this evidence. It's known as the J.E.T. Argument.

Jerusalem - It's indisputable that the Jesus movement began in Jerusalem shortly after his death. The disciples boldly preached the resurrection of Jesus in the streets of Jerusalem and at the Temple (See: Acts 2:22-24; 3:15; 4:2, 33). It would be difficult (if not impossible) to do this if Jesus' tomb w as still occupied! Notice what Peter said in Acts 2:22-24a,

50. Tacitus, Annals, 15.44; Josephus, 18.3.3. For a book on this topic see: Wallace, J. Warner. Cold Case Christianity. (Colorado Springs, David C. Cook Publishing.) 2013.
51. For more on this fact see: http://www.reasonablefaith.org/independent-sources-for-jesus-burial-and-empty-tomb; http://www.reasonablefaith.org/grounds-for-scepticism-concerning-jesus-burial-and-empty-tombw

Men of Israel, hear these words: Jesus of Nazareth, a man attested to you by God with mighty works and wonders and signs that God did through him in your midst, as you yourselves know — this Jesus, delivered up according to the definite plan and foreknowledge of God, you crucified and killed by the hands of lawless men. God raised him up, loosing the pangs of death, because it was not possible for him to be held by it.

-Acts 2:22-24 (ESV)

It's It's clear that Peter was speaking to eyewitnesses of Jesus' death, and it's equally clear his message assumed the tomb of Jesus was empty. The Jesus movement would have never gotten off the ground especially in Jerusalem without an empty tomb.

Enemy Attestation- Sometimes the best witness to a fact in history comes from a source that is hostile to the event. For example, when you ask the losing team about the game last night, they probably won't exaggerate the score. They admit they lost but certainly aren't prone to embellish their defeat.

In the gospel of Matthew, we read that the Jewish leaders who pushed to execute Jesus admitted his tomb was empty. We read,

And when they had assembled with the elders and taken counsel, they gave a sufficient sum of money to the soldiers [13]and said, "Tell people, 'His disciples came by night and stole him away while we were asleep.'

-Matthew 28:12-13 (ESV)

Notice, the Jewish leaders didn't even try to suggest the tomb was occupied. They know it isn't. So, they're forced to come up with an explanation. The fact they tried to promote a "Stolen Body Conspiracy" is actually evidence the tomb must have been empty.

Testimony of women- It is easy to overlook a final important detail in the Easter morning events that supply powerful evidence for the empty tomb. Every gospel account recorded that the first witnesses to the empty tomb were women (See: Matthew 28:1-7; Mark 16:1-7; Luke 24:1-11; John 20:1-3). At first glance this doesn't seem important. However, if we consider that in the first century, women were not regarded as credible witnesses, it's remarkable that the gospels admit that women were the first to find the tomb empty. This is the sort of detail that cause historians to pay close attention because the text is admitting something that is culturally embarrassing. In the first century, this admission would have been met with scorn. Nevertheless, the gospel accounts faithfully record that female disciples were the first to come to the empty tomb, because that is exactly what happened!

FACT #4:

The disciples of Jesus fearlessly proclaimed the resurrection of Jesus in Jerusalem.

This fact is indisputable. The record that Luke gave us in the book of Acts confirms that they "filled Jerusalem" with the message of Jesus' resurrection" (See: Acts 5:28). This is even corroborated by the Roman historian Tacitus (56 AD – c. 120 AD). In a passage where he recounted the burning of Rome, he suggested that the Emperor Nero was actually responsible but that Nero blamed local Christians. Notice what Tacitus said:

> Nero fastened the guilt ... on a class hated for their abominations, called Christians by the populace. Christus, from whom the name had its origin, suffered the extreme penalty [crucifixion] during the reign of Tiberius at the hands of ... Pontius Pilatus, and a most mischievous superstition, thus checked for the moment, again broke out not only in Judaea, the first source of the evil, but even in Rome.[52]

This passage corroborates the crucifixion of Jesus, the role Pilate played, and that this teaching, called a "mischievous superstition", "broke out" in "Judaea," the very province where Jerusalem is located.

As all of the gospels record, the disciples shamefully abandoned Jesus upon his arrest with Peter denying that he even knew him (See: Matthew 26:56; 69-75; Mark 14:50; 66-72; Luke 22:54-62; John 18:17-18, 25-27). In the minds of his disciples, Jesus' public crucifixion effectively ended any claim of being Israel's long-awaited Messiah. They fled and hid behind a locked door (See: John 20:19). They'd seen what had happened to other groups who ended up on the wrong side of Roman justice and so were in hiding.

So what explains the spectacular change in these disciples? They're now radically bold despite persecution and threat of martyrdom (See: Acts 7:54-60; 12:2-3). The only plausible answer is they believed death had been defeated! They knew Jesus had confirmed his promise. Jesus had said, "Whoever believes in me, though he die, yet shall he live, and everyone who lives and believes in me shall never die" (John 11:26 ESV). The fact these disciples fearlessly proclaimed Jesus' resurrection in Jerusalem at the cost of their own lives powerfully supports the fact they believed Jesus did in fact rise from the dead!

FACT #5: The conversion of Paul and James.

The final historical fact we will examine is the conversion of Paul and James. Both men were not followers of Jesus prior to his resurrection, in fact much the opposite. James was a scoffing half-brother of Jesus who rejected his brother's claims. Paul was a Jewish Pharisee that believed the Jesus movement was blasphemous. So what explains their conversion?

---

52. Tacitus, Annals 15.44, cited in Strobel, The Case for Christ, 82

Let's start with James. He is listed in Mark 6:3 as a member of Jesus' family. As Jesus ministered in his hometown and surrounding areas, some scoffed and said he was crazy (See: Mark 3:20). In a culture that placed a high value on family honor, it's easy to see how Jesus' behavior could cause a problem for his brothers (and sisters).[53] The clearest example of this is in John 7:1-5:

> After this, Jesus traveled around Galilee. He wanted to stay out of Judea, where the Jewish leaders were plotting his death. But soon it was time for the Jewish Festival of Shelters, and Jesus' brothers said to him, "Leave here and go to Judea, where your followers can see your miracles! You can't become famous if you hide like this! If you can do such wonderful things, show yourself to the world!" For even his brothers didn't believe in him.
>
> -John 7:1-5 (ESV)

It's clear that Jesus' brothers were not among his disciples. Nevertheless, Jesus continued to claim he was Israel's messiah. In fact, this was the official charge brought against Jesus and directly led to his crucifixion as the titulus, "King of the Jews," placed above his cross indicated (See: Matthew 27:28-30, 37; Mark 15:26; Luke 23:38; John 19:19-22).

It would seem that the crucifixion of Jesus would confirm what James and the other brothers had been saying—Jesus was crazy and now his delusions got him killed. However, the opposite happened. Luke recorded that, shortly after Jesus' death, James was leading the Jesus movement in Jerusalem (See: Acts 15:13)! So, what explains his conversion? In I Corinthians 15:7, Paul recounted the specific individuals that saw Jesus after his crucifixion, and here we read, "Then he [the resurrected Jesus] was seen by James and later by all the apostles."

This appearance must have had quite an impact on James. He not only lead the early Jesus movement for the next 30 years, but also his death in Jerusalem as a martyr for Christ is recorded in two non-biblical ancient sources.[54] There is simply no other reasonable explanation for the conversion of James—he believed he saw the risen Jesus and was convinced that Jesus was, in fact, Israel's Messiah.

Paul's conversion is even more remarkable. Prior to seeing the resurrected Jesus, he was called "Saul" and violently persecuted the early church (See: Acts 8:1-3; 9:1-2; 26:9-11; Galatians 1:1

53. Some may be surprised to learn that Matthew 13:55, Mark 3:20, 6:4, John 7:3-5, Galatians 1:16 mention that Jesus had siblings. Some have suggested that Joseph had a previous marriage and brought children into his marriage with Mary. Others have suggested the translation should be "cousins". Neither option is very convincing and seems to ignore the natural reading and translation of the text. Matthew 1:25 seems to indicate Mary and Joseph had normal sexual intimacy after the birth of Jesus and so it is unsurprising that Jesus had siblings.

54. James' martyrdom is without doubt. The Jewish historian Jospehus and church historian Eusebius both record the same event occurring in Jerusalem around AD. 62. Their account of the event has been analyzed to have come from independent sources which further substantiates the historicity of the event.

3-14; Philippians 3:6; I Timothy 1:12). Paul recounted his own encounter with the risen Jesus in Galatians 1:13-16. Here's an excerpt:

> For you have heard of my former life in Judaism, how I persecuted the church of God violently and tried to destroy it… But when he who had set me apart before I was born, and who called me by his grace, was pleased to reveal his Son to me, in order that I might preach him among the Gentiles, I did not immediately consult with anyone.

-Galatians 1:13-16 (ESV)

Paul's conversion is detailed in Acts 9:3-16, repeated in Acts 22:3-10, and again recounted in Acts 26:12-18. God did indeed have a special calling for this young man. Over his ministry of probably 30 years, Paul led missionary teams that planted churches throughout the Mediterranean basin. He also penned 13 letters (known as epistles) to churches that are included in the New Testament.[55]

Prior to meeting Jesus, Paul (Saul) had no reason to become a Jesus follower. By his own admission, he was confident in his former life in Judaism (See: Philippians 3:4-6). But when he met Jesus, he realized everything he had served prior to Jesus was worthless! He wrote,

> But whatever gain I had, I counted as loss for the sake of Christ. Indeed, I count everything as loss because of the surpassing worth of knowing Christ Jesus my Lord. For his sake I have suffered the loss of all things and count them as rubbish, in order that I may gain Christ.

- Philippians 3:7-8 (ESV)

As Paul declared, this decision to follow Jesus cost him the loss of all things, eventually, including his own life. Paul died as a martyr in Rome around A.D. 67. What changed this zealous Pharisee? Why would this man radically change the direction of his life, only to suffer so much for it (See: Acts 14:19-22; 16:16-24; 21:13,30; II Corinthians 11:16-33)? There is only one explanation for the conversion of Paul; he believed he saw the risen Jesus!

---

55. There are 27 books in the New Testament. As we've learned the first four are gospel-biographies of the life of Jesus. The book of Acts is the history of the early church and it's spread throughout the Roman Empire. The remaining books are letters written by church leaders to various churches, with the exception of Revelation, which is an apocalyptic book about the end of times and return of Jesus. Paul is believed to have written 13 of these "epistles," which is a remarkable contribution to the New Testament. While some scholars are uncertain of his authorship of some of the letters, 7 are "indisputably Pauline." All of these letters are invaluable to us, because they give us specific teaching about important issues from those who were the close associates of Jesus. Much of the Church's official doctrines are founded upon the teaching in the New Testament epistles.

History's Mystery

As we wrap up this lesson, it might be helpful to look at the early Jesus movement as a sort of historical puzzle. How did this Jewish Messiah movement survive the public, humiliating death of its leader? The Jewish Messiah was supposed to deliver the Jews from her enemies. But clearly, Jesus was the one delivered over and killed by the Romans. Why would any Jew (much less Gentiles) ever believe in Jesus?

Let's review the facts we've covered. Jesus of Nazareth existed. Jesus boldly claimed to be Israel's Messiah and deliverer. Jesus was crucified for that claim. Jesus was buried in a tomb near Jerusalem. His tomb was found empty a short time later. His disciples fled and hid at first, but then they were suddenly and spectacularly transformed into bold proclaimers of Jesus' victory over death. This claim led all of them to either horrible persecution or violent deaths, with none ever recanting. Additionally, even non-disciples like James and Paul claimed to see Jesus alive after his crucifixion; and they too died horribly for it. Lastly, the Jesus movement quickly spread after his death, boldly proclaiming the unlikely message that Jesus was, in fact, Israel's Messiah.

So how did the Jesus movement survive the humiliating public death of its leader? How could Christians continue to claim Jesus was the promised Messiah after he had clearly died? Further, why would men like James and Paul change their minds about Jesus and even give their lives for him? Even more incredibly, how has this peasant from an obscure village in Galilee, made a bigger mark on the human race than any king, nobleman, inventor or statesman? And why have billions of people over the past two millennia found their lives radically transformed by placing their faith in Jesus the Messiah? There is only one reasonable answer to these questions: Jesus of Nazareth rose again from the dead.

He is Heaven's champion, the victor over death, and has been installed as Lord over all.

While no historical event can be proven to absolute certainty, (in fact, very little in life can), I believe we've seen enough to conclude that the evidence for the resurrection of Jesus is beyond reasonable doubt. Since this book is only meant as a brief introduction, I could only give some of the evidence for the resurrection, much more could be said on this topic. However, it's my hope that you'll continue your study by examining the resources mentioned below.

IN CONCLUSION:

The bodily resurrection of Jesus is the most significant event in human history. It brings hope to our dying race. Jesus has defeated death. The resurrection of Jesus vindicates his life and message. It proves once and for all that Jesus was God's son. His claim to offer forgiveness from sin and offer life to those who believe is legitimate. The resurrection of Jesus is the linchpin of the Christian faith. If it were untrue, there is absolutely no reason to follow Jesus. However, if true, there remains no doubt that Jesus is Lord over all.

BIBLE STUDY [Answer the following questions to enhance your learning.]

What is a major difference between Christianity and other religious systems? Explain why this difference is important?

Which of the historical facts regarding the resurrection of Jesus did you find most important? Why?

Explain the "J.E.T." argument.

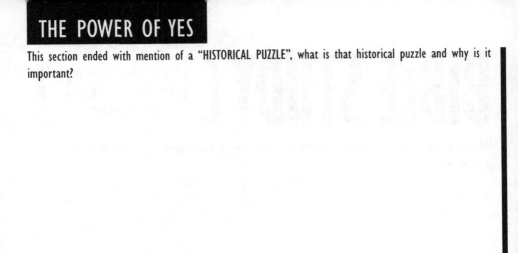

This section ended with mention of a "HISTORICAL PUZZLE", what is that historical puzzle and why is it important?

What was the most significant thing you learned in this section?

Pray over what you've learned in this lesson. Write out a summarizing prayer below.

MEMORY VERSE:

"And if Christ has not been raised, your faith is futile and you

are still in your sins."

- I Corinthians 15:17 (ESV)

FOR FURTHER RESOURCES ON THIS TOPIC:

Gary R. Habermas, and Michael R. Licona. The Case for the Resurrection of Jesus. Grand Rapids: Kregel Publications, 2004.

Lee Strobel. Case for Christ. Grand Rapids: Zondervan, 2016.

J. Warner Wallace. Cold Case Christianity. Colorado Springs, David C. Cook Publishing, 2013.

N.T. Wright, Surprised by Hope: Rethinking Heaven, the Resurrection, and the Mission of the Church. New York: HarperOne, 2014.

LESSON #7: Our Future Hope—The Resurrection (Part 2)

Life changes when someone you've always known passes away. The first time I experienced this was when my grandmother died. She'd fought colon cancer and spent her final months receiving hospice care in my parent's home. However, that last week of her life something extraordinary happened. Near the end, my grandma began sleeping a lot. She was too weak to be conscious for very long.

But one day, things changed. My mother had just come home from work and stopped to speak with the hospice nurse who had also just arrived. Not knowing my grandma was awake, my mom took her time getting back to see her. When she finally arrived in the bedroom, my grandma was slightly irritated. "Why didn't you come back sooner?" Somehow my grandma knew she'd been home awhile. She even repeated details of the conversation my mom had with the nurse! All this seemed impossible since my grandma was very sick and my mom and the nurse had been too far away to be overheard.

But my grandma quickly dismissed all of this as unimportant, she wanted to tell my mom of the incredible day she just had. She recounted what sounded like an out of body experience. With energy my mom hadn't seen in weeks, she gave vivid details of what she saw on "the other side." Her eyes flashed with an infectious smile, as she spoke of the indescribable colors she'd seen in heaven. Then she described loved ones who had long been dead. After a while she started to grow tired, and she laid back down. Then suddenly, she sat back up with the last bit of energy she could muster and looked directly into my mom's eyes and said. "Sue, it's all true. Every word of it is true. It's all true!" Then she laid back, closing her eyes, repeating that phrase, "It's all true."

That was the last real conversation she had. After this, she slipped into a semi-coma like state and passed away that Sunday afternoon. At my grandma's funeral, many people spoke about how she loved others and Jesus. They shared stories of how her faith impacted them and about the mark that she left on their lives. She was an incredible elementary teacher, mom and "Grammy." There wasn't any doubt in anyone's mind that my "Grammy" was in heaven with Jesus.

When Jon died, it was so different. He hadn't been in pain battling cancer for years as my grandma had. Instead, he was a 27-year-old young man, in relatively good health—now suddenly gone—leaving behind two little kids and a young wife. But there were some similarities too. Both Jon and my grandma followed Jesus. No, not perfectly, who does that? But they both had placed their faith in Jesus and knew that he had died for them.

As I mentioned in the last lesson, Jon died just after I had taken the course on the resurrection. It was one thing to see my cancer-stricken grandma pass away, it was another to see my younger brother's body in a casket. Both were terrible, but Jon's death was shocking. As I said in the previous lesson, his death took the textbook material I'd been studying off the pages and burned those truths right into my heart. The preciousness of Jesus' resurrection took on a whole new meaning. I've never been the same.

I remember standing before a huge crowd of friends, families and strangers at Jon's funeral. I wept, but through my tears I had confidence. There was an assurance I hadn't known before. I was able to boldly say that Jon Griffin's life hadn't ended February 28, 2010. I told that crowd that since I was absolutely sure that Jesus had defeated death, I was also sure he had the power to give eternal life to all who believed in him. I looked at that group of weeping people and through my own tears, quoted Jesus' powerful words, "Whoever believes in me, though he die, yet shall he live, 26and everyone who lives and believes in me shall never die" (John 11:25-26 ESV).

In this lesson, I want to reflect on what the resurrection of Jesus means for us today. We're going to see that the resurrection doesn't just validate Jesus as God's son and Israel's messiah, it's also the foundation for our every hope. As the early Church faced a hostile world and endured terrible persecution, they were able to confidently declare that God was good and that death wouldn't have the final word. Since they knew Jesus had defeated death, they believed they too would share in his victory (See: I Thessalonians 4:13-17).

Jesus' Bold Claims about Death

Even before his death, Jesus made a string of startling claims and promises to those who followed him. As I just mentioned, he said things like, "I am the resurrection and the life. Anyone who believes in me will live, even after dying. Everyone who lives in me and believes in me will never ever die" (John 11:25-26. NLT). He claimed that, "If anyone would come after me, let him deny himself and take up his cross and follow me. For whoever would save his life will lose it, but whoever loses his life for my sake and the gospel's will save it" (Mark 8:34-35 ESV). Right up to the night before his death, he said, "I will not leave you as orphans; I will come to you. Yet a little while and the world will see me no more, but you will see me. Because I live, you also will live" (John 14:18-19 ESV).

Whenever Jesus would speak of his eventual dying and rising again, his disciples were often confused (See: Mark 8:31-33, 9:10; 32-33; Luke 18:34; John 16:19). He was an extraordinary rabbi and rabbis often said things that went over the heads of their students. So at the time, Jesus' disciples must have chalked these statements up to being heavenly metaphors or some esoteric truth.

Of course, it wasn't until after the resurrection that his disciples realized the true meaning of what Jesus had been saying all along. He had really come "to destroy the works of the devil" (I John 3:8). He was sent to defeat sin, satan and death itself (See: Isaiah 61:1-2; Luke 4:18-19; John 8:32-26). So, on Easter Sunday when the Father raised the Son back to life, everything changed. As the book of Acts tells us, the disciples began boldly preaching that Jesus had won the victory over darkness. Heaven's Champion was victorious!

I Corinthians 15
The Resurrection Changes Everything

There's probably no clearer passage in the New Testament that spells out the implications of the resurrection of Jesus than I Corinthians 15. The entire chapter is a tightly argued unit that aimed to help the Corinthians understand what the resurrection of Jesus meant for them personally. Let's look at this chapter section by section.

First, Paul reminded the Corinthians that the good news of Jesus' resurrection is either true or it isn't. He wrote, "It is this Good News that saves you if you continue to believe the message I told you—unless, of course, you believed something that was never true in the first place" (I Corinthians 15:2 NLT). Everything that follows in this chapter hinges on if the good news about Jesus is true. In other words, the resurrection of Jesus gives the believer a solid foundation for their faith.

Second, Paul cited an oral creed that summarized the gospel. (Memorizing this is recommended.)

> I passed on to you what was most important and what had also been passed on to me. 'Christ died for our sins, just as the Scriptures said. He was buried, and he was raised from the dead on the third day, just as the Scriptures said. He was seen by Peter and then by the Twelve. After that, he was seen by more than 500 of his followers at one time, most of whom are still alive, though some have died. Then he was seen by James and later by all the apostles.'[56] Last of all, as though I had been born at the wrong time, I also saw him.
>
> - I Corinthians 15.3—8 (NLT)

This creed emphatically states that the death, burial and resurrection of Jesus is "of most importance" to Christian faith. The mention of many eye-witnesses to the risen Jesus is critical. Interestingly, Paul included himself among those witnesses. This implies that if there were any doubt about Christ's resurrection, the eyewitnesses were still around to verify it.

Third, Paul used this foundation to address a false teaching that must have been spreading in the Church—there will be no resurrection of the dead. We're not sure of the details but Paul combated this. He asked, "Why are some of you saying there will be no resurrection of the dead?[57] For if there is no resurrection of the dead, then Christ has not been raised either" (I Corinthians 15:12-13 NLT). He pushed further. "And if Christ has not been raised, then all our preaching is useless, and your faith is useless. And we apostles would all be lying about God—for we have said that God raised Christ from the grave. But that can't be true if there is no resurrection of the dead" (I Corinthians 15:14-15 NLT).

As you can see, Paul went "all in" on the resurrection of Jesus. It either happened or it didn't. If it didn't, then Christian preaching and faith is "useless." However, if Jesus did rise, then other resurrections are possible! All of our hope rests on the resurrection of Jesus.

---

56. The single quotation marks indicate where I assume the preexisting oral creed starts and stops as Paul incorporated it into his letter to the Corinthians. Scholars have dated this creed to within 5 years of the resurrection of Jesus. Oral creeds were important to the early church as many didn't have access to expensive copies of written documents and were uneducated and so couldn't read them anyway. Oral cultures, such as ancient Palestine, relied much on memory and mnemonic devices to aid in recall. For a book on the dating of this oral creed see: Habermas, Gary. "Tracing Jesus' Resurrection to Its Earliest Eyewitness Accounts," God is Great, God is Good (InterVarsity Press, 2009). For a book on the oral culture of Palestine and how they preserved oral history remarkably well see: Bauckham, Richard. Jesus and the Eye Witnesses. (Wm. B. Eerdmans Pub., second ed. 2016)

57. The resurrection of Jesus is the best attested ancient miracle in human history. However, today, the prevailing worldview in the West is naturalism. This is the idea that only the physical world exists and that things like miracles are impossible. However, if it can be shown that Jesus did, in fact raise from the dead, then naturalism is false. There can be no compromise between Christianity and naturalism. Either we live in a universe electrified by mystery designed by God with real hope for life after death, or we live in a cold, brutal, hopeless world where we simply exist for a blink of time, look around and then vanish into the nothingness from which we came. Jesus' victory over death also represents the ultimate defeat of naturalism.

Fourth, Paul suggested that the resurrection of Jesus opens the door for humanity to escape Adam's curse. He wrote,

> So you see, just as death came into the world through a man, now the resurrection from the dead has begun through another man. Just as everyone dies because we all belong to Adam, everyone who belongs to Christ will be given new life. But there is an order to this resurrection: Christ was raised as the first of the harvest; then all who belong to Christ will be raised when he comes back.
>
> - I Corinthians 15:21-23 (NLT)

When we are united to Christ through faith we can share in his victory over death. This echoes what Jesus himself said in John 11:25-26 (see above). We have assurance of our personal resurrection in the future because of the resurrection of Jesus in the past. His resurrection guarantees mine!

This is precisely what Paul told another church who had written to him about the loved ones in their church who had died. He wrote, "But we do not want you to be uninformed, brothers, about those who are asleep, that you may not grieve as others do who have no hope. For since we believe that Jesus died and rose again, even so, through Jesus, God will bring with him those who have fallen asleep" (I Thessalonians 4:13-14 ESV). Paul was able to tell this church that their funerals should be markedly different from the funerals of non-believers. We should not grieve "as others do who have no hope." Why? Because, "Jesus rose again!"

Fifth, Paul's willingness to suffer and endure hardship in his preaching is directly connected to his confidence in Jesus' resurrection. Notice what he said,

> And why should we ourselves risk our lives hour by hour? For I swear, dear brothers and sisters, that I face death daily. This is as certain as my pride in what Christ Jesus our Lord has done in you. And what value was there in fighting wild beasts— those people of Ephesus —if there will be no resurrection from the dead? And if there is no resurrection, "Let's feast and drink, for tomorrow we die!
>
> - I Corinthians 15:30-32 (NLT)

Once again, the resurrection is everything. If it didn't happen, then why not just "feast and drink?" The resurrection of Jesus motivates us to keep on keeping on because we know this life isn't all there is! There's hope ahead.

Sixth, Paul addressed the skeptics of the resurrection who couldn't imagine what a resurrected body would be like. He wrote,

> But someone may ask, "How will the dead be raised? What kind of bodies will they have?" What a foolish question! When you put a seed into the ground, it doesn't grow into a plant unless it dies first. And what you put in the ground is not the

plant that will grow, but only a bare seed of wheat or whatever you are planting. Then God gives it the new body he wants it to have. A different plant grows from each kind of seed... It is the same way with the resurrection of the dead. Our earthly bodies are planted in the ground when we die, but they will be raised to live forever. Our bodies are buried in brokenness, but they will be raised in glory. They are buried in weakness, but they will be raised in strength. They are buried as natural human bodies, but they will be raised as spiritual bodies. For just as there are natural bodies, there are also spiritual bodies... What I am saying, dear brothers and sisters, is that our physical bodies cannot inherit the Kingdom of God. These dying bodies cannot inherit what will last forever.

- I Corinthians 15:35-38, 42-44, 50 (NLT)

Paul told us bodies are similar to a seed placed in the ground but "raised" as something radically different. There is an organic connection between what was planted and what is raised. And so, it is with our bodies. We are "planted" in death but our resurrected bodies will be radically different. Our future resurrected body will be glorious, sustained by the Spirit and like the resurrected body Jesus had (See: Philippians 3:21). The resurrection of Jesus gives us hope that our eternal existence will be vastly better than any existence we have ever experienced under Adam's curse.

Finally, Paul finished this magnificent chapter highlighting the hope and reward the resurrection of Jesus gives the believer.

But let me reveal to you a wonderful secret. We will not all die, but we will all be transformed! It will happen in a moment, in the blink of an eye, when the last trumpet is blown. For when the trumpet sounds, those who have died will be raised to live forever. And we who are living will also be transformed. For our dying bodies must be transformed into bodies that will never die; our mortal bodies must be transformed into immortal bodies. Then, when our dying bodies have been transformed into bodies that will never die, this Scripture will be fulfilled: "Death is swallowed up in victory. O death, where is your victory? O death, where is your sting?" For sin is the sting that results in death, and the law gives sin its power. But thank God! He gives us victory over sin and death through our Lord Jesus Christ. So, my dear brothers and sisters, be strong and immovable. Always work enthusiastically for the Lord, for you know that nothing you do for the Lord is ever useless.

- I Corinthians 15:22-26; 51-58 (ESV)

Here Paul tied everything together. Since Jesus defeated death, we will too. We will receive a glorious new body and enter a glorious eternal existence. Death does not have the final word over a believer's life. And because of these truths, we must stay strong and keep going. The resurrection of Jesus gives our life ultimate purpose, because we have ultimate hope!

Christ's Resurrection Points to Creation's Renewal

The personal implications of the resurrection are always what we tend to focus on first. What is going to happen to me and to those I love after death? But before we end this lesson, it's important to understand that Jesus' resurrection doesn't just affect humans but, in fact, all of creation.

An important passage that connects how the resurrection of Jesus affects both humanity and the creation is Romans 8:18-23. Again, Paul is the author and was writing to the church at Rome:

> Yet what we suffer now is nothing compared to the glory he will reveal to us later. For all creation is waiting eagerly for that future day when God will reveal who his children really are. Against its will, all creation was subjected to God's curse. But with eager hope, the creation looks forward to the day when it will join God's children in glorious freedom from death and decay. For we know that all creation has been groaning as in the pains of childbirth right up to the present time. And we believers also groan, even though we have the Holy Spirit within us as a foretaste of future glory, for we long for our bodies to be released from sin and suffering. We, too, wait with eager hope for the day when God will give us our full rights as his adopted children, including the new bodies he has promised us.
>
> -Romans 8:18-23 (ESV)

God created humanity as His representatives (image bearers) over creation, but when we sinned, we brought creation itself under the same bondage and decay that we experience. Jesus, as the new Adam, broke that curse, and now creation waits along with humanity for God to complete what He began that first Easter morning (See: Romans 5:12-20; I Corinthians 15:21-28).

It's common today for Christians to think that God will destroy the earth one day and that we will live in Heaven for eternity. But that is not the whole story. While it's true that believers who die prior to the final resurrection will depart and immediately enter God's presence,[58] Heaven is not our final destination. Remember, human beings were designed and created to live on earth. We're meant to rule and reign with God over creation; and that is exactly what will happen again when Jesus returns (See: I Corinthians 15: 24-28; Ephesians 1:20-23; Philippians 2:9-11; Hebrews 1:4-9). Jesus will set things right. He promises to make all things new and wipe away every tear (See: Revelation 21:4-5). The creation will be redeemed and heaven and earth will be forever joined (See: Isaiah 11:6-16; Revelation 21-22). Our final destination is to rule on a New Earth with Jesus as our King.

The resurrected Jesus is the beginning of New Creation (See: Revelation 3:14). There will be a resurrection of all who ever lived either to eternal life or eternal death (See: John 5:25-29). The creation itself will be.

---

58. See: Acts 7:59-60; II Corinthians 5:1-4; Philippians 1:23; Hebrews 12:1-2

resurrected into a New Heaven and a New Earth (Revelation 21:1-2). Those who've followed Jesus will enter an eternal existence that will be absolutely glorious! As Paul teased, "That is what the Scriptures mean when they say, "No eye has seen, no ear has heard, and no mind has imagined what God has prepared for those who love him" (I Corinthians 2:9 NLT). The details of our future existence are obscure, but we know enough to be eagerly anticipating Christ's return (See: Mark 8:38; I Corinthians 6:2; 15:58; Galatians 6:9)

THE SUMMARY:

We believe in the return of our Lord Jesus Christ (See: John 14:3; Acts 1:11; Hebrews 9:28). The resurrection of Jesus is the basis for our belief that all of humanity will be resurrected in the final day of Judgment. When our Lord returns, a resurrection of both the just and the unjust will occur (See: John 5:28-29; Acts 24:15; I Thessalonians 4:14-18). The just are those who have been made right by trusting in the sacrifice of Jesus Christ on the cross (See: Romans 5:1, 9; Galatians 3:13). The just will be bodily resurrected unto eternal life; the unjust will be bodily resurrected unto eternal death and separation from the Father (See: Revelation 20:5-6,12-15).

BIBLE STUDY [Answer the following questions to enhance your learning.]

List a short summary of the seven things the resurrection of Jesus should do for the believer based on I Corinthians 15.

It's understandable that we focus on what the resurrection means for me personally, but summarize the significance of resurrection of Jesus for creation?

What was the most significant thing you learned in this section?

Pray over what you've learned in this lesson. Write out a summarizing prayer below.

MEMORY VERSE:

"For I delivered to you as of first importance what I also received: that Christ died for our sins in accordance with the Scriptures, that he was buried, that he was raised on the third day in accordance with the Scriptures, and that he appeared to Cephas, then to the twelve. Then he appeared to more than five hundred brothers at one time, most of whom are still alive, though some have fallen asleep."

-I Corinthians 15:3-6 (ESV)

FOR FURTHER RESOURCES ON THIS TOPIC:

Don Thorsen. An Exploration of Christian Theology. Grand Rapids: Baker Academic, 2010. (Ch. 27)

N.T. Wright, Surprised by Hope: Rethinking Heaven, the Resurrection, and the Mission of the Church. New York: HarperOne, 2014.

LESSON #8: The Church

Church Church planting is hard work! I know from experience. Our church has been at it for almost 15 years. The Church at Lake Mead is a miracle story of God's grace and provision. It was a dream long before it became reality.

I remember being in a grocery store parking lot, talking on the phone to Eddie McGath in Florida, trying to convince him to come out here to start a church. Pastor Mike and I had been working with my mom and other teachers to provide Bible studies for interested families that had students in Lake Mead Christian Academy.

We had another teacher, Jeremy Goad, who was good with a guitar and was already acting as a youth pastor to many of the students. So as I saw it, we had a church staff ready to go. The only problem was none of us knew what to do next! That's why I was on the phone with Eddie. He was much older and more experienced than the rest of us. He'd actually pastored a church for two whole years! Wow! I know what you're thinking, and I agree, none of us really knew what we were getting into.

Looking back over these years, church planting has been incredibly important and rewarding work. Church work is connected to the up and down rhythms of life. Some days we're walking with a family suffering through difficult times. Other days, we're celebrating weddings and baby dedications. Through it all, we get a front row seat as we watch Jesus transform our lives and the lives of people in our church. One of the things I cherish most is the strong Jesus-centered community that has grown here. There's more to do and there's much more transformation Christ wants to do in our Church, but I am so excited about what God has already accomplished!

So as we get into today's lesson, I want to ask some important questions: 1.) What is the church? 2.) What does the Bible teach about church? 3.) Why is going to church so important? 4). And finally, what are the marks of a healthy church community?

What Is the Church?

As we get started answering the first question, it is important to note that Jesus came up with the idea of the church—it all started with him (See: Matthew 16:18; 18:17)! As Jesus ministered in and around Palestine, a group of devoted followers gradually grew around him. Some he called to follow him. Others asked if they could join. And while all were welcomed, all were given the same requirement: total surrender to Jesus (See: Luke 14:25-32).

It's also clear Jesus expected his disciples to love and treat one another in the exact same way he had loved them (See: John 13:34-35, 15:12; 17:1, 21). So if we're going to study what the Church is supposed to be like, we must begin by looking at three important features of the early Jesus movement itself.

First, the Jesus movement was shockingly egalitarian. When Jesus launched his Church, human society was hopelessly stratified. Rigid divisions existed between men and women, rich and poor, slave and free, Jew and Gentile, Roman and barbarian. Everywhere one looked, people were divided and segregated. The Jesus movement was radically different. Jesus intentionally welcomed social outcasts (called "sinners") into his fellowship. Rich, poor, men and women were equally invited to follow him. This was utterly unique in Jewish culture!

Yet when we look closely at the descriptions of the crowds listening to Jesus (see: Luke 15:1-2), the people sharing meals with Jesus (compare Luke 7:36-50 to Luke 19:5-10), or types of people elevated as examples of faith by Jesus (see: Luke 7:44-48; 8:45-48; 10:25-36; 16:19-31; 21:1-4), we see earth-shattering social equality. He was just as likely to publicly praise the faith of a prostitute, as he was to encourage the honest questions of a religious leader (Compare Luke 7:47-48 to Mark 12:34). Men and women were equally invited to "sit at his feet" and learn (Luke 8:1-3; 10:38-41).[59]

Second, the early Jesus movement was completely centered on Jesus himself.

> And he said to all, "If anyone would come after me, let him deny himself and take up his cross daily and follow me. For whoever would save his life will lose it, but whoever loses his life for my sake will save it.
>
> - Luke 9:23-24 (ESV)

KING OF KINGS

As we saw in the lesson on the resurrection, his disciples came to understand Jesus as their long awaited Jewish king. He had ushered in God's kingdom. So their relationship to him is best understood in terms of allegiance to a king. Jesus was "master" (See: John 13:13-16); they were "servants" (See: Luke 6:46; John 15:15). But Jesus was a radically different kind of master! This leads us to our last distinctive feature of the Jesus movement.

Third, Jesus taught that leadership in his kingdom was "upside down." He famously taught that the first would be last, and that the greatest among them would be a servant to all (See: Matthew 23:11; Luke 22:24-27; John 13:15). These weren't just words—he lived servant leadership.[60] In fact, just before his death, Jesus gathered his disciples and completely redefined power and leadership with a final, powerful object lesson.

> When he had washed their feet and put on his outer garments and resumed his place, he said to them, "Do you understand what I have done to you? You call me Teacher and Lord, and you are right, for so I am. If I then, your Lord and Teacher, have washed your feet, you also ought to wash one another's feet. For I have given you an example, that you also should do just as I have done to you.
>
> -John 13:12-15 (ESV)

59.The careful reader may have noticed that many of the references that support Jesus' special care for the marginalized are from the book of Luke. It seems that one of Luke's special concerns was to demonstrate Jesus' inclusion of all, especially women. This highlights a fact about the ancient gospel-biographies themselves. Each gospel presents the life and ministry of Jesus from slightly different angles, perhaps intended for different audiences and written around different important themes. Luke, for example, has given special care to present Jesus as the "savior of the world" including the commoner and minority. Luke's message: "Everyone is welcomed to become Jesus' disciple!"

60.For a fascinating study that demonstrates Jesus of Nazareth introduced humility as a virtue see: Dickson, John Humilitas: A Lost Key to Life, Love, and Leadership. (Grand Rapids, Zondervan) 2011.

After this stunning display of humility and love, Jesus shocked his followers with one final command:

> A new commandment I give to you, that you love one another: just as I have loved you, you also are to love one another. By this all people will know that you are my disciples, if you have love for one another.
>
> -John 13:34-5 (ESV)

These features of the Jesus movement: radical social egalitarianism, Jesus as Lord of Heaven and Earth, and servant-leadership had a profound impact on the shape and development of the early Church.

After the resurrection and ascension of Jesus, the Holy Spirit fell and the church was born. The disciples of Jesus spilled on to the streets of Jerusalem boldly preaching Jesus' resurrection. That first day over 3,000 people were baptized (See: Acts 2:41)! Now the Jesus movement was transformed. No longer was Jesus directly leading. It was Spirit-filled men and women who were preaching and teaching, prophesying and healing all in Jesus' name. Leadership had been transferred to imperfect humans. Yet with all of its missteps and mistakes, the Jewish Jesus movement slowly flowered into the global Christian Church. Now, 2,000 years later, the radical seeds that Jesus planted continue to transform our world!

The Church's Role in Our Life

As we noted earlier, the disciples traveled beyond Jerusalem and started churches throughout the Roman Empire. The letters written to these churches preserved in the New Testament give us a solid foundation for the role that church should play in a believer's life today. Here are three important truths about the role of the church. These truths answer our last three questions: What does the Bible teach about church? Why is going to church so important? And what are the marks of a healthy church community?

First, in the New Testament letters, disciples of Jesus are pictured as members of a "body." Paul wrote: "Now you are the body of Christ and individually members of it" (I Corinthians 12:27). Earlier, in this passage, Paul taught that each individual disciple of Jesus is given special "spiritual gifts" that contribute to the "common good" of the body (See: I Corinthians 12:4-11; See also: Romans 12:3-6). Today, it's common to find Christians who do not regularly attend a church body, much less use their gifts in service to that body. This was unheard of in the New Testament. Each Jesus follower should be connected to a local church and using their spiritual gifts.

Second, the Church is regularly described as a spiritual family. Throughout the New Testament, family terms like brothers, sisters, fathers and mothers are used. This underscores the new social arrangement that the church of Jesus provided. In the ancient world, regardless of how one was known outside the church, inside they were family. Again, this reflects the way Jesus treated his followers. The radical egalitarianism Jesus offered was reflected in the early church. Sadly, these values haven't always persisted throughout history. The lessons of equality and servant leadership that Jesus taught have been difficult to hold on to. Even as Martin Luther King Jr. tragically observed in 1963, "At 11:00 on Sunday morning... we stand at the most segregated hour in this nation." It is obvious we still have much to learn and overcome in living out Jesus' vision for the church. Difficulties notwithstanding, the church should be a diverse spiritual family welcoming every believer.

Finally, the New Testament assumed that the church provides vital spiritual leadership and biblical instruction for all believers. Paul stated that God appoints leaders in the church.

> Now you are the body of Christ and individually members of it. And God has appointed in the church first apostles, second prophets, third teachers, then miracles, then gifts of healing, helping, administrating, and various kinds of tongues.
>
> - I Corinthians 12:27-28 (ESV)

When Paul addressed a young pastor who was planting a church, he reminded him, "This is why I left you in Crete, so that you might put what remained into order, and appoint elders in every town as I directed you."

> - Titus 1:5 (ESV).

Peter was addressing church leaders when he wrote,

> Shepherd the flock of God that is among you, exercising oversight, not under compulsion, but willingly, as God would have you; not for shameful gain, but eagerly; ³not domineering over those in your charge, but being examples to the flock.
>
> - I Peter 5:2-3 (ESV)

Paul clearly outlined the job of spiritual leadership in the church. He wrote,

> And he gave the apostles, the prophets, the evangelists, the shepherds and teachers, to equip the saints for the work of ministry, for building up the body of Christ, until we all attain to the unity of the faith and of the knowledge of the Son of God, to mature manhood, to the measure of the stature of the fullness of Christ, so that we may no longer be children, tossed to and fro by the waves and carried about by every wind of doctrine, by human cunning, by craftiness in deceitful schemes.
>
> - Ephesians 4:11-14 (ESV)

As these passages indicate, the church must be a place where Christians are under spiritual leadership and protection from false teaching and the enemy's schemes (See: Matthew 18:17-20; I Corinthians 5:4-5,12). As a pastor, I've sadly witnessed the ruin that happens to a believer's faith when they stop connecting to a local church.

Today, the church Jesus established exists in every nation on Earth. While there are still some who have never heard, the spread and influence of Jesus is larger than any other religious movement on the planet. For the Jesus follower, church is not optional. It's to provide believers a place to use their spiritual gifts. It's to be a diverse spiritual family nurturing and growing believers and fostering spiritual leadership to train and protect. It isn't perfect. And the history of the church is marked by both progress and regress, incredible love and regrettable hate. But for all her flaws and defects, the Church remains the hope of the world. For it is in and through the church of Jesus that the Spirit of God is doing His eternal work of rescue and redemption. Later in the book, we'll talk in more detail about our connection to Christian community.

THE SUMMARY:

Our church's statement of faith summarizes this lesson nicely: "We believe in the spiritual unity of believers in our Lord Jesus Christ (Romans 8:9; II Corinthians 12:12-13; Galatians 3:26-28). We believe in one holy universal church (Romans 12:5; Ephesians 4:4-6)." The Church is a vital community for Christian growth and unity.

BIBLE STUDY [Answer the following questions to enhance your learning.]

List a short summary of the distinctive features of the early Jesus movement.

Which of these features did you find most interesting and why?

List a short summary of the distinctive features of the Church that were listed in this section.

Which of these features did you find most interesting and why?

What was the most significant thing you learned in this section?

Pray over what you've learned in this lesson. Write out a summarizing prayer below.

MEMORY VERSE:

"A new commandment I give to you, that you love one another: just as I have loved you, you also are to love one another."

-John 13:34 (ESV)

FOR FURTHER RESOURCES ON THIS TOPIC:

Dietrich Bonhoeffer. Life Together. New York: Harper & Row, 1954.

Scot McKnight. Fellowship of Differents. Grand Rapids: Zondervan, 2016.

Don Thorsen. An Exploration of Christian Theology. Grand Rapids: Baker Academic. 2010, (Ch. 24)

LESSON #9: Community Practices

This is the last lesson in our first section. Congratulations for getting this far! As you finish this lesson, I want to encourage you to take a spiritual inventory of all that you've learned in the previous weeks of study. Today, we're going to talk about Christian baptism and communion. If you've never been baptized, it is our prayer that after this lesson you'd feel informed, confident and ready to make that decision.

So let's dive in. There are two church practices that we celebrate today that trace their origin back to the first century: Baptism and Communion. Both traditions reinforce the family ties of the Church. Both serve as different ways to remember our connection to Jesus and to each other. And both involve physical actions that mediate spiritual realities into our lives as Jesus followers.

Baptism

Before Jesus entered the scene publicly, John the Baptizer was already calling Israel to repentance and baptism (See: Matthew 3:1-2; Mark 1:2-8; Luke 3:2-3; John 1:6, 19-28). As people came confessing their sins and receiving baptism out in the Judean wilderness, John's preaching and ministry presented a clear rival to the Jewish Temple system. After all, the Temple, not the Jordan River, was the place for Israel to find forgiveness and offer confession.

Understandably, John's activity caused quite a stir among the Jewish religious leadership (See: Matthew 3:7-12). As his movement gained more followers, clashes with the religious establishment became more common. Eventually, John's preaching got him killed (See: Matthew 14:1-12; Mark 14:1-5; Luke 3:19-20), but the clash with the Jewish leaders didn't end there. In fact, things were just getting warmed up. As John said of himself, he was only the forerunner of the One who would be the Lamb of God (See: John 1:29).

This gives us the context for how baptism was understood in the first century. It was an initiation and identification. It was a public act of allegiance with John's message—Israel needed renewal; the temple was corrupt. So, when Jesus entered the baptismal waters, it would have been seen as an act of solidarity with John's message. But the story takes a turn. John tells Jesus that he should baptize him (See: Matthew 3:14)! As we know, Jesus wasn't another disciple coming for repentance but was, in fact, the fulfillment of everything John had been pointing to (See: Mark 1:3; Luke 1:17; John 1:30).

As the disciples later came to understand, Jesus had come to replace the Temple. He was the place of forgiveness. He was God's sacrificial lamb. His blood would be shed for their sin and his body broken for their salvation. Jesus' mission was to call Israel (and the larger world) to repentance and faith in him. He alone was the sacrifice for human sin. Jesus alone was the place where God and humanity could meet and be reconciled (See: 1 Timothy 2:5).

It's also significant that all four gospels record that it was at Jesus' baptism that the Holy Spirit descended upon him in bodily form (See: Matthew 3:16-17; Mark 1:10; Luke 3:21-22; John 1:31-33). It was there Jesus' true identity was announced as "the Lamb of God who takes away the sin of the world" (See: John 1:29) and "the beloved son" (See: Matthew 3:17; Mark 1:11; Luke 3:22). You could say, it was at his baptism that everything got started.

After Jesus' baptism, John continued his ministry until he was killed by Herod a year or so later. However, as Jesus started his ministry his disciples had begun baptizing new followers as well (See: John 4:1-3). So, baptism continued to play an important role even after John's death. It seems to have always been the way people connected to the Jesus movement.

Baptism's significance is further underscored after Jesus' death and resurrection.[61] As Jesus gathered his disciples together for the last time, he gave explicit instructions about what to do next. Once again, baptism was to play an important role.

> And Jesus came and said to them, "All authority in heaven and on earth has been given to me. [19]Go therefore and make disciples of all nations, baptizing them in the name of the Father and of the Son and of the Holy Spirit, [20]teaching them to observe all that I have commanded you. And behold, I am with you always, to the end of the age.
>
> - Matthew 28:18-20 (ESV)

As Jesus followers took the message of salvation to the streets of Jerusalem, baptism continued to be the identifier for all new disciples. Notice what happened immediately after Peter preached his first public message in Jerusalem,

> Brothers, what shall we do?" And Peter said to them, "Repent and be baptized every one of you in the name of Jesus Christ for the forgiveness of your sins, and you will receive the gift of the Holy Spirit.
> - Acts 2:37-38 (ESV)

After this sermon, we're told that 3,000 people were baptized and became a part of the Jerusalem church (See: Acts 2:41-47). This pattern repeats throughout in the book of Acts: the disciples preach, people repent, confess allegiance to Jesus and get baptized (See: Acts 8:12; 8:34-39; 9:18; 10:48; 16:14-15; 16:31-34; 18:8; 19:2-7; 22:14-16).

Today, baptism continues to play this function. Simply put: Jesus followers get baptized. It's what Jesus commanded, and it's how we're initiated into God's family (See: Galatians 3:26-29). Baptism has always been the universal identifier for disciples of Jesus for nearly 2000 years! Notice what Paul said about baptism in his letter to the Romans. He wrote,

> Do you not know that all of us who have been baptized into Christ Jesus were baptized into his death? We were buried therefore with him by baptism into death, in order that, just as Christ was raised from the dead by the glory of the Father, we too might walk in newness of life. For if we have been united with him in a death like his, we shall certainly be united with him in a resurrection like his.
>
> - Romans 6:4-6 (ESV)

---

61. As scholar Douglas Moo observes, "Baptism, then, is not the place, or time, at which we are buried with Christ, but the instrument (dia) through which we are buried with him."- Douglas J. Moo, The Epistle to the Romans, New International Commentary on the New Testament. Accordance electronic ed. (Grand Rapids: Eerdmans, 1996), p. 364.

Baptism joins us to Christ's death, burial and resurrection. Of course, baptism is meaningless apart from Christian faith and that's why baptism alone doesn't save or justify the believer. However, Paul was arguing here that baptism is a powerful spiritual event in a Jesus follower's life. To those of us raised in the West, it might be difficult to understand how certain rites would carry spiritual power, but it's clear that is what Paul was saying. So, while we might not fully understand why or how immersion in water joins us to the work of Christ on the cross, it does. This is why baptism is essential, and we can't ignore it.

Communion

Just before Jesus died, he celebrated one final Passover meal with his disciples (See: Matthew 26:17-29; Mark 14:12-25; Luke 22:14-23; John 13). The Passover meal was highly significant for the Jewish people, as it commemorated their national freedom from slavery in Egypt (See: Exodus 12:1-26). This would have been similar to our 4th of July celebrations.

However, in Jesus' day, Israel hardly had anything to celebrate. They weren't free. Another foreign power, in a long string of foreign powers, was ruling over them. So for many Jews, the Passover meal generated mixed emotions as they reflected on a time when God had delivered Israel. What many couldn't see at the time is that Jesus had come to do exactly that (See: Luke 4:16-21; John 8:31-38; 1 Corinthians 5:7)! His death would bring freedom, not from Rome, but from sin and death itself.

So, during this last supper, Jesus told his disciples that this meal would now be transformed. This wasn't the first time Jesus reoriented a Jewish symbol around himself and mission, but this was perhaps the most powerful.[62] The bread and wine of the Passover meal would now represent his body and blood. And after his death, whenever they broke bread and shared wine, they were to remember it was his body and blood that was shed for their freedom. Notice what Jesus said,

And he took a cup, and when he had given thanks he said, "Take this, and divide it among yourselves. [18]For I tell you that from now on I will not drink of the fruit of the vine until the kingdom of God comes." [19]And he took bread, and when he had given thanks, he broke it and gave it to them, saying, "This is my body, which is given for you. Do this in remembrance of me." [20]And likewise the cup after they had eaten, saying, "This cup that is poured out for you is the new covenant in my blood.

- Luke 22:17-22 (ESV)

---

62. Throughout Jesus' ministry, he provocatively reoriented Israel's national symbols around himself and movement. He intentionally set himself up as a new Moses whose mission was to lead a new Israel to new freedom. In other ways, Jesus embodied the nation of Israel itself. For instance: his baptism symbolized Israel's crossing the Red Sea, his 40 days of testing in the wilderness, repeated Israel's 40 years in the same wilderness. Further, Jesus gathered 12 disciples around him (later known simply as "the Twelve") and Israel was comprised of 12 tribes. Jesus "was" Moses and the nation of Israel, with one significant difference: He remained faithful to YHWH [Yahweh] (the formal name for Israel's God) and to Israel's covenant with Yahweh. Jesus didn't fail in the wilderness temptation, and he didn't fail at the cross! Whereas, the Old Testament records Israel's repeatedly failures (see: Exodus 34-36; Numbers 11; 14; 16; 25), Jesus was faithful. He became the "Suffering Servant" of Isaiah 53 and took the full consequence of Israel's (and humanity's) rebellion and idolatry. Jesus is our Champion who represented Israel (and humanity) perfectly and was victorious.

There is no good trying to be more spiritual than God. God never meant man to be a purely spiritual creature. That is why He uses material things like bread and wine to put the new life into us. We may think this rather crude and unspiritual. God does not: He invented eating. He likes matter. He invented it.[63]

So when we celebrate communion in our churches, we're performing a powerful spiritual act. Communion brings us together as disciples. We're corporately remembering Jesus' body and blood as we eat and drink together (See: Acts 20:28; I Corinthians 6:20; 7:23). And yet communion is even more than just remembering. Like baptism, it's a powerful spiritual act that joins us to Jesus. There's mystery here to be sure, but what is clear is that communion unleashes new grace in our lives for his service.

Both baptism and communion are important community practices that reinforce our connection to our church family. Christianity isn't just about believing certain things. It's about doing things as well. Baptism and communion visibly declare invisible realities. They're to be done within the spiritual family of the church and remind us of our need for each other in our journey as a Jesus follower. So, next time you witness a baptism or participate in a communion service, consider the deeper, spiritual reality happening in front of you. Grace is pouring out. Heaven and earth are meeting as the church gathers in Jesus' name!

THE SUMMARY:

Christian baptism is the immersion of a believer in water in the name of the Father, the Son, and the Holy Spirit. Baptism is the public declaration of the believer's allegiance to King Jesus. It's a vital spiritual moment that joins the believer with the crucified, buried and risen Savior (See: Romans 6:3-6; Colossians 2:12). The old life of sin is gone and the new life as a disciple of Jesus Christ begins (See: Matthew 28:19-20; Acts 2:38-42; Romans 6:1-11).

Communion is an act of obedience whereby followers of Christ, through partaking of the bread and the fruit of the vine, remember the death of Jesus and his victory over Satan, sin and death. In celebrating the Lord's Supper, we anticipate, in faith, his victorious second coming and the consummation of all creation under his rule (See: Luke 22:14-21; I Corinthians 10:16; 11:23-26).

---

63. Lewis, C. S. Mere Christianity. (New York, Harper Collins), 1952 p. 63-64

BIBLE STUDY [Answer the following questions to enhance your learning.]

How did the earliest disciples view baptism?

What was the reason John gave for why he was baptizing in the wilderness? (You may need to look up these passages to find out: Matthew 3:1-2; Mark 1:2-8; Luke 3:2-3; John 1:6, 19-28.)

What was the pattern that is evident in the book of Acts regarding baptism?

Explain the original significance of the Jewish feast of passover. (Consult Exodus 12:1-26 if needed).

Read I Corinthians 11:17-34. There was disunity and a lack of love for each member in the Corinthian church, how was this church misusing the "Lord's supper?" (Notice v. 21-22). How did Paul want the Corinthians to address this problem? (Notice v. 28-34).

BONUS QUESTION:

Read the footnote in this section about how Jesus reworked the story of Israel around himself and his movement. Which of the national symbols did you find most interesting? If you are familiar with the Bible, can you think of any other things Jesus did that implied his identity and mission?

MEMORY VERSE:

"And when he had given thanks, he broke it, and said, "This is my body, which is for you. Do this in remembrance of me."

- I Corinthians 11:24 (ESV)

FOR FURTHER RESOURCES ON THIS TOPIC:

Don Thorsen. An Exploration of Christian Theology. Grand Rapids: Baker Academic, 2010. (Ch. 26)

THOUGHTS & REFLECTIONS:

Take some time to do a spiritual inventory. Have you made any Spiritual commitments? Are you ready to take any significant steps in your walk with Jesus? Write these out and discuss them with someone.

FOLLOWING JESUS

As we said in the beginning of this book, it all starts with saying "Yes" to Jesus. When we say "Yes", his power is unleashed in our lives. The earliest disciples started to experience this when they decided to respond to Jesus' invitation, "follow me." Jesus was on the move and life on earth would never be the same.

Jesus always lived with the Father's ultimate mission in his mind (See: Luke 19:10; John 8:29). His life was always moving toward that direction. As Jesus followed his Father, his disciples followed him. It's the same for us now. As we follow Jesus, we're joining the Father's great work of redemption. We're invited to join Him in His work and to see, "His Kingdom come and his will done on Earth as it is in Heaven" (See: Matthew 6:10; John 15:1-8). As we'll learn in this section, following Jesus matures us so his mission can be accomplished through us (See: Philippians 2:13).

Unfortunately, many believe Jesus came to simply take us to "Heaven" when we die. This has caused people to think that the Christian life is simply about believing certain things and then going on with life as normal. For them, Jesus is a sort of "insurance policy" for things to be OK when they die.

This isn't why Jesus came. And this isn't what following Jesus can be reduced to! As we said in the introduction of this book, Jesus called us to "take up our crosses daily and follow him" (See: Luke 9:23). His only offer is total surrender. And when this happens, changes start to take place in our lives. Notice how Paul talked about these changes,

...Do you not know that the unrighteous will not inherit the kingdom of God? Do not be deceived: neither the sexually immoral, nor idolaters, nor adulterers, nor men who practice homosexuality, [10]nor thieves, nor the greedy, nor drunkards, nor revilers, nor swindlers will inherit the kingdom of God. [11]And such were some of you. But you were washed, you were sanctified, you were justified in the name of the Lord Jesus Christ and by the Spirit of our God.

- I Corinthians 6:9-11 (ESV)

In this second part of the book, we want to take a look at the life of a Jesus follower. What does it really look like to say "yes" in everyday life? At first glance, following Jesus can seem difficult, and there is some truth there. Following Jesus isn't always easy. But as we'll learn, it's his love that motivates us and transforms us. He doesn't force us into saying "yes." As we follow Jesus, we begin to see that the changes he wants to make in our lives are always for our good and his glory. It's been often said, God takes us just as we are, but He loves us too much to leave us that way.

We'll cover practical things like how we should pray, read our Bible, and how to hear God's voice in our lives. We'll study how God develops Christ-like character in our lives and how to have victory over our sinful nature. This process of growing in holiness is called "sanctification." And that's God's ultimate purpose for us—to become just like Jesus (See: Romans 8:29; I Peter 2:21). May God bless you as you begin.

LESSON #10: Transforming Love (Part I)

My My wife and I earned a Master's degree in "Disney Princess Studies" as we've raised our three girls. As a boy growing up, I didn't pay much attention to the Princess stories. But now that I've been forced to watch them over and over (and over) again as an adult, I've realized how much I missed (insert sarcasm here).

All kidding aside, I must admit, as I've watched each of the stories, the life-lessons woven into the narratives and plot lines are worthwhile. And while some of the princesses show more character than others, and for some reason nearly all of them have mommy-issues, the story of The Beauty and the Beast is truly remarkable.

The story begins with a spoiled wealthy prince who shows terrible unkindness to a disguised enchantress. He is cursed for his deed and so is transformed into a beast (because that is what he truly is on the inside). The only way for the Beast to break his curse is for the prince to learn true love and find love in return. All this must happen before his 21st birthday or his curse is permanent.

After some time passes, an old man seeking shelter during a terrible storm finds the enchanted castle. The Beast's servants show compassion and let him in. But when the Beast finds out, he's furious. Still a "Beast", the prince imprisons the old man for trespassing. Eventually, the old man's horse finds its way home, alerting his beautiful daughter, Belle, that something terrible has happened.

After a frantic search, Belle finds the castle. She quickly learns that the Beast is holding her father prisoner and the only way to save him is to take his place. And so the beautiful young Belle does just that! Before her father could stop her, she trades herself and becomes the beast's new prisoner.

Belle's sacrificial love for her father begins to have a transforming effect on the cursed prince. Over the next days and weeks, the Beast's interactions with Belle show him the true depth of his selfishness and pride. Slowly, his heart begins to open. And to his surprise, he discovers that he genuinely cares for her.

Then the story takes a turn. Belle learns that her father is once again in danger. She needs to be set free or her father will die. But what she doesn't know is that the Beast's birthday is drawing near, and after this, his curse will be permanent. The Beast knows Belle is his only chance to break the curse, but he also knows he can't keep her his prisoner. So, he does what would have been unimaginable weeks earlier, he sets her free. He forfeits his future for hers. You can watch the movie for how all of this plays out (I know you want to!), but the important truth we can learn from this story is: Love transforms the human heart.

What I love about that story is that it mirrors the story of God. In fact, that's why I think we love, love stories. Every love story is an echo of the great story God is writing. The entire cosmos declares His love. At two points in The Beauty and The Beast, we see sacrificial love—Belle for her father and the Beast for Belle. We learn true love can't be forced. Coercion and love can't coexist. It was the Beast's love for Belle that compelled him to set her free even at great personal cost. This mirrors how God made us.

In love, He created us, giving us freedom. Yet this freedom provides the opportunity to rebel or obey. And as we've seen in the previous lessons, humanity chose to rebel. And we've suffered the awful consequences of life without God ever since!

But then Love came. The Apostle Paul wrote about it beautifully,

> Once we, too, were foolish and disobedient. We were misled and became slaves to many lusts and pleasures. Our lives were full of evil and envy, and we hated each other. But— When God our Savior revealed his kindness and love, He saved us, not because of the righteous things we had done, but because of his mercy. He washed away our sins, giving us a new birth and new life through the Holy Spirit.
>
> - Titus 3:3-5 (ESV)

Jesus was the embodiment of God's love (See: Romans 5:8-10; Ephesians 2:4-5; 1 John 4:7-10). And when we look at the relationship that Jesus had with his disciples, we see that his love profoundly transformed their lives.

Every time I read the   gospel of John, I imagine the author, now an old man sitting down to write about things that happened decades before. But even then as he's writing, his emotions still overwhelm him. Notice how John introduced the final hours of Jesus' life. "Now before the Feast of the Passover, when Jesus knew that his hour had come to depart out of this world to the Father, having loved his own who were in the world, he loved them to the end" (John 13:1-2 ESV).

Did you catch it? As John turned the reader's attention to the events leading to the cross, he reminisced. He couldn't help but comment on the powerful way Jesus loved! The years he spent with Jesus had forever changed him. Jesus' love transformed him.

Actually, one of the most striking examples of this special love relationship is found in a conversation that happened after the crucifixion of Jesus. Before we look at it, we need to get some context. At the last Passover meal, Jesus suddenly turned to his disciples and announced that every one of them would abandon him that very night.

It's clear that the disciples didn't quite understand (See: Mark 9:32; Luke 18:31-34). But Peter spoke up, "Though they all fall away because of you, I will never fall away" (Matthew 26:34 ESV). Jesus then gave Peter the sorry news. His defection would be the worst. He would even deny knowing Jesus three times before the rooster's crowing that next morning.

As the evening events played out, Peter did in fact deny knowing Jesus (See: Matthew 26:69-75; Mark 13:66-72; Luke 22:54-62; John 18:15-18, 25-27). After Jesus was crucified and was raised again, we can only imagine Peter's self-loathing as he remembered his foolish boast that fateful night (See: Luke 22:33).

But that isn't how the story ends. Thankfully, John recorded one final conversation between Peter and Jesus after these horrible events. The disciples had returned to Galilee as Jesus instructed them (See again: Matthew 26:32; also Matthew 28:7). They hadn't seen the resurrected Jesus for a while and not knowing what to do next, Peter announced that he was going back to fishing (John 21:3). So, the others joined him. They worked all night but didn't catch anything. However, early in the morning a solitary figure on the shore called out to them asking if they had any fish. They answered no. Then the person on the shore said that they should throw their net on the other side (See: John 21:6). To their astonishment, their net was soon filled with fish.

It was Jesus! And even more significant for Peter, this was exactly what Jesus did three years earlier just before he invited Peter to follow him (See: Luke 5:1-11). Now we come to the conversation I mentioned earlier.

> When they had finished breakfast, Jesus said to Simon Peter, "Simon, son of John, do you love me more than these?" He said to him, "Yes, Lord; you know that I love you." He said to him, "Feed my lambs." He said to him a second time, "Simon, son of John, do you love me?" He said to him, "Yes, Lord; you know that I love you." He said to him, "Tend my sheep." He said to him the third time, "Simon, son of John, do you love me?" Peter was grieved because he said to him the third time, "Do you love me?" and he said to him, "Lord, you know everything; you know that I love you." Jesus said to him, "Feed my sheep.
>
> - John 21:15-17 (ESV)

There are several remarkable things about this conversation. First, Jesus uncharacteristically addressed Peter very formally. "Simon, Son of John..." I think this sets a serious tone for their conversation. But then somewhat surprisingly, Jesus simply wanted to know if Peter "loves" him. Evidently, love was a dead serious topic for Jesus. Peter replied, "Yes, Lord; you know that I love you." Then Jesus told him to, "Feed my lambs." Then, again a surprise, Jesus asked Peter the same question two more times. Many believe Jesus asked three times because Peter denied three times and that's probably right. However, what's truly fascinating isn't how many times Jesus asked the question. Rather, it's the question itself.

Do you love me? What a powerful question! But in that setting, it's so unexpected. Consider what other questions Jesus could have asked Peter that morning? Maybe, "Hey Peter, do you now know who I am!?!" This would have been appropriate given what had happened. After all, Peter had failed to acknowledge that he knew him that awful night. Or perhaps, Jesus could have asked, "Peter, are you sorry!?!" Once again Jesus would have been justified——he was owed an apology. No doubt Peter's shame and guilt had made it difficult for him to even speak to Jesus. Or maybe worst of all, Jesus could have just launched into how his failure had disqualified him from any future leadership. But Jesus didn't do any of that. He ignored all of it. He simply asked, "Do you love me?"

Of all of the things that could be said at that critical moment, all Jesus wanted to know was, "Peter, do you love me?" Why? Because the love relationship between Peter and Jesus was the only thing Jesus cared about. He had always loved Peter. But now their relationship was broken, and he wanted to know Peter's next move. Was he going to run? Or would he let the fierce love of God melt away his shame? Sometimes we choose to hide even if we know hiding is just as terrible as facing the shame. Sometimes we just don't feel worthy of love.

But there's something else even more profound about this question. If you think about it, this question actually opened Jesus up to Peter rejecting him once more. When Jesus reached out and asked Peter, "do you love me?", he was extending his heart. We usually only ask that question of people we love, and when we do, we risk their rejection. So, in Peter's greatest moment of shame, Jesus reached out to him with radical vulnerable love. When he could have come to Peter in strength, rebuking him for his failure, he extended his heart.

One final point from this passage. Jesus wasn't just content to restore Peter, but wanted to give him a whole new life-calling. As you'll notice, Peter started that day a fisherman but ended it a shepherd. Consider again exactly what Jesus said to Peter, the order is important. 1.) "Do you love me?" 2.) "Yes, Lord." 3.) "Feed my sheep." You see for Jesus, love precedes performance. Jesus wasn't going to give Peter a new responsibility until he knew his heart. This is the same for us, our relationship with God comes before the work we do for God. Jesus wants his love to transform us so profoundly that everything we do flows from that love relationship.

Jesus explicitly said this in another place when he was speaking to all the disciples, "If you love me, you will keep my commandments." (John 14:15 ESV). Jesus followers love first, then obey. He wants our obedience to flow from our love for him, and not from a sense of obligation to him. So for a follower of Jesus when we struggle to obey or to deny ourselves, we must go back to the foundation of our discipleship—love (See: Revelation 2:4-5).

Jesus' leadership is radically different. Other leaders and kings demand allegiance from their servants. They use various means to control those who follow them. Instead, Jesus simply loved his disciples. He won their hearts; he didn't force himself into their lives. Notice carefully what Jesus said.

> This is my commandment, that you love one another as I have loved you. Greater love has no one than this, that someone lay down his life for his friends. You are my friends if you do what I command you. No longer do I call you servants, for the servant does not know what his master is doing; but I have called you friends, for all that I have heard from my Father I have made known to you.
>
> -John 15:12-15 (ESV)

83

Jesus extended genuine friendship to his followers. He was their leader, make no mistake, but he didn't choose to keep them at arm's length. He embraced them. He loved them. And it changed their lives.

This is the foundation of Christian discipleship—love for Jesus that motivates our love and service to others. He first loved us. He rescued us; now we belong to him. His love is kind and genuine. His love is complete and unconditional. When we fail, his love restores. When we find obedience difficult, his love motivates. When temptation to sin is strong, we can find that his love is stronger.

As the Apostle Paul put it once, "My old self has been crucified with Christ. It is no longer I who live, but Christ lives in me. So I live in this earthly body by trusting in the Son of God, who loved me and gave himself for me" (Galatians 2:20 NLT). Paul lived a difficult missionary life, but underneath it all was a white-hot love for the one who died for him. I can imagine Paul repeating those words often whenever following Jesus was difficult and costly. This too, must be our motivation. Jesus gave everything for us. We give everything for him!

THE SUMMARY:

The furious love of Jesus is what conquers us. It's the foundation of Christian discipleship. Our love relationship with Jesus is what everything else hinges upon. Before he leads us anywhere on this journey, he insists that we are rooted in his love. It was the love that he demonstrated for us that started this relationship, and it is our love for him that fuels our obedience. Everything starts and ends with love. You could summarize the entire journey of the Christian disciple as a life, birthed, matured and completed in love. Here's Christian maturity captured in a single sentence: Jesus' love has transformed me from a selfish beast into a new creation who is in the process of becoming Love.

BIBLE STUDY [Answer the following questions to enhance your learning.]

Reflect on "Transforming Love." Write a thoughtful reflection on the power of love to transform a human heart.

Why did Jesus lead with love? How did his leadership style compare with leaders in your life?

In what ways is it "risky" to lead the way Jesus did?

Read John 15:12-15. Write a paragraph as if you were explaining what Jesus was teaching here to a new believer.

What was the most significant thing you learned in this section?

Pray over what you've learned in this lesson. Write out a summarizing prayer below.

MEMORY VERSE:

"If you love me, you will keep my commandments."

- John 14:15 (ESV)

FOR FURTHER RESOURCES ON THIS TOPIC:

Clyde Cranford. Because We Love Him: Embracing a Life of Holiness. Sisters, OR: Multnomah Publishers, 2002.

LESSON #11: Transforming Love—Leads to Loving Well (Part 2)

One of my favorite moments of Jesus' recorded life is when Jesus received a dinner invitation from Simon, a religious Pharisee. In this culture, hospitality for travelers was customary. For Jesus to accept Simon's dinner invitation was an act of good-faith. Conversely, it would have been a great honor for Simon to host a rabbi like Jesus. What may be fascinating from our modern-day perspectives is that unlike the private dinners we have now in our culture, a dinner like this one would have been semi-public. Others from the community would have gathered just to listen to the conversation between these two religious teachers. (No one had Netflix to occupy their evenings!)

However, this dinner got controversial quickly. The problems actually began as soon as Jesus arrived. Luke wrote that when Jesus arrived at the house he simply "took his place at the table" (Luke 7:36 ESV). At first glance, this doesn't seem like anything significant. However, in a culture that highly valued hospitality, several important traditions were being neglected by Simon. It was a subtle signal to Jesus and others watching that Simon had not intended to pay Jesus respect as a rabbi. Interestingly, Jesus ignored these insults and simply seated himself.

As dinner was served, Simon's disrespect for Jesus became more apparent. Luke informed us throughout his gospel that the religious group to which Simon belonged, the Pharisees, constantly opposed Jesus and his message (See: Luke 5:15-24; 30; 6:1-10). Obviously, Jesus knew this going into the dinner. Perhaps, he hoped Simon would be different. Maybe Simon would be open to his message of love and forgiveness. Or maybe Jesus was demonstrating once again his willingness to open himself to ridicule in service to his Father's mission. Regardless, Jesus patiently endured Simon's disrespect.[64]

Now the story really gets interesting! Remember, I told you that this dinner would have been semi-public with other non-invited guests watching? Well, evidently a prostitute from that town was in the room that evening.

We're not told much about her, but we can imagine that she must have met Jesus earlier that day. We know this because Luke wrote that she had brought a flask of ointment to anoint Jesus' head (a customary way of showing great honor). The woman had obviously noticed how Simon was treating Jesus. One of Simon's subtle insults was that he had not appointed a servant to wash the feet of his invited guests. So when the woman saw Jesus' unwashed feet, she was overcome with emotion!

This prostitute began to weep. And what's more, her tears began to wet Jesus' feet (See: Luke 7:38). This gives us an idea of how near she was to the dinner table. What she did next was spontaneous. Seeing that her tears had landed on his dirty feet, she removed her hair pin and began to wipe his feet with her hair. Let's read how Luke recorded this:

---

64. It's impossible to know Simon's motives, maybe he had invited Jesus in order to straighten out this Galilean rabbi or perhaps use his position as host to disgrace Jesus and bring shame to his followers. While we can't be sure, it is interesting how many times the gospels note that Israel's religious leaders consider Jesus a friend to "sinners" in an effort to discredit him and his movement. (See: Matthew 9:9-13; 11:19; Luke 5:29-32; 7:33-34; 15:1-2

...she began to wet his feet with her tears and wiped them with the hair of her head and kissed his feet and anointed them with the ointment. Now when the Pharisee who had invited him saw this, he said to himself, "If this man were a prophet, he would have known who and what sort of woman this is who is touching him, for she is a sinner."

-Luke 7:38b-39 (ESV)

In Jewish culture, a woman's hair was always to be covered and veiled (See: I Corinthians 11:6). In fact, if a woman "let her hair down" in public it would have been seen as sexually suggestive. Yet here she was publicly wiping Jesus' feet with her hair and even kissing them for good measure!

This confirmed Simon's notions about Jesus. He must have been a fraud. If he were a prophet he would have known who this "sinner" was and certainly wouldn't have allowed this lavish and improper affection![65]

Here Jesus seized the moment to have some good fun with Simon and to make a serious point about the relationship between true faith and love. Up till this moment, he ignored Simon's insults and for the moment ignored the absolutely ridiculous exhibition happening at his feet. In a scene that would fit perfectly in a slapstick comedy, the text tells us that Jesus knew Simon's thoughts and addressed them directly.

He said, "Simon, I have something to say to you." The Pharisee, absurdly trying to pretend that dinner was going along normally, answered, "Say it, Teacher" (Luke 7:40 ESV). Then Jesus began to tell a story of two men who owed a lender two different sums of money. The first man owed over a year's wages, while the second owed a modest two months' worth. The creditor decided to forgive each man his debt. Then Jesus asked Simon, "Now which of them will love him more?" (Luke 7:42 ESV). Simon answered, "The one, I suppose, for whom he canceled the larger debt" (Luke 7:43 ESV).

Remember, all of this is happening while this "sinful" woman was washing and kissing Jesus' feet. Then Jesus said (and I've got to believe it was with a suppressed smile), "Do you see this woman?..." (Luke 7:44 ESV). I can only wonder if Jesus paused for just a second. Of course, he had seen this woman (along with everyone else at dinner)! He'd seen this woman and what Jesus had been allowing! But now the jig was up. Jesus had ignored Simon's insults, and he'd ignored the woman's lavish affection long enough. It was time to teach the real lesson that evening. Notice what Jesus said,

...When I entered your home, you didn't offer me water to wash the dust from my feet, but she has washed them with her tears and wiped them with her hair. 45You didn't greet me with a kiss, but from the time I first came in, she has not stopped kissing my feet. 46 You neglected the courtesy of olive oil to anoint my head, but she has anointed my feet with rare perfume.47"I tell you, her sins—and they are

---

65. Many of the cultural insights that I mention here are from the excellent book: Jesus Through Middle Eastern Eyes. by Kenneth E Baile (Downers Grove: Ill. InterVarsity Press Academic) 2008.

many——have been forgiven, so she has shown me much love. But a person who is forgiven little shows only little love." [48]Then Jesus said to the woman, "Your sins are forgiven.

- Luke 7:44-48 (NLT)

The stunning contrast between Simon's disrespect and the woman's lavish love provided Jesus the perfect opportunity to explain a profound spiritual truth: when we've really experienced God's love, it shows! The love we show reflects the forgiveness we've received. This works in both directions. If our pride blinds to our real need of God's forgiveness, that shows too. As Jesus' parable taught, when we foolishly believe our sins are small, we think we've been "forgiven little" and so we "love little." The size of our love reveals the true state of our heart. The point here is that true transformation only begins after a deep experience of God's amazing grace.

> "The love we show, reflects the forgiveness we've received."

The sinful woman in this story had experienced the shocking love of Jesus and that love transformed her. That night she showed up prepared to anoint Jesus with expensive oil. This was a lavish expression of love for the one who had first loved her us. Jesus saw this and told her, "Your sins are forgiven." (Luke 7:48 ESV). Don't miss the irony. She was the biggest sinner in the room and yet she was publicly elevated as the example of someone who loved well! Her love revealed her transformation.

This truth shows up in our relationships with others as well. I love others best when I'm aware of God's forgiveness most. Notice this powerful point John made,

> We love each other because he loved us first. If someone says, "I love God," but hates a fellow believer, that person is a liar; for if we don't love people we can see, how can we love God, whom we cannot see? And he has given us this command: Those who love God must also love their fellow believers.
>
> -1 John 4:19-21 (ESV)

John saw a connection here: Loved people, love people. When we experience the love of God, we love others! This became the foundation for perhaps the most difficult command Jesus ever gave his disciples——to love one's enemies. When Jesus told us we must love and forgive those who have hurt us (See: Matthew 19:25), it's not because they deserve it. They don't. It's because Jesus deserves it. Jesus' love for us is shocking. What he endured to secure our complete forgiveness from sin is beyond words. He deserves it.

Our Christian struggle is real! Unlearning years (or decades) of selfishness isn't easy. Yet, that is exactly what Jesus came to do. He came to completely transform us. He does this as we surrender to his love. He frees us from our slavery to sin and selfishness (See: John 8:34-36).

The Apostle Paul said that followers of Jesus are "new creations" (II Corinthians 5:17 ESV) and that "...

we all, with unveiled face, beholding the glory of the Lord, are being transformed into the same image [the image of Christ]" (II Corinthians 3:18). When Paul had heard reports of a church that had some defections from the gospel, he wrote with concern, "My little children, for whom I am again in the anguish of childbirth until Christ is formed in you!" (Galatians 4:19 ESV).

You see there's an expectation that disciples of Jesus experience a transformation that turns them into little copies of Christ. His image, his Spirit, is to be formed in the life of every believer. Luke recorded Jesus plainly teaching this. Jesus said, "A disciple is not above his teacher, but everyone when he is fully trained will be like his teacher" (Luke 6:40).

We are to go through training as disciples of Jesus. This training implies a process, a journey. It takes time to become "like Christ" (See: I Corinthians 11:1; Ephesians 5:1-2; I Thessalonians 1:6). Some things can happen quickly, other areas will take more time. But what's clear is that we don't instantly become "fully trained" disciples.

The rest of the lessons in this section are designed to break down this journey of discipleship into smaller, bite-sized lessons. However, it all starts with firmly anchoring ourselves in the transforming love of God as revealed in Jesus Christ. Sadly, it's easy to forget how much Christ has forgiven. It's too easy to become like Simon, and see others as "sinners" forgetting that we ourselves are in desperate need for God's forgiveness. We should never forget who we were before Love came. As Pastor Tim Keller put it, "We're far worse than we've ever imagined, but far more loved than we could ever realize."

THE SUMMARY: Learning to say "yes" to Jesus starts with love. We love well when it flows from a deep appreciation of all we've been forgiven. Sadly, it's easy to forget and to let prideful self-righteousness replace humble gratitude. The sinful woman at Simon's house taught everyone there how to love well. Her heart exploded in lavish love for the one who had rescued her. Whether we'd like to admit it or not, we're all just as sinful as that prostitute. It's only our pride that obscures that insight. And it's only our pride that keeps us from loving as she did! The foundation of our discipleship is captured by what the Apostle Paul said of himself: "Christ Jesus came into the world to save sinners—and I am the worst of them all" (I Timothy 1:15b). Clear-minded appreciation of the enormous debt that was paid for us serves to keep our love pure and our will surrendered.

BIBLE STUDY [Answer the following questions to enhance your learning.]

What was your favorite insight from the dinner at Simon's house?

Explain in your own words the spiritual law that Jesus taught Simon (and the rest of the dinner party) that night. Why is it so important to anchor your efforts to follow Jesus in his "transforming love?"

Why is it so important to anchor your efforts to follow Jesus in his "transforming love?"

What was the most significant thing you learned in this lesson?

Pray over what you've learned in this lesson. Write out a summarizing prayer below.

MEMORY VERSE:

"For God so loved the world, that he gave his only Son, that whoever believes in him should not perish but have eternal life. [17]For God did not send his Son into the world to condemn the world, but in order that the world might be saved through him."

- John 3:16-17 (ESV)

FOR FURTHER RESOURCES ON THIS TOPIC:

Clyde Cranford. Because We Love Him: Embracing a Life of Holiness. Sisters, Oregon: Multnomah Publishers, 2002.

LESSON #12: A Kingdom of Love

There is a scene in Mel Gibson's The Passion of the Christ that perfectly captures the epic conversation between Pilate and Jesus. After a sleepless night of cruel mocking and false accusation, the Jewish leadership brought Jesus to Pontius Pilate, the Roman prefect of Judea. Early that morning Caiaphas, the Jewish high priest, demanded that Pilate execute Jesus. The Jews evidently weren't authorized to carry out capital punishments, and since Jesus was found "guilty" before the Jewish Sanhedrin, it was now up to Pilate to carry out the execution.

In dramatic Hollywood brilliance, the camera zooms in on a beleaguered Roman governor who had clearly endured a long and difficult battle to keep these rebellious Jews under Roman control. Now Caiaphas once again threatened a riot if his wishes weren't carried out. So, Pilate reluctantly agreed to examine the accused, and Jesus was brought into his headquarters. As the scene shifts, Jesus is now face to face with Pilate.

> "Are you the King of the Jews?" Jesus answered, "Do you say this of your own accord, or did others say it to you about me?" Pilate answered, "Am I a Jew? Your own nation and the chief priests have delivered you over to me. What have you done?"
> -John 18:33b-35 (ESV)

Pilate was aware of the buzz around Jesus—the claim that he was "King of the Jews." In fact, the term "Christ" means messiah, another way of saying "King." So when the crowd won dered if Jesus could be "the Christ" (John 7:26), they were wondering if Jesus was the long awaited king that would finally deliver them. Notice what Jesus said to Pilate next,

> Jesus answered, "My kingdom is not of this world. If my kingdom were of this world, my servants would have been fighting, that I might not be delivered over to the Jews. But my kingdom is not from the world." Then Pilate said to him, "So you are a king?" Jesus answered, "You say that I am a king. For this purpose I was born and for this purpose I have come into the world— to bear witness to the truth. Everyone who is of the truth listens to my voice.
> - John 18:36-37 (ESV)

After the interrogation, Pilate knew that Jesus was innocent. However, Caiaphas manipulated the crowd into a riotous frenzy shouting, "Crucify him, Crucify him!" (John 19:15 ESV). Pilate shouted back, "Shall I crucify your king?" And in bitter irony, these Jewish leaders sealed Jesus' fate (and theirs) as they shouted, "We have no king but Caesar."

Pilate relented, and the execution order was given. However, in a final prophetic moment, Pilate insisted that an inscription be made identifying the condemned man as, "Jesus of Nazareth, the King of the Jews" (John 19:19 ESV). So as Jesus hung, seated on a cross, with a crown of thorns framing his brow and an inscription identifying him as "King" in vivid display overhead, it would have unmistakably appeared as if a royal figure was dying. And in fact, that's exactly true.

Pilate had it right, Jesus is king. Shortly after his resurrection, the announcement of the once-dead-now-alive"crucified king" filled the streets of Jerusalem (See: Acts 2:14-40; 5:27). As the Jesus movement evolved into the Church, and as the Apostles and other witnesses wrote what is now the New Testament, we can see clear evidence that early Jesus followers considered Jesus their king. First, the early disciples constantly referred to Jesus as "Lord." This was a common title for Caesar and likely a semi-subversive act by Christians to remind themselves of their true Lord. Additionally, the frequent use of the title "Jesus Christ" (more accurately "Jesus the Christ") in the New Testament demonstrated they viewed Jesus as the Christ or their king.

We can see an example of this in Paul's letter to the Philippians,

> Therefore God has highly exalted him and bestowed on him the name that is above every name, so that at the name of Jesus every knee should bow, in heaven and on earth and under the earth, and every tongue confess that Jesus Christ is Lord, to the glory of God the Father.
>
> - Philippians 2:9-11 (ESV)

So it's without doubt that the disciples believed that Jesus had been appointed king and "Lord over all" (See: Acts 10:36; See also: Romans 10:12). It's also clear they viewed themselves as citizens of his kingdom (See: Ephesians 2:19; Philippians 3:20). Now consider this, since the four gospels were written sometime after the Church was established and after it was settled that Jesus of Nazareth was "The Christ," the four gospel writers would have been recording Jesus' teachings with his kingship in mind. To them, his teachings wouldn't have simply been wise sayings from a now dead Jewish rabbi. No! They would have been intended as royal commands to citizens of a heavenly kingdom.[66] For them, Jesus was their king and they were waiting with obedient anticipation for his return. Then Jesus would fully establish his rule on earth, as it is in heaven.[67]

With these insights in mind, the teachings of King Jesus can take new shape for us. We, too, must see his teachings as the way the King intended his disciples to live. And although the world has not yet been fully brought under his rule, we live as if his future rule is our present reality (See: Hebrews 2:8). Let's work our way through some of Jesus' teaching and see how that changes the way we should live in the here and now.

Kingdom Ethics[68]

When we read the Sermon on the Mount (Matthew 5-7), we need to remember that Matthew wasn't recording every word Jesus spoke that afternoon. Rather, we're reading a collection of Jesus' teachings

---

66. It is true that in the gospels the writers make it clear his disciples didn't fully know Jesus' identity until after his resurrection, nevertheless the reader is given special insight about Christ's identity in the beginning of each account. (See: Matthew 1:1,21,23; Mark 1:1; Luke 1:35,43; John 1:1-18)

67. Bible scholars have identified a consistent pattern in the New Testament that addresses this strong conviction that Jesus is King but also recognized that life on earth has not yet been fully brought under his rule. This is known as the "already but not yet" motif. Understanding this helps the modern Bible student reconcile interesting paradoxes that exist in the New Testament. How, for example, could Paul so confidently preach that Jesus was Lord from Caesar's prison cell? The "already but not yet" understanding of reality convinced him and the early disciples that Jesus was just the "firstfruits" (I Corinthians 15:20, 23) of what God was going to do. They were to live as faithful servants in God's kingdom until he returned. (See also: Parable of the Mina- Luke 19:11-26

carefully composed to teach us what life in his kingdom is supposed to look like.

If you've read the Sermon before, you've probably noticed the phrase, "You have heard that it was said... but I say to you." (See: Matthew 6:21-22; 27-28; 31-32; 38-39; 43-44). This is Jesus' way of comparing how the Jews were living then with how life is to be lived under his rule and in his Kingdom (See: Colossians 1:13).

For example, Jesus said, "You have heard that it was said to those of old, 'You shall not murder; and whoever murders will be liable to judgment.' But I say to you that everyone who is angry with his brother will be liable to judgment..." (Matthew 5:21-22 ESV). A few verses later he says, "You have heard that it was said, 'You shall not commit adultery.' But I say to you that everyone who looks at a woman with lustful intent has already committed adultery with her in his heart" (Matthew 5:27-28 ESV).

Here's one final example, Jesus noticed they lived by the rule, "'You shall love your neighbor and hate your enemy'" (Matthew 5:43 ESV) but Jesus said in his kingdom his disciples would "Love [their] enemies and pray for those who persecute [them]." These are radical reversals to instinctual human tendencies!

We don't have space to look at each of Jesus' corrections and commands from his sermon about life in his kingdom.[69] However, what's clear even from our brief glance is that Jesus expected his followers to go beyond a mere outward obedience to the Law. Instead, we are to experience a life transformed by a radical renovation of the heart.

Christian Philosopher Dallas Willard comments on this process of transformation. He writes, "Spiritual formation for the Christian basically refers to the Spirit-driven process of forming the inner world of the human self in such a way that it becomes like the inner being of Christ himself."[70] Willard's point? Our walk with Jesus transforms us on the inside so that we begin responding to people and circumstances, just like Jesus did. In essence, Jesus changes us from the inside out.

Notice what Jesus said, "A good person produces good things from the treasury of a good heart, and an evil person produces evil things from the treasury of an evil heart. What you say flows from what is in your heart" (Luke 6:45 NLT). This is why Jesus' teachings in the Sermon on the Mount focused on the interior life of his disciples. He isn't interested in just "cleaning the outside" of our life (See: Matthew 23:25-26). In order to really live under Heaven's rule, we must be changed from the inside out.

Our Role in Transformation

A common mistake that we can make is to think that this transformation is something that just happens

---

68. Gushee, David P., Stassen, David P. Kingdom Ethics: Following Jesus in Contemporary Context 2nd edition (Grand Rapids: InterVarsity Press) 2016
69. It is important to understand how the original audience would have heard some of the statements in the Sermon. Scholarly work on the teaching methods of Jewish rabbis reveal that use of hyperbole was a common and effective way of making a point. Jesus would have followed this tradition as a Jewish teacher in Palestine. So, we should not assume that Jesus is literally advocating self-mutilation (Matthew 5:29-30) or that you should never defend yourself (Matthew 5:39). He is simply making an extreme point to emphasize the radical nature of how life is his kingdom is to be lived. We have totally different values and so live by different rules.
70. Willard, Dallas. Renovation of the Heart (Colorado Springs, Co. NavPress) 2002.

to us after we begin to follow Jesus. Unfortunately, that's not the case! We still live in bodies that have been conditioned to sin. We still have minds that easily drift away from God. So our "spiritual formation," this transformation we've been talking about, takes effort on our part. We must willfully surrender ourselves to the Holy Spirit's control.

This is what Paul was talking about in Galatians 5:19-25.

> When you follow the desires of your sinful nature, [kingdom of darkness living] the results are very clear: sexual immorality, impurity, lustful pleasures, idolatry, sorcery, hostility, quarreling, jealousy, outbursts of anger, selfish ambition, dissension, division, envy, drunkenness, wild parties, and other sins like these. Let me tell you again, as I have before, that anyone living that sort of life will not inherit the Kingdom of God. ve before, that anyone living that sort of life will not inherit the Kingdom of God. But the Holy Spirit produces this kind of fruit in our lives: love, joy, peace, patience, kindness, goodness, faithfulness, gentleness, and self-control.
> [kingdom of Heaven living] There is no law against these things! Those who belong to Christ Jesus have nailed the passions and desires of their sinful nature to his cross and crucified them there. Since we are living by the Spirit, let us follow the Spirit's leading in every part of our lives.
>
> - Galatians 5:19-25 (ESV)

There are actually several places in the New Testament where we read strong warnings against allowing our former life to dominate our new life as Christians (See: Romans 6:6-22; Ephesians 4:17-24; I Peter 4:1-11). The fact these warnings exist tells us that Christians are still capable of sinning. (That probably isn't news to you!) But these warnings also assume that we don't automatically and instantly become transformed into the image of Christ. We have a role in this process.

Let's be clear, the Holy Spirit ultimately produces these changes in our life, but we must submit to His control. God's plan is to shape us into the image of "his dear son" (Romans 8:29 ESV). But we must "give [our]selves to be slaves to righteous living so that [we] will become holy" (Romans 6:19 NLT). We must learn to place ourselves in a space of full surrender so the Holy Spirit can refine and transform our hearts and minds. We develop rhythms, habits, and daily choices that continually set God's kingdom and the kingdom way of living before our minds. These are regular practices that "train" us in holiness (See: Titus 2:11-12; Hebrews 5:14).

Throughout the history of the church, Christians have used these "Spiritual Disciplines" to draw near to God in order to experience His transforming presence in their life. Recently, Dallas Willard and others have written extensively in an effort to reemphasize spiritual disciplines as "training tools." Since God doesn't violate our freewill, we must surrender to him and these spiritual practices help us do just that. Willard lists things such as: solitude, silence, fasting, Sabbath, Bible reading, worship, and prayer. Since the purpose of this book is to only introduce these concepts, I won't be able to elaborate further. But

I'll include several book suggestions for further reading at the end of this lesson.

One note of caution here: Scot McKnight reminds us that "spiritual disciplines don't make us holy, nor do they make us more loving." It's easy to think that just because I'm praying more or going to church now that I'm automatically a better person. Growing as a disciple doesn't work that way. It's always God who makes us holy. McKnight goes on to say that spiritual disciplines are simply "practices that are designed to make us open to the Spirit and open to the presence of God..."[70] Doing "spiritual" things doesn't give us extra points with God, nor is it the goal for the Christian life. That kind of thinking leads to pride and arrogance. Instead, the Christian life is about inside out transformation. It's about becoming love. Essentially, it's about our core self becoming like Jesus.[72]

Transformed to Love

Growing in holiness is the expectation for every believer (See: Matthew 5:48; Romans 8:28-30; I Corinthians 10-15). This is what it means to "consider yourselves dead to sin and alive to God..." (Romans 6:11 ESV). Before we end our lesson, let's see what this transformation actually looks like when it begins to take root in our lives. Paul described this perfectly in his famous poem, If I could speak all the languages of earth and of angels, but didn't love others, I would only be a noisy gong or a clanging cymbal. If I had the gift of prophecy, and if I understood all of God's secret plans and possessed all knowledge, and if I had such faith that I could move mountains, but didn't love others, I would be nothing...Three things will last forever—faith, hope, and love—and the greatest of these is love.

- I Corinthians 13:1-2,13 (ESV)

It all starts and ends with love. "God is love" (I John 4:16 ESV). God's love is why he sent his Son into the world to rescue us (See: Romans 5:8; Galatians 2:20; I John 3:16). It's what transforms the human heart (See: I John 4:19). Love is the supreme proof of Christian discipleship. It's how Jesus would live if he was living your life.

It's easy to get this wrong. It's easy to measure ourselves by things like Bible knowledge, spiritual disciplines, church attendance, spiritual experiences, or even acts of service. However, when life is over the only thing that will matter is, did we learn to love well? Were we transformed into love? Ultimately, the only reliable mark of Christian maturity is our love (See: I John 4:11-13).

THE SUMMARY: It's all about love. We've been rescued by the King of love and brought into his kingdom of love. However, we still have an old nature that will struggle against our new nature. As disciples of Jesus, we've been set free from sin and now we must learn to walk in that freedom. This process takes time. We need to continually surrender ourselves and say "yes" to the Holy Spirit. This allows him to transform us from the inside out. Spiritual disciplines are important habits and routines that Christians have used for 2,000 years to discipline themselves to "think on things above" (Colossians 3:2 KJV). The only true mark of Christian growth and transformation is how well a Christian's life is oriented to love God and others. This is the aim and goal of the Christian life (See: I Timothy 1:5).

---

71. McKnight, Scot and Dave Ferguson. Open to the Spirit: God in Us, God with Us, God Transforming Us. (New York: WaterBrook, 2018),15
72. In Luke 18:9-14, Jesus taught a parable warning about the pride that can occur surrounding spiritual disciplines.

BIBLE STUDY [Answer the following questions to enhance your learning.]

Based on this lesson, summarize how the early church viewed Jesus? Include evidence for your answer.

How does this understanding of Jesus change the way we might look at his teaching?

Reread the section on "Kingdom Ethics", write an insight that challenged you.

Consider your role in transformation. What is a spiritual discipline that you plan to incorporate into your life? (Remember these practices don't make you holy, they only serve to fix your heart and mind on the One who does the transformation.)

"The greatest of these is love" (I Corinthians 13:13). Are there real changes?

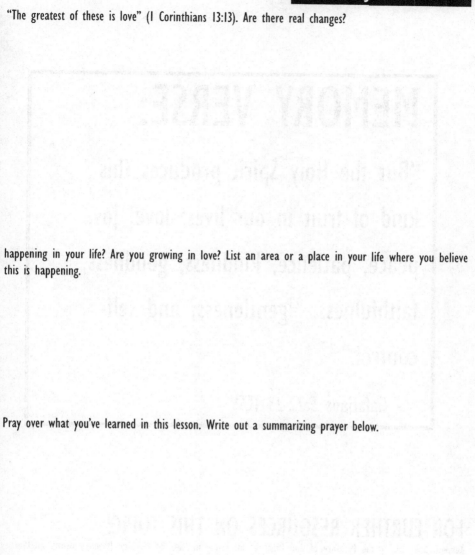

happening in your life? Are you growing in love? List an area or a place in your life where you believe this is happening.

Pray over what you've learned in this lesson. Write out a summarizing prayer below.

MEMORY VERSE:

"But the Holy Spirit produces this kind of fruit in our lives: love, joy, peace, patience, kindness, goodness, faithfulness, [23]gentleness, and self-control."

- Galatians 5:22-23 (ESV

FOR FURTHER RESOURCES ON THIS TOPIC:

Kenneth Boa. Life in the Presence of God Practices for Living in Light of Eternity. Downers Grove. InterVarsity Press, 2017.

Henry Cloud and John Townscend, How People Grow: What the Bible Reveals About Personal Growth. Grand Rapids, Zondervan, 2001.

Richard Foster, Celebration of the Discipline: The Path to Spiritual Growth. New York, HarperCollins, 1998.

John Ortberg, Soul Keeping: Caring For the Most Important Part of You. Grand Rapids, Zondervan, 2014.

N.T. Wright. After You Believe: Why Christian Character Matters. New York, HarperCollins, 2010.

Dallas Willard, Renovation of the Heart. Colorado Springs, Co. NavPress, 2002.

Dallas Willard, The Spirit of the Disciplines: Understanding How God Changes Lives. 2nd edition. New York, Harper Collins, 1998.

LESSON #13: Learning to Listen Well

Earlier we looked at the remarkable conversation that Jesus had with Peter on the Galilean sea shore. Recall how Jesus beautifully loved Peter at his lowest point. I'm sure Peter never forgot how intensely Jesus loved him, even when he failed. However, we didn't finish looking at the conversation, and there's one final lesson that Jesus taught Peter that will introduce this lesson's topic.

Let's get acquainted with the context. Jesus had just asked Peter, "Do you love me?" for the third time. And it was that symbolic third question, that "grieved" Peter. It's probably with a quivering voice that he said, "Lord, you know everything. You know that I love you" (John 21:17 ESV). It was only then that Jesus dropped a bombshell.

> I tell you the truth, when you were young, you were able to do as you liked; you dressed yourself and went wherever you wanted to go. But when you are old, you will stretch out your hands, and others will dress you and take you where you don't want to go." Jesus said this to let him know by what kind of death he would glorify God. Then Jesus told him, "Follow me."   - John 21:18-19 (ESV)

Jesus pointed out that Peter was a strong, young man, accustomed to doing as he liked. Yet one day, years from then, Peter would find himself in a very different experience. His hands would be "stretched out."[73] John specifically stated this was a prophecy about Peter's martyrdom, probably crucifixion. But notice Jesus' final words: "Follow me." Jesus told Peter where the journey would eventually take him—to his death, and still Jesus leaned in and said, "Follow me."

"You follow Me."

At that point in that semi-private conversation, Peter noticed another disciple who was following them as they walked and talked. It was the mysterious "beloved disciple" who has been narrating the entire gospel[74] of John. Peter, never shy, asked, "What about him, Lord?" (John 21:21 NLT). Notice Jesus' powerful reply, "If it is my will that he remain until I come, what is that to you? You follow me!" (John 21:22). It's as if Jesus grabbed Peter by the shoulders, looked deep into his eyes and said, "Don't worry about him. In fact, don't worry about anything else. Here's the one thing I want you to worry about. You follow me!" Interestingly, the first words Jesus said to Peter (Mark 1:17), became the last—follow me!

Last words are important things. People don't waste them. They convey final thoughts. They aren't forgotten. Many times they capture what is most important. But what can Jesus possibly mean when he said, "Follow me"? This was easy to understand when Jesus first approached this fisherman three years earlier. It meant leave your current job and become my disciple; start following me. At that point, however, Jesus was leaving. He was going to ascend to his Father (See: Luke 24:50-52; John 14:1-5; 16:6, 17-28; Acts 1:2,6-11). How was Peter to "follow" now? It's obvious that Jesus expected to keep leading Peter.

---

73. The phrase to have one's hands stretched out was a common euphemism for crucifixion.
74. One of the unique features of the book of John is that the author never identifies himself by name but instead simply calls himself, "the one whom Jesus loved." (See: John 13:23,25; 19:26; 20:2; 21:7, 20,24).

This implies that he would have needed to learn how to follow an unseen Jesus. Their relationship would continue but now it would be radically different.

This is what this chapter is about: learning to hear the voice of Jesus and follow him. Peter lived for the next thirty years doing exactly that. He faithfully followed a Jesus he could no longer see. In many ways, his relationship with him became exactly like ours.

This is what Jesus meant when he said, "My sheep hear my voice, and I know them, and they follow me. I give them eternal life, and they will never perish, and no one will snatch them out of my hand" (John 10:27-28 ESV). The assumption here is that we will know how to hear his voice. However, for a lot of us this can be a source of frustration. As Dallas Willard observed in his book Hearing God, "On the one hand we have massive testimony to and widespread faith in God's personal, guiding communication with us... [But] on the other hand we also find a pervasive and often painful uncertainty about how hearing God's voice actually works..."[75]

So how do we learn to hear the voice of the Shepherd? Throughout the history of the Church, Christians have believed that Jesus guides the believer in four basic ways: the inner leading of the Holy Spirit (in rarer occasions, dreams and visions), the word of God, the leading of the Spirit within the local church, and in the circumstances that God orchestrates in one's life. We will consider each of these as a "voice" in a choir. When they sing in harmony, we'll be able to hear the Shepherd's voice clearly. Learning to hear the Shepherd takes skill and patience; and waiting to hear each of these voices properly will help us listen well.

The Spirit's Voice

The first voice we need to talk about is the voice of God's Spirit. Jesus told his disciples that after his departure a "helper" would come (See: John 14:16, 26; 15:26; 16:7-14; 20:22; Acts 1:4, 8; 2:4). This promised "helper" was the Holy Spirit. Notice what Jesus said, "When the Spirit of truth comes, he will guide you into all the truth, for he will not speak on his own authority, but whatever he hears he will speak, and he will declare to you the things that are to come" (John 16:13 ESV). So Jesus promised his disciples that the Holy Spirit would come and "speak" to them, giving them guidance.

We see this taking place throughout the book of Acts (See: Acts 2:4; 8:29, 39; 10:19; 11:12; 16:7; 20:22; 21:4). For example on one occasion, Paul and his missionary team wanted to go into an area that today is in modern Turkey. But the text tells us that, "the Spirit of Jesus did not allow them" (Acts 16:7 ESV). However, shortly after this, Paul had a vision at night of a Macedonian man crying for help (See: Acts 16:8). Clearly, the early church regularly experienced the Spirit's guidance just as Jesus promised.

I can remember reading these accounts and wondering if I was missing something in my Christian life. How could I know for sure if I was "hearing" the Spirit like the early disciples did? I can remember many times in my life, agonizing over important decisions just hoping for the Spirit to guide me. I would try to quiet my mind and patiently wait for God to speak, but I would wonder if the thoughts in my head were coming from me or from God. How can we know!?! It can be frustrating.

75. Willard, Dallas. Hearing God. (Downers Grove, Ill. InterVarsity Books) 1999. p.25

Let me end this section by saying I firmly believe the Spirit still guides us today just as He did the disciples in the book of Acts. I think He still authors dreams and visions (See: Acts 2:17) although I don't think this is His common way of guiding us. What I've come to believe is that the problem lies with us. Many of us aren't trained on how.

The Scripture's Voice

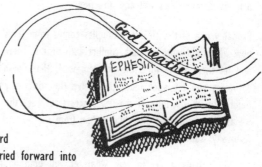

The Holy Scriptures have always played a major role in guiding Jesus' disciples. Jesus himself quoted extensively from the Old Testament, citing it as an authoritative source for knowledge and wisdom. Additionally, the ancient Jews had always believed that God had spoken through prophets, giving them His word and instruction. This same assumption was carried forward into the early church. Paul wrote, "All Scripture is breathed out by God and profitable for teaching, for reproof, for correction, and for training in righteousness, that the man of God may be complete, equipped for every good work" (II Timothy 3:16-17 ESV).

This follows the Jewish tradition that the "oracles of God" (See: Romans 3:2) were given to God's people as a great and precious gift. The Scripture was God's wisdom, God's light, a treasure for God's children. They gave guidance on what was true, how one should live and what one should do (See: Deuteronomy 30:1-20; Psalm 119).

In the New Testament, the words of the Apostles were treated with the same authority (See: II Peter 3:15-16). The letters to the churches commanded the attention of all Jesus followers. In these letters, we see examples of judgments that Paul and other Apostles made about various situations that were seen and accepted as "the will of God" (See: Matthew 18: 18-20; Acts 15:19-21; I Corinthians 5:3; Philippians 4:2-3; James 2:1-5; I Peter 5:1-5).

Peter summarized this nicely,

> "Knowing this first of all, that no prophecy of Scripture comes from someone's own interpretation. For no prophecy was ever produced by the will of man, but men spoke from God as they were carried along by the Holy Spirit."
>
> - II Peter 1:20-21

After the books of the New Testament were written, the early church began making hand written copies (called manuscripts). These copies were spread throughout all the churches, and Christians everywhere soon recognized their authority. From ancient times up to the present moment, followers of Jesus have looked to the Old and New Testament for guidance and discernment about God's will and direction for their lives. So it is clear, the Bible must be one way for us to discern God's voice in our life. We will spend an entire lesson looking at how to read and understand the Bible in a later chapter.

The Church's Voice

God intends for us to walk in community with other believers. We are collectively referred to as, "the body of Christ" (See: Romans 12:5; I Corinthians 12:12). Our fellowship with one another is vital to our growth and discipleship. What's more is that the Bible clearly teaches that God uses other believers to help us discern God's will and direction.

Probably one of the clearest examples comes from Jesus' own teaching in Matthew 18. He was discussing how we should work through conflict with others. There he instructed us to first go to the person alone and let them know what the problem is. If that doesn't resolve the issue, we are to take one or two witnesses and try once more to resolve the conflict. Finally, if that fails, we are to bring the offense before the church (one of the few places Jesus uses the term, "church"). If this last resort doesn't work, we are to remove the offending person from the fellowship of the believers (See: Matthew 18:15-17). Then Jesus says something very interesting,

> Truly, I say to you, whatever you bind on earth shall be bound in heaven, and whatever you loose on earth shall be loosed in heaven. Again I say to you, if two of you agree on earth about anything they ask, it will be done for them by my Father in heaven. <u>For where two or three are gathered in my name, there am I among them.</u>

-Matthew 18:18-20 (ESV)

In this context, Jesus is promising to be "present" when a group of believers are gathered seeking direction in making a tough decision.[76] In difficult times, when conflict has threatened the unity of the church, Jesus promises to lead and guide us as we gather together in his name.

We also see an example in Acts,

> While they were worshiping the Lord and fasting, the Holy Spirit said, "Set apart for me Barnabas and Saul for the work to which I have called them." Then after fasting and praying they laid their hands on them and sent them off.

-Acts 13:2-3 (ESV)

As the church body gathered, God gave guidance and direction for Saul (Paul) and Barnabas. The mighty missionary movement was launched when a group of believers were gathered together praying and fasting.

Finally, we see this again in Paul's letter to Corinth. Here we get a fascinating look into what the ancient house church was like in that city. Near the end of the letter, Paul was addressing some of the bad habits that had developed in this church during its gatherings. He described a chaotic scene where everyone wanted to "show off" their spiritual gifts. One person would start speaking in tongues and then someone else would interrupt them, all with no interpreter. Meanwhile everyone would just be in the dark about

---

76. Unfortunately, these verses are sometimes interpreted to mean that God only hears us when we pray in a group of "two or three." Other times, these verses are thought to be teaching that there is more "spiritual power" when a group of people pray together. The context here is about having several believers joining together in agreement about the difficult decision to remove an offending member from the church. Jesus is telling us that major decisions should be made as a group and in that setting Jesus will recognize the decision we come to.

what was going on (See: I Corinthians 14:1-3, 6, 9-11). In addition to the rude behavior, Paul was very concerned about what non-believers who were visiting would think (See: I Corinthians 14:23)! However, he suggested that if the church services were orderly and if those with the gift of prophecy had a chance to speak, that would have a powerful impact on everyone.

He wrote,

> "But if all of you are prophesying, and unbelievers or people who don't understand these things come into your meeting, they will be convicted of sin and judged by what you say. As they listen, their secret thoughts will be exposed, and they will fall to their knees and worship God, declaring, "God is truly here among you."

> - I Corinthians 14:24-25 ESV

As we can see here, it was in the corporate setting where Paul said people could hear God's As we can see here, it was in the corporate setting where Paul said people could hear God's Spirit speak. In this same chapter, Paul said that the church is edified (instructed and built up) when they hear those with the gift of prophecy (See: I Corinthians 14:29-31). This underscores the role other believers should play in helping us discern the Lord's voice.

> "It's a sign of healthy church community when we allow others to speak into the decisions we're making."

In my life, I can think of so many examples of trusted friends and mentors praying with me about decisions I needed to make. Sometimes they received thoughts and impressions that we discerned was a leading from God. Other times, I've shared my thoughts and impressions with them, and they helped me discern how God was leading. It's a sign of a healthy church community when we allow others to speak into the decisions we're making. If we really believe that God's Spirit is present in them, we should be willing to listen to what others have to say.

The Voice of Circumstance

The final voice that helps discern Jesus' leading is in the circumstances of our life. As is true with each "voice" we've been discussing, it's important that we don't read too much into this one voice. However, if we believe that God is at work in our lives (See: Romans 8:28) then we should be able to sense His direction in our life's events.

Throughout the Bible, the people of God have assumed that His leading could be discerned in the circumstances they faced. Notable characters in the Old Testament such as Moses, David and Daniel all saw God's hand in their circumstances. The problem is that it's just as easy to see circumstances in the wrong light as well. When David was being mercilessly chased by king Saul, David had many chance opportunities to kill his enemy (See: I Samuel 24:4; 26:8). In fact, on more than one occasion, David's soldiers believed that God had orchestrated the circumstances so that he could kill Saul and become king. But of course, David knew that wasn't true. Instead, he saw these as opportunities to demonstrate faithfulness and trust in God. David knew God wouldn't orchestrate circumstances for him to murder his way into the throne.

In addition to trying to see God's leading in circumstance, we must also understand that many times God uses circumstances to get our attention! Sometimes it is a painful experience that wakes us up. Other times a new opportunity brings us to a major crossroad in life, and we need to seek God's guidance and direction. Here it can be tricky. It's easy to see all "open doors" as evidence that God is trying to move us in a different direction. The problem is that Satan opens doors too (See: Matthew 4:8-9; Luke 4:5-7). This is why we must not depend on circumstances alone to guide and direct us. We need to utilize all four voices we've discussed to hear the Shepherd's voice.

Throughout my life, I've seen God's providential hand in my circumstances most clearly from the rear view mirror. That is, it's not until after the fact that I've been able to discern God's guidance from the events in my life. Sometimes, I sit and think about how a certain setback actually forced me to take another route which led to a great opportunity. That's usually how we most clearly can see God in our circumstances. It's comforting to know that even when I don't always get it right, God is still able to help me out from my self-imposed mess. Although I don't see this until after the fact, I have hope for the things I'm going through now. God's faithfulness in my past, builds my faith in the present.

Loving God Leads the Heart

St. Augustine (A.D. 354-430) had some timeless wisdom about understanding God's will. He famously said, "Love God, then do what you please."[77] What he meant was those who genuinely love God will make good decisions. In fact, in many cases God doesn't want to tell us specifically what to do. He'd rather leave most things up to us. God isn't a general who loves to give orders; He's a Father who loves to see us mature and grow.

This reminds me of Jesus' answer when someone asked him what the most important command was. Jesus said, "'You must love the LORD your God with all your heart, all your soul, and all your mind.' This is the first and greatest commandment. A second is equally important: 'Love your neighbor as yourself.' The entire law and all the demands of the prophets are based on these two commandments" (Matthew 22:37-40 NLT).

Jesus simplified the Law—love God, and love others. If we do this consistently our decisions will line up with God's will. This is what Jesus had in mind when he said, "You can ask for anything in my name, and I will do it, so that the Son can bring glory to the Father. Yes, ask me for anything in my name, and I will do it!" (John 14:13-14 ESV). Jesus is telling his disciples that if they ask "in his name" that he will do it. This means that their desires are in line with his will. Essentially they want what he wants. So when we pray for Kingdom-oriented requests, we're praying according to "God's will be done..." (Matthew 6:10 ESV).

This really gets us to the heart of the lesson. The voice of Jesus is heard by those who really want to hear it. When we pursue him, when we seek him, we find him (See: Matthew 6:33; 7:7; Luke 11:9-10; 12:31; Hebrews 11:6). Here's a hard truth: we're as close to Jesus as we want to be. Since, he doesn't play "favorites" (See: Acts 10:34-35; Romans 2:11), he will draw near to anyone who draws near to him. (See: James 4:8).

---

76. From St. Augustine's Sermon on the First Epistle of John 4:4-12

That's really the issue, will we "draw near" to God? Our life as disciples should be lived in close intimacy with Jesus. God doesn't want to direct the small details of our life. Rather, He's interested in the big picture. What kind of person am I becoming? To state it bluntly: loving people generally make loving decisions. When we're in love with God, we're going to do the right kinds of things. That's how David knew it wasn't God's will to kill Saul even though it looked like it might be. Remember, the final thing Jesus asked Peter, "Do you love me?" Why did he ask that? Because that is really all that matters.

Sadly, it's easy to neglect our relationship with Jesus. We might spend days or weeks without really giving God our attention and then wonder why we don't sense His presence or experience His guidance. Here's the good news, today you can make the decision to order your life with Jesus at the center. You can determine to be a sheep that hears. It all starts with the decision to surrender daily to Jesus and to determine to love God with your heart, soul, mind and strength (See: Mark 12:30).

So as we follow Jesus, we must listen to the four voices that God uses to speak to us. We must consider what we believe the Spirit is saying to us internally. We must stay connected to a local church and seek God's direction as He speaks to other believers. We need to stay rooted in God's word and allow the Bible to shape our thinking and direct our life. Finally, we must consider the circumstances we face as yet another voice God uses to direct and guide us. However, let's not forget what is most important—loving and following Jesus. We can be confident that our lives will hear the Shepherd's voice as we pursue loving intimacy with Jesus daily! This is how we learn to "listen well."

THE SUMMARY: Jesus said, "My sheep hear my

voice..." (John 10:27). This implies that his disciples will receive his instruction throughout their lives. This should be the experience of every Christian. As we say "yes" to Jesus we will experience his voice more. There are four primary ways or "voices" that God uses to guide and direct us. They are: the Spirit, the scripture, the church, and circumstances. When these voices speak in harmony, our sense of God's leading grows stronger and stronger. When we seek God, we find him! God cares more about who we are than what we do. As we follow Him, our lives are transformed into the kind of people who do the right kind of things. When a believer genuinely loves God, they find their desires are ordered by that love. As we pursue our relationship with God, our confidence grows stronger. We will learn to listen well. We gain a confidence that comes from knowing Him and knowing we're doing His will (See: I John 3:21).

BIBLE STUDY [Answer the following questions to enhance your learning.]

What do you think was the most difficult thing for Peter to learn as he followed the risen and ascended Jesus?

Which of the "voices" do you think is the most difficult for you to listen to? Why?

Reflect on the statement: "I'm as close to Jesus as I choose to be." How close is your relationship with Jesus right now? What steps could you take to draw a little nearer?

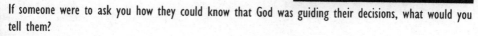

If someone were to ask you how they could know that God was guiding their decisions, what would you tell them?

Pray over what you've learned in this lesson. Write out a summarizing prayer below.

MEMORY VERSE:

"The thief comes only to steal and kill and destroy. I came that they may have life and have it abundantly. [11]I am the good shepherd. The good shepherd lays down his life for the sheep."

- John 10:10-11 (ESV)

FOR FURTHER RESOURCES ON THIS TOPIC:

Bill Hybes, The Power of a Whisper: Hearing God, Having the Guts to Respond. Grand Rapids, Zondervan, 2012.

Dallas Willard, Hearing God. Downers Grove, Ill. InterVarsity Books,1999.

Sermon series: "God's will is whatever" by Pastor Steven Furtick

https://www.youtube.com/playlist?list=PLl3cs80o6bOBX5mR8OGZT3Ys0oZPtvCSW

LESSON #14: Learning to Pray

Prayer is a universal human activity. Humans pray. Surprisingly, this even applies to those who don't believe in God. A recent Pew Research poll found that 11% of agnostics/atheists pray at least monthly.[76] Perhaps, that's not as surprising as it should be, knowing what we do about human beings. I remember a professor I had in grad school telling us that humans shouldn't have been classified Homo sapien (wise man) since at times we're not all that wise. Rather, he said, more appropriately, we should have been Homo religiosus (Religious man). His training was in world religions, and he said that if there is one universal trait among humans—modern and ancient—it is that we are extremely religious. It's a fact, as a race, we have an undeniable, innate desire to connect to a higher power.

This is exactly what Jesus came to do—connect us with God. "Jesus told him, I am the way, the truth, and the life. No one can come to the Father except through me (John 14:6 NLT). This was the belief of the earliest Christians as well. Paul said, "For, There is one God and one Mediator who can reconcile God and humanity—the man Christ Jesus. 6He gave his life to purchase freedom for everyone..." (I Timothy 2:5-6 NLT). Jesus alone revealed the Father to the human race. He alone is the one who can connect us to God.

In this lesson, we want to talk about prayer from two angles. First, as Jesus followers, we need to understand why Jesus prayed and what he specifically taught his disciples about prayer. This will bring unique shape to our prayers. As we just noted above, just about everyone on the planet prays, but how does our unique relationship to God as Jesus followers change the way we pray? Second, we want to look at practical ways to increase our prayer life. How can we get better at praying? How do we develop better prayer habits?

Kingdom Prayer[79]

One of the things Jesus' disciples noticed was Jesus' peculiar practice of spending long uninterrupted times in private prayer (See: Matthew 14:23; 26:36-39; Mark 1:35; 6:31-32,46; Luke 2:49; 5:16; 11:1; 22:39; John 4:34). In the Jewish culture, prayer was a corporate, public event. Congregational, recited prayers occurred in the synagogues each Sabbath. Pious Jews would draw attention to themselves on the street corners as they prayed (See: Matthew 6:5; Luke 20:47).

Jesus' prayers were different. He taught his disciples to pray in secret and to be particularly careful not to draw attention to themselves (See: Matthew 6:6). It's not that Jesus never prayed in public, he did (See: Matthew 14:19; John 11:41-42). It's just that his public ministry was fueled by a private relationship with the Father. When Jesus did anything in the public eye, a deep intimate prayer life supported it all.

So it's not surprising that one day, his disciples came to him and asked, "Lord, teach us to pray..." (Luke 11:1 NLT). What followed is the famous "Lord's Prayer" recorded in both Luke and Matthew. And as we look at Matthew's version, we need to keep in mind that Jesus didn't see himself as a religious teacher or an enlightened guru. Instead, he claimed to be Israel's king initiating God's Kingdom "on Earth as it is in Heaven." Therefore, we should see the "Lord's Prayer" in this light. It's instruction from the King of Heaven to his citizens about how they should address their Father in Heaven while living on Earth (See: Matthew

---

78. The Pew Research Center found that 6% of atheists/agnostics admitted to praying everyday and another 11% pray at least monthly. http://www.pewforum.org/files/2012/10/NonesOnTheRise-full.pdf p. 52 (Accessed 5/2/18)

79. You may want to read Matthew 6 in preparation for this lesson.

6:5-13). This "Kingdom-prayer" should radically shape the prayers we pray and the priorities we hold.

Let's read through it and then break it down a bit.

> And when you pray, do not heap up empty phrases as the Gentiles do, for they think that they will be heard for their many words. Do not be like them, for your Father knows what you need before you ask him. Pray then like this: "Our Father in heaven, hallowed be your name. Your kingdom come, your will be done, on earth as it is in heaven. Give us this day our daily bread, and forgive us our debts, as we also have forgiven our debtors. And lead us not into temptation, but deliver us from evil.
>
> - Matthew 6:7-13 (ESV)

The King's prayer begins with, "Our Father in heaven..." Jesus followers acknowledge their true Father. In a world with many pretenders, we acknowledge our true authority. But this heavenly authority isn't a distant deity but instead He is "Father." Jesus has made it possible for us to become sons and daughters of God (See: John 1:12; Galatians 4:5-7)!

It continues, "...hallowed be your name." We set his name apart in reverence. Although God is our Father, we hold Him in utmost reverence. This will shape how we live and the decisions we make. We recognize that we're not our own, instead we've been bought with a price (See: I Corinthians 6:20: Acts 20:28). God radically loved us and gave his Son to save us (See: John 3:16-17; Titus 3:4; I John 4:9-10). So we of all people on Earth, reverence his mighty name (See: I Timothy 6:15-16).

Now comes the key for Kingdom living. "Your kingdom come, your will be done, on earth as it is in heaven." Jesus is teaching us to pray that God's rule would come to earth. We pray that God's will would be done on earth, as it's already happening in heaven. This is the essence of the Christian life. Our obedience to Christ's commands ushers in God's kingdom and expels the kingdom of darkness (See: Luke 10:17-19; 11:17-23; Romans 16:20).

Now for the second half of the prayer. "Give us this day our daily bread..." (Matthew 6:11 ESV). Here the prayer addresses things that we need: "daily bread." In our modern culture, we can forget how unstable resources were for people in Jesus' day. Daily bread was a real concern. However, this phrase serves as a placeholder for the general needs that all of us have in life. In this light, the prayer is very relevant. Billions of people pray each day for things they need. However, even here, we find a stark difference. We're asking for "daily bread" as kingdom citizens. We're looking to our Father to provide for us.

In this same passage a bit later, Jesus reassured his disciples about their daily needs. Read this passage carefully.

> Therefore I tell you, do not be anxious about your life, what you will eat or what you will drink, nor about your body, what you will put on. Is not life more than food, and the body more than clothing? Look at the birds of the air: they neither

sow nor reap nor gather into barns, and yet your heavenly Father feeds them. Are you not of more value than they? And which of you by being anxious can add a single hour to his span of life? And why are you anxious about clothing? Consider the lilies of the field, how they grow: they neither toil nor spin, yet I tell you, even Solomon in all his glory was not arrayed like one of these. But if God so clothes the grass of the field, which today is alive and tomorrow is thrown into the oven, will he not much more clothe you, O you of little faith? Therefore do not be anxious, saying, 'What shall we eat?' or 'What shall we drink?' or 'What shall we wear?' For the Gentiles seek after all these things, and your heavenly Father knows that you need them all.

- Matthew 6:25-32 (ESV)

Jesus is assuming that there will be a vast difference between how his disciples pray and how the "Gentiles" pray. Our Father knows our needs. He is a good, good Father! We can live without the anxieties that stress those who don't know God.

But then Jesus completely reorients our perspective. He says we must simply, "seek first the kingdom of God and his righteousness, and all these things will be added to you" (Matthew 6:33 ESV). In effect, Jesus is saying, since we're trusting our Father for our daily needs, we're free to devote ourselves to seek first his kingdom. When we find ourselves anxious about life, it's a telltale sign that our focus is away from God's Kingdom. In other words, earthly anxieties flee when we're Kingdom focused (See: I Peter 5:7). This is a very un-instinctual way to live. That's why learning to practice the spiritual disciplines mentioned in lesson 12 are so important. They help us "seek first" God's kingdom when we're so tempted to worry about our daily needs (See: Philippians 2:12-13; Colossians 3:1-2).

Jesus' prayer continues, "forgive us our debts, as we also have forgiven our debtors" (Matthew 6:12 ESV). Jesus alone forgives our sins and imperfections. Since God has forgiven us, we must "also forgive our debtors" (Matthew 6:12,14). Citizens in the kingdom of light refuse to let bitterness and unforgiveness dominate their relationships with others. Again, this is unique to Christianity. Jesus calls us to love our enemies (See: Matthew 5:44) and to not seek revenge on those who've hurt us (See: Matthew 5:38-42; Romans 12:17-21). We trust that our Father will judge, so we don't have to. We're free to love!

Finally, we must remain vigilant, always aware of the enemy's desire to destroy us. So, Jesus finished the prayer with, "And lead us not into temptation, but deliver us from evil" (Matthew 6:13 ESV). We have a real enemy that uses temptation to undermine our effectiveness in God's kingdom. Sin can still enslave us, and it still brings real consequences into our lives. We must not fight it alone. God is our protection. He gives us strength to stand against the tempter's traps (See: II Corinthians 11:1-3; Ephesians 6:10-18).

This prayer reminds us that the life of a disciple is really an "on-earth-as-it-is-in-heaven" way of living. We choose to live now as if Jesus is presently ruling, because for us, he is!

Making Progress in Prayer

Now that we've studied Jesus' Kingdom prayer. I want to look at some ways to develop good prayer habits in our life. The first thing that needs to happen is that we must decide to be disciplined about a regular prayer routine. When I asked Pastor Eddie about this, he said, "Until prayer becomes a priority, it will never become a part of our life."[80] This is just like other things we value in life. We all know a good parent is someone who's decided to make their children a strong priority. They spend time with them even when they're tired or busy. The same goes for a spouse who places the needs of their partner ahead of their own (See: I Corinthians 7:3-5; Ephesians 5:21). So like most things, progress depends on priority.

After deciding to be disciplined about your prayer life, it's important to find a regular time to pray. If you fail to decide when you'll pray, you'll never develop the prayer habit. For me, I've found it helps to tie my prayer time around the things that are constant in my life each day. For example, I used a prayer journal and wrote out my prayers each morning with breakfast. Other people I know decide to pray immediately after getting up in the morning. They drop down next to their bed for a few minutes and pray. Since we all get up at some point every day, that's a consistently recurring thing we can tie our prayer to. Another idea is to pray every lunch hour, or every drive into work, or really any other regular activity where you can be praying. More recently, I've decided my best prayer times are before I go to bed. I try to make it a personal rule not to sleep until I've spent time with my Father.

The next thing we need to do is to keep our prayer times fresh. One of the most discouraging things about prayer is how easily our minds can wander off when we're supposed to be praying. It's crazy! So for me, I've tried to do things to keep my focus on God as I pray. As I mentioned, I used to keep a prayer journal. My regular habit was to read my Bible in the morning and then journal my prayers on my computer. Typing out what I was praying helped to keep my mind on prayer.

But after several years, I realized that even this was growing stale. So, I began nightly prayer walks. And since I'm praying at night before bed, the walking helps keep me awake and alert. I've enjoyed getting out of the house and finding something almost mystical about the beautiful night sky. As I look up into the heavens and pray to the One who holds the stars in his hands, I'm reminded of all God has made and how small I am (See: Isaiah 40:12)!

Finally, I think we need to change the way we pray from time to time. I'm going to give a few suggestions on how to do this. However, before I do, please remember, prayer is primarily about getting to know God. It's about being with Him. Prayer is a two-way conversation. We talk to Him, but we also must quiet ourselves so we can hear from him. The goal in every prayer is to spend time with the Father. If we keep remembering this, I believe words will come naturally. All the same, here are a few ways to help get the conversation going.

Suggestion #1: Pray the Lord's prayer: As we saw in the section earlier, when Jesus taught his disciples how to pray he gave them the "Lord's Prayer." This can serve as a kind of prayer outline for us. Each phrase becomes a new heading or section for your prayers.

I. "Our Father in heaven, hallowed be your name." - We begin our prayer with reverence, gratitude and humility. Take a few minutes to think about who it is you are addressing!

II. "Your kingdom come, your will be done, on earth as it is in heaven."- We now begin to pray for God to move. We ask for His mighty will to be done in this broken world. In this section, we pray that God would bring his power into situations and problems that we face on earth. We want God's rule here as it is in heaven!

III. "Give us this day our daily bread..."- Here we transition to pray for things we need personally. We pray for His provision. He is who we look to for our needs and desires.

IV. "Forgive us our debts, as we also have forgiven our debtors"- Now we turn our attention to our relationship with God and others. First, we pray to restore our relationship with God. We reflect on anything that may have dishonored our relationship with Jesus. We humble ourselves and repent. We also consider any-one we're harboring resentment toward. We ask God to help us forgive others.

V. "And lead us not into temptation, but deliver us from evil."- Finally, we pray for strength to resist temptation. We ask God to protect us. We acknowledge that we're no match for our enemy. We need God to deliver us and keep the ones we love safe.

Suggestion #2: Pray the "A.C.T.S. Outline"- Adoration, Confession, Thanksgiving, Supplication. Begin your prayers with praising God (Adoration). Then confess any known sin in your life and consider any relationships in your life that are troubled. Follow this with a time to thank God for all He's done in your life and in the life of others. Finally, end the prayer time asking God for things you need or want (Supplication).

Suggestion #3: Pray the Word of God. Another way to keep prayer fresh is to pray scripture back to God. Many times reading a Psalm during your prayer is a powerful way to connect to God. For centuries both, Jews and Christians have considered the Psalms a "prayer book" for believers. In fact, most of the psalms are just that, recorded prayers. But they're not just for us to read, they also can help us to pray to our Father. Sometimes the prayers of others can give voice to our thoughts especially when we don't know quite what to say. For many Christians in more formal denominations, written prayers are widely used. This can be an effective way to communicate to God and pray prayers that you probably wouldn't have ever considered before.

Connect with God

As I said, the purpose of prayer is to connect with God in a personal intimate way. As you begin developing your own prayer life, remember that God wants to connect with you. Experiment. It's okay to keep trying new things until you feel like you've really connected. For me, sometimes, I need to settle my heart with worship music before I try to pray. At times, life can be so noisy and busy, so it might take a little time to prepare to enter His presence. Other times, I might not do anything at all. I just need to sit in silence before Him and quiet my heart.

To be honest, there are many times I don't feel like praying. My desire to pray just isn't there. So my first prayer is, "God help me to pray!" It's amazing how God can change our desires when we ask.[81] In fact, Paul told us the Holy Spirit is specifically our helper in prayer. He wrote,

> And the Holy Spirit helps us in our weakness. For example, we don't know what God wants us to pray for. But the Holy Spirit prays for us with groanings that cannot be expressed in words. And the Father who knows all hearts knows what the Spirit is saying, for the Spirit pleads for us believers in harmony with God's own will.
>
> - Romans 8:26-27 (NLT)

As we pray, the Holy Spirit helps us communicate with the Father. We're entering into a holy conversation with God the Spirit and God the Father where truly powerful things can happen. We're spiritually entering the courts of Heaven each time we come to God in prayer (See: Hebrews 4:16). So, it's important to pray as if that is actually happening. Sometimes, when I think of what all Jesus has done so that I could approach the Father, and I realize how hard the enemy fights to keep me from praying, it fires me up. I'm reminded that prayer is a spiritual battle. In these moments, I pray with more fierceness and passion. When I pray like this, I can feel the enemy retreat, and the kingdom of darkness fall (See: Luke 10:17-20; Romans 16:20). But this takes faith. You aren't actually seeing Satan retreat. You don't know how God is hearing you. You don't know for certain how these prayers might be answered. But you pray. You pray because you know God is good, and you know God hears! We must remember that it's the prayer of faith that can heal the sick or even stop the rain (See: James 5:13-18)! So pray!

We need to see prayer as a great gift God has given to us. We're not meant to carry heavy burdens (See: Matthew 11:28-30). Instead, we pour out our hearts to God and shout to the heavens (See: I Peter 5:6-7; Psalm 47:1; 148:1-14). Prayer stirs the mighty resources of Heaven for us in our time of need (See: Psalms 37:39-40; 59:1-10). Only in eternity will we fully realize the power and importance of our prayers. For reasons, I don't fully understand, God has planned that some things won't happen until we pray (See: Exodus 32: 9-14; Job 42:10; Luke 18:1-8; James 5:16-18)!

So get started. Pray! Pray when you're alone. Pray with your family. Pray with other believers. Make it a priority. Every time you eat, pray. Every time you're in the car alone, pray. Every time you get worried, pray. Before every challenge you face, pray. Every day God gives you, pray (See: I Thessalonians 5:17)! May we all become people who pray!

THE SUMMARY: Everyone prays. Humans are hardwired to connect to their Creator. As Jesus followers, our prayers are shaped by the relationship we have with God through Jesus. As we pray, what we believe about God, our purpose in this world and what is important shows through. We must pray "Kingdom prayers" that are aligned to God's will. Prayer must be a priority in the life of a Jesus follower. As we pray, we must remember that it's primarily about connecting and developing our relationship with God. Prayer is about being with him even more than it is about getting anything from Him. Prayer is a daily "yes" to Jesus.

---

81. Thankfully God even changes our desires sometimes when we don't ask. I believe God's grace works primarily at this "desire" level in our consciousness. Have you ever had the sudden desire to pray, go to church, read your Bible, or minister to someone? This should be recognized as evidence of God's Spirit ministering grace to us in that moment. These "holy desires" don't originate apart from God. Therefore we must see them as invitations from God to obey and grow. When we find these desires absent it is appropriate to pray for God's grace to change our heart and give us the desire to obey. (Acts 10:10-48)

BIBLE STUDY [Answer the following questions to enhance your learning.]

How would you describe the differences between how a Jesus follower prays and how someone else might pray?

Go back and look up the passages where Jesus prayed. Read the context a bit. What insights did you notice about Jesus and his habit of prayer?

What new things did you learn about "The Lord's Prayer?"

What time of day do you pray? Are you able to make a new commitment to pray in your life? If so, what is that commitment?

Pray over what you've learned in this lesson. Write out a summarizing prayer below.

119

MEMORY VERSE:

"and whatever we ask we receive from him, because we keep his commandments and do what pleases him.."

- I John 1:22 (ESV)

FOR FURTHER RESOURCES ON THIS TOPIC:

Jim Cymbala, and Dean Merrill. Fresh Wind, Fresh Fire: What Happens When Gods Spirit Invades the Heart of His People. Grand Rapids, MI: Zondervan, 2018.

Bill Hybes, Too Busy Not to Pray: Slowing down to Be with God. Grand Rapids, MI: Zondervan, 2013.

Paul E. Miller, A Praying Life: Connecting with God in a Distracting World. Colorado Springs, CO: NavPress, 2017.

LESSON #15: Learning to Read Well

I'll never forget trying to read my Bible cover to cover as a kid. The churches in which I grew up all emphasized the importance of daily Bible reading. And each new year, it seemed like everyone I knew made the resolution to read through the whole Bible before the year's end. I would try too. I remember starting out reading in Genesis. Things would go just fine. There were lots of great stories with all of the right elements to capture the attention of a young man—an epic flood, bloody battles and beautiful girls. Then I'd hit Exodus. I mean, after we get everybody out of Egypt safely, it got real boring real quick. And don't get me started on Leviticus!

Then, when I was around 16, our church challenged us to not only read through the entire Bible but to also journal on every chapter we read. We were supposed to write a summary of the chapter, then a "personal application" and finally a prayer that asked God to help us live out what we had read. That sounded like a great goal. I knew this would take longer than a year, so I thought maybe I could cut myself a little slack and give myself more time so I could potentially make it past Joshua!

After about a year or so into it, I was trying to plod through the book of Ezekiel. And that's when I'd had it! I threw up my hands in exasperation. I couldn't summarize it. I couldn't apply it. Because I HAD NO IDEA WHAT IT WAS TALKING ABOUT! I remember telling my pastor. He laughed at first then saw that I was serious. I was probably the only teenager he'd met that was struggling with Ezekiel! Trust me, I was no angel. I had the typical teenage issues, but this was a goal I was determined to finish. I just felt completely overwhelmed. Looking back, I laugh now too. I can get a bit intense. As frustrating as that was at the time, I am so glad I was taught the importance of reading my Bible. So as we begin this lesson, let me start out by encouraging you to become a student of the Bible. I know it's a big book and parts of it can seem obscure and intimidating, but it's worth it!

The Most Unique Book Ever!

When you think about it, there's no other book in the world like the Bible. When you compare it to all other books (ancient or modern), it's in a class of its own. It's by far the most translated, the most sold and the most read book of all time.[82] As an ancient text, our modern Bible is supported by thousands of early manuscripts. This fact is astounding when one realizes just how few manuscripts exist for other ancient documents.[83] When we consider it as literature, there is simply no other book with more influence upon our culture than the Bible. Everything from our sense of morality and justice, to the names we

---

82. As of October 2017, the Wycliffe Global Alliance says that the complete Bible has been translated into 670 languages, the New Testament is in 1,521 languages and portions of the Bible into 1,121 languages. This places the total number at over 3,300 languages that have some scripture.

83. Virtually everything we know from ancient history comes from the written records left behind. Ancient authors like, Josephus, Tacitus, and Pliny wrote extensively about life in the Roman empire in and around the time of Christ. However, since these writings are nearly 2000 years old, we no longer have the original drafts of what was written, rather we have the surviving ancient manuscripts or copies. For the authors just mentioned, historians are relatively pleased with the number of copies we possess. For instance, we have 33 copies of Tacitus's writings, about 130 for Josephus and around 200 for Pliny. However, the number of manuscripts isn't the only important factor. Historians also prize early copies. The closer the time gap between the original draft and the oldest copies should be as short as possible. For these authors, the time gap between their writing and the oldest copy is several hundred years. Even so, historians are fairly confident that what these authors has written has been preserved. However, here's another example of the utter uniqueness of the New Testament. With over 5800 ancient manuscripts and a time gap within 50 years for its earliest fragments, the New Testament is in a class of its own! If we expand our comparison to all ancient literature, Homer's Iliad comes in at a distant second, with approximately 1757 ancient copies or fragments, and a time gap of over 400 years. Clearly, there's just no comparison for the textual support the New Testament enjoys. There is absolutely no reason to doubt whether or not we have an accurate copy of the original writing of the New Testament I will include a few books for more reading on this topic at the end of this chapter.

give our children, to some of our ideas about human nature are pulled from the characters, stories and teachings found exclusively in the Bible. When we think about it as a religious text, we can identify it's supernatural power. Whether we're considering fascinating prophecies long fulfilled or reading predictions about the future, we can find evidence that it is inspired by God.

Perhaps most compelling, is its authority. In particular, the words of Jesus are especially weighty. During his life, people everywhere, including his enemies, recognized his spiritual authority (See: Matthew 13:54; Mark 1:22; 6:2; 11:18; Luke 4:32; John 7:46). Still less prejudiced hearers found their hearts examined and exposed by his soul-piercing words (See: Matthew 7:28-29; John 4:29;39-42). Today, the words of Jesus are as powerful as ever. Whether we consider the timeless parables he told, his famous Sermon on the Mount or simply the way he beautifully loved the outcast, the gospels that record Jesus' life and message are unique in all of human literature. When we go on to think about the rest of the New Testament and then the entire Bible itself, it's indisputable; the Bible is powerfully unique and uniquely powerful.

It's because the Bible is so unique and so powerful that it's regularly misread and misused. For example, some believe that simply reading it earns them extra points with God. For them, the Bible becomes a Christian rabbit's foot which promises to give them good luck throughout their day. Others see reading it as a religious exercise; something that good Christians are "supposed" to do. These folks dutifully read it, but easily slip into the habit of treating it as a task on a religious checklist. Still others treat it almost like a holy Weegee board, consulting it only when they need guidance. They might randomly open it, reading the first place their eye falls, and then believe this to be a special word from God to them.

I can understand why people tend to approach the Bible these ways. For instance, I definitely think regular Bible reading should be apart of our daily routine. It is an important spiritual habit. And while I don't think reading the Bible brings you good luck, I do think meditating on it is a great way to shape our day. And for sure, there have been times when a random Bible verse has felt like a special word from Heaven guiding and leading me. So I understand these approaches to the Bible, really I do. But as a rule, these aren't good reasons for reading the Bible.

In this lesson, we'll discuss the primary reasons we should read our Bibles and the proper way we should interpret scripture. This is important so that we can avoid misusing the Bible and (what may happen even more frequently) misreading the Bible! Sadly, wars have been fought, cults started, and churches divided all because the Bible was misused and misread. That is why we, as disciples, must learn to read well.

Why Should We Read the Bible?

Let's look first at why a follower of Jesus should read the Bible. As just mentioned, the Bible's historical influence, moral insights, and supernatural power would be reason enough to read it with interest. But as impressive as this is, this isn't primarily why a disciple of Jesus should read the Bible. We should fundamentally read the Bible for the purpose of meeting and knowing God. This means we approach scripture humbly, looking for God to use His word to "speak" and reveal Himself to us. Interestingly, as we come to know God through His word, we also come to know ourselves.[84] Theologian

---

84. The great theologian John Calvin 1509-1564) said, "Nearly all the wisdom we possess, that is to say, true and sound wisdom, consists of two parts: the knowledge of God and of ourselves." Institutes 1.1.1-2.

Kelly Kapic observes, "Growing in our knowledge of God changes our view of everything else. It is not that we lose sight of all except God, but rather that we view everything in light of God."[85]

This leads us to the second reason we should read the Bible—to know truth. In the Jewish culture, a disciple was one who sat and learned from a Master. So as disciples of Jesus, it's expected that we study God's word and learn His teaching. Jesus boldly told his disciples that he had given them the truth. Listen to Jesus' prayer to the Father, "I have given them your word, and the world has hated them because they are not of the world, just as I am not of the world...Sanctify them in the truth; your word is truth" (John 17:14,17 ESV). Paul pointed out the danger of not learning truth in his letter to the Ephesians. He warned, "So that we may no longer be children, tossed to and fro by the waves and carried about by every wind of doctrine, by human cunning, by craftiness in deceitful schemes" (Ephesians 4:14 ESV). The apostle knew that well-trained disciples would be less prone to "human cunning" and "deceitful schemes."

Today is no different. Our modern culture preaches a message that runs counter to what the Bible says. So, it is vital that we know God's truth and develop a biblical worldview. The Bible must play a foundational role in our lives. In fact, this has been assumed throughout this book. This is why we've studied through so many biblical passages and referenced so many verses in our lessons.

This brings us the final reason I'll mention for reading the Bible—to know how we should live. What good is knowing truth if we're not going to apply it? Notice what Paul said, "All Scripture is breathed out by God and profitable for teaching, for reproof, for correction, and for training in righteousness, that the man of God may be complete, equipped for every good work" (II Timothy 3:16-17). The Bible is not only our foundation for teaching and training but also our foundation for reproof and correction. As disciples, we're not called to be, "good just for goodness sake." But instead, our lifestyle must match our message. If you think about it, no one really expects an atheist to love their enemies, although they might. But everyone knows how a Christian is supposed to live. So if our morality doesn't match our message, we miss our mission. It's for this reason, Paul says that scripture sometimes corrects us. Therefore, it plays both an instructive and corrective role in our lives. This is how it equips us to accomplish the good work to which God has called us.

How Should We Read the Bible?

So far we've discussed just how unique the Bible is and looked at a few reasons why we should read it, but now we come to the heart of this lesson, "How should we read the Bible?" Or to phrase the question differently, "Are there ways to avoid misinterpreting what the Bible says?"

Some people might push back on this. They might say, "Hey, I'm just going to start reading and let the Holy Spirit guide me. Why complicate matters?!?" I certainly agree, let's get to reading, and I definitely believe the Spirit guides us. As we've already said, the Bible is a powerful book, but it has often been misused. It's not a sign of spiritual maturity to ignore time-tested rules of biblical interpretation; it's just pride. This is a bit of a sore spot for me, so I won't say more!

Since, I'm just giving an introduction in this book, we're going to look at just three basic rules that will greatly help us as we read and study the Bible. As in the other lessons, if you'd like to read more on this topic, please see the resources listed at the end of the lesson.

85. Kapic, Kelly M. Little Book for New Theologians: why and how to study theology. (Downers Grove, IL: InterVarsity Press) 2012. p. 26

RULE #1 Approach the Bible as Literature

It's important that we approach the Bible as it has been given to us—as a book. It's a unique book, a powerful book, an inspired book, but it's obvious God chose a book to reveal himself to us (See: II Peter 1:20-21). So, if we think of the Bible as a book, we must consider the rules about book reading.

Here I might have just lost some of you! For all you "rule-breakers" out there, the sheer mention of the word "rule" might be a trigger! Or maybe this is starting to sound too much like school all over again. But the simple fact is: everyone who reads a book, automatically interprets it. And that's the problem, not all interpretations are created equal—just ask any literature teacher! This is why we need "reading rules."

It's just true; all readers are interpreters. Whenever we read a book and comprehend its grammar, we automatically interpret it. There's no way around it. If you tried to read something in a foreign language, your eyes might scan the letters. However, since there isn't any comprehension, there's no interpretation (haha—maybe that's how some of you are feeling about my book!). This was actually one of the reasons Church leaders in the middle ages resisted translating the Bible into the common language of the people. They felt, if people read it, they might interpret it incorrectly. While I understand that fear, it's always better to teach people how to read it than to keep people from reading it.

Some might push back at this point and ask, "Isn't it true that God speaks to us through scripture? So how can we say someone's interpretation of the Bible is wrong? Isn't this just a way to censor what someone feels God has said to them?!"

If you're feeling that way, please don't misunderstand me. I absolutely believe the Holy Spirit illuminates the Bible and gives us incredible insights that we may not have noticed before. It's probably one of the most thrilling things in my Christian experience. But what I am cautioning against is approaching Scripture as if the normal rules governing literature don't apply. We must not twist a verse to "mean" something that the original author never meant. In their book, How to Read the Bible for All Its Worth, Gordan Fee and Douglas Stuart state, "On this one statement, however, there must surely be agreement. A text cannot mean what it could never have meant... Or to put that in a positive way, the true meaning of the biblical text for us is what God originally intended it to mean when it was first spoken or written. This is the starting point."[86]

Perhaps things could be helped if we distinguish the difference between interpretation and application. Interpretation is my attempt to understand what the text means generally. Application is my attempt to understand how the text applies to me personally.

Let's discuss interpretation for a minute. Interpreting a biblical passage is sometimes relatively easy. For example, when we read about the story of Jarius in Luke 8, it's a pretty straightforward account of a

86. Fee, Gordon D., and Douglas K. Stuart. How to read the Bible for all its worth: a guide to understanding the Bible 4th Edition. (Grand Rapids, MI: Zondervan) 2014. p. 34-35

desperate father trying to get Jesus to quickly come to the bedside of his dying daughter. Understanding what's happening in that story is fairly easy.[87]

However, other portions of scripture have some elements that are less clear but still have a relatively simple overall message that is easy to interpret. The account of Jesus and Nicodemus in John 3 is a good example. There are some obscure parts of that conversation. What exactly did Jesus mean when he said, "...Truly, truly, I say to you, unless one is born of water and the Spirit, he cannot enter the kingdom of God. 6That which is born of the flesh is flesh, and that which is born of the Spirit is spirit" (John 3:5-6 ESV). Scholars have debated for centuries what it means to be "born of water." Is it baptism? Is it physical birth? However, when we read the entire passage, obscure parts notwithstanding, we have a pretty clear understanding of what Jesus is telling him: "Nicodemus, you need a spiritual rebirth that only comes through believing in God's Son."

Still other parts of scripture are extremely hard to interpret because of it's difficult genre (more on that in a minute). When we think about the book of Revelation for example, there are portions in that book where there is little agreement about its meaning. There can also be portions of scripture where we understand the genre just fine but there's still disagreement about a passage due to theological or philosophical reasons.

Application on the other hand is where we personalize the Bible. We say things like, "This is what I got out of my Bible reading this morning..." or "I feel like God is telling me...". The caution here comes when we forget that this is a personal application and begin assuming that our application necessarily applies to others. Perhaps the Spirit is using scripture to guide you personally in your life and your application might be helpful to others, but we shouldn't assume that our application applies beyond ourselves.

I do want to offer one caveat here. I believe that the spiritual gifts of teaching and pastoring use scripture to make relevant applications for a group of people. A Spirit-gifted Pastor/teacher must first correctly interpret a text but then offer an application to an entire congregation The Spirit uses men and women with these gifts to bring important insight and fresh conviction to the church. In my own life, I can think of numerous times where Spirit-anointed preaching greatly shaped my Christian walk. It's the powerful intersection of biblical interpretation and Spirit-led application that God uses in our life to shape, correct, instruct and guide us.

---

87. However, I must add even though there is a fairly straightforward interpretation of this story, there is still a lot going on here. It seems Luke, especially, has intentionally introduced us to two desperate people who are at both ends of the social spectrum. While Jesus is being rushed to go to the house of a prominent leader named Jarius' to heal his dying daughter, a poor anonymous woman suffering with a chronic gynecological condition touches Jesus's tunic as he passes by and is healed. Interestingly, we're told that the woman's condition has lasted 12 years, and that Jarius' daughter is 12 years old. When Jarius approaches Jesus it's public and he bows down before him. Meanwhile, the woman approaches privately from behind. There are even more comparisons, but I mention these facts to demonstrate that even "simple" passages contain subtleties that are easy to miss. Even the fact Jesus pulls the woman from the shadows and commends her faith publicly shows his commitment to treat her with dignity. (See: Luke 8:48). Since the text doesn't explicitly tell us what to make of these similarities and differences, we must speculate about the intended message. I believe this passage emphasizes Jesus's mission to all people rich, important men and obscure women. In fact, texts like these speak powerfully to our modern sensitivities for the marginalized and forgotten. The message of Jesus is still speaking to us today. He doesn't forget the forgotten.

RULE #2 Context Is King

I love how Christian scholar Greg Koukl phrases this reading rule. For a bit of shock value he says, "Never read a Bible verse."[88] What he means, of course, is that we shouldn't just read a single verse. We need to read more; we must read several verses, or the entire chapter, or maybe the whole book to get the context. Failing to do this is a sure way to misunderstand scripture.

This is foundational to good interpretation. We shouldn't take verses out of their context.[89] Bible readers have ignored this rule all the time. As we've said, the Bible has been misused and abused for thousands of years. We even see evidence of this in the first century.

> And remember, our Lord's patience gives people time to be saved. This is what our beloved brother Paul also wrote to you with the wisdom God gave him— [16]speaking of these things in all of his letters. Some of his comments are hard to understand, and those who are ignorant and unstable have twisted his letters to mean something quite different, just as they do with other parts of Scripture. And this will result in their destruction.
>
> - II Peter 3:15-16 (NLT)

Peter pointed out how some people have "twisted" Paul's letters "to mean something quite different." Obviously, some of what Paul had written had been taken out of context and twisted. Further, Peter was pointing out that these people had misinterpreted Paul's original intent and suggested that they did this with "other parts of Scripture." In other words, they were bad interpreters! They weren't following the reading rules.

Interestingly, Satan did this too. During Jesus' temptation in the wilderness, Satan tempted Jesus to throw himself off the pinnacle of the Temple. Satan quoted Psalms 91:11-12, "For he will command his angels concerning you to guard you in all your ways. 12On their hands they will bear you up, lest you strike your foot against a stone" (ESV). Satan suggested these verses in Psalms promise God's unfailing protection, no matter what. What better way to put God's "promise" to the test, than to jump? Jesus wisely understood that this wasn't what the context was teaching. So he responded to Satan's temptation with another passage explicitly commanding us not to test God (See: Deuteronomy 6:16). Jesus knew that it wasn't our place to test God; that's arrogance, not faith.

It's surprising just how many misunderstandings of scripture are cleared up if we read the entire context of a troubling or unclear passage. Over the years, I've had many conversations with Mormons or Jehovah's Witnesses, and as we talk through areas of theological disagreement, inevitably we end up discussing

---

88. Koukl, Gregory. Never read a Bible verse: "The most important thing I could ever teach you ". Signal Hill, CA: Stand to Reason. 2000
89. Sometimes the chapter divisions and verse markings are a distraction from really understanding the passage. These markers weren't in the original writings, in fact, they weren't inserted until the late middle ages. There's nothing special about the chapter or verse divisions and so we shouldn't assume that each verse expresses a complete thought. For example, Ephesians 1:3-14 is one sentence in the original Greek language. If we were studying through that text it would be important to constantly read those 11 verses to understand Paul's thought.

verses taken out of context used to support a false teaching. This also applies to many of the disagreements between Christians. In my experience, so much of what divides the church could be helped with more attention to the context! As I mentioned a minute ago, this is a pretty basic rule. So why does this happen so much with the Bible? I think it goes back to the uniqueness of the Bible. It's God's word. It's inspired! Therefore, we somehow think that the normal rules of reading don't apply. But they do. We must keep context king. If we don't, we'll end up twisting the scripture to say anything we want (See: II Corinthians 2:17; II Timothy 3:5-7; Jude 1:4).

RULE #3 We Must Understand the Genre

Imagine scrolling through your news feed on your phone or computer and you come across the following article: "Lions massacre defenseless Texans."[90] There's two different things this headline could mean. It could be about a tragedy in Texas involving ferocious lions and innocent residents from the state of Texas. Or it could be a sports writer having some fun talking about Sunday's football game. The difference between whether or not you interpret this as a national tragedy or just the results of a game is a matter of genre. If this was a news article, the genre would be reporting an actual massacre. If the genre is sports, then we know this is just about football. (It still may be a tragedy if you're a Texan fan, but I haven't met many of those!)

When we think of the Bible, it's easy to think that since all 66 books are in one big book that it's all the same. But it's not. The Bible has two major sections: the Old and New Testament. In both sections, we have portions that are historical (non-fiction genre). We have long poetry sections (e.g. Job, the Psalms, Song of Solomon). There are prophetic books and apocalyptic books. There are proverbs and parables. The Bible is a diverse collection of writings from many different authors expressed in many different genres. Explaining how we should read and interpret each of these genres would take us too far from the purpose of this book. My purpose here is to just introduce you to these ideas. The only point here is to show you the way a genre can (and should) affect interpretation.

As we bring this lesson to a close, I can imagine that you might feel like reading the Bible has just become a whole lot more complicated. Fear not! We are so fortunate to live in a time when there are so many wonderful resources to help us read and study our Bible. Here is where a good study Bible will help you. Study Bibles have commentaries that accompany the text itself. My favorites are the Life Application Study Bible or the ESV Study Bible. Also, I believe every serious disciple of Jesus should get acquainted with at least a couple of good commentaries to help with biblical interpretation.

---

90. Professor Walt Russell uses this creative way to explain how genres affect interpretation. For more on this see: Russell, Walt. Playing with fire: how the Bible ignites change in your soul. (Colorado Springs, CO: NavPress) 2000.

Good commentaries take the context and genre into account as they explain the text. For a general audience, I recommend the NIV Application Commentary series or The Story of God Commentary series. These individual commentaries can be expensive but start out with a book of the Bible you want to intensely study and just buy that one! The rewards of studying your Bible are immeasurable.

I'd like to end with some simple advice about reading your Bible. First, read a book from start to finish. Don't play "Bible roulette", you'll be reading out of context if you do. Second, read every day for at least 10 minutes. Usually, you'll be able to read a chapter or two during that time. For me, I like to read while listening to an audio Bible. This tends to keep my mind focused. Third, read actively. Ask questions. Another word for this is, study! Don't read just to read, read to comprehend. Finally, once a month set more time aside to really dig into a passage. Whether you're using a Bible study book or you're just going through a passage with a commentary, make it a habit once a month. Don't let the size of the Bible intimidate you. Read through the New Testament first. That's a very doable goal. Now, it's time to get to reading!

THE SUMMARY:

The Bible is God's incredible revelation of Himself to humankind. Without the Bible, we would have an incomplete and inadequate picture of God. We wouldn't know of His great love for us and the amazing rescue that He achieved in Christ's death on the cross. The Bible is a powerful book that can be used for great good or misused for great evil. It's important that we learn how to interpret the Bible correctly so that we can learn the truth for ourselves. Further, training in proper biblical interpretation methods help us discern when someone else has misinterpreted scripture. The Bible should shape our Christian faith. As disciples of Jesus we must have a worldview that is based solidly upon scripture.

BIBLE STUDY [Answer the following questions to enhance your learning.]

What fact about the Bible's uniqueness was most interesting to you? Why?

Which reason for reading the Bible most connected with you? Why?

Have you ever misunderstood and misinterpreted a passage in the Bible? Have you ever thought that someone else did that and tried to mislead you?

Explain something that you learned from this lesson about the "rules for reading."

Pray over what you've learned in this lesson. Write out a summarizing prayer below.

MEMORY VERSE:

"Sanctify them in the truth; your word is truth"

- John 17:7 (ESV)

FOR FURTHER RESOURCES ON THIS TOPIC:

Francis Chan. Multiply Disciple-making for Ordinary People. Colorado Springs, Co.: David C Cook, 2012.

Gregory Koukl, Never read a Bible verse: "The most important thing I could ever teach you." Signal Hill, CA: Stand to Reason, 2000.

Walt Russell, Playing with fire: how the Bible ignites change in your soul. Colorado Springs, CO: Nav-Press, 2000.

Gordon D Fee and Douglas K. Stuart. How to read the Bible for all its worth: a guide to understanding the Bible fourth Edition. Grand Rapids, MI: Zondervan, 2014.

LESSON #16: The Holy Spirit

I've often thought about what it must have been like to be in the Church in the very beginning. Imagine the chaos: Jerusalem abuzz with controversy after Jesus' tomb was found empty (See: Matthew 28:11-15; Acts 2:29-41), the Jewish leadership trying in vain to keep the disciples from preaching and teaching (See: Acts 4:18; 5:20-40), and then Peter and John healing a lame man right in front of the Temple (See: Acts 3:1-10)! From the perspective of the Jewish leaders, things were quickly spiraling out of control. But this was what Jesus had promised, the Holy Spirit descended and the Church was born. Christ's disciples were filled with the Spirit's power, and they immediately began preaching the gospel to everyone who would listen (See: Acts 2:1-41).

As the church rapidly grew, the Jewish leadership felt increasingly threatened, and it didn't take long for their opposition to turn violent. After we read about the arrest and beating of some of the Apostles (See: Acts 5:40-41), the story in Acts turns our attention to a young leader named Stephen. He was described as, "full of grace and power, [who] was doing great wonders and signs among the people..." (Acts 6:8 ESV). We're told that he debated with some of the Jews, but they couldn't, "withstand the wisdom and the Spirit with which he was speaking" (Acts 6:10 ESV). Steven's Spirit-filled preaching infuriated the Jews, and so they falsely accused him of trying to turn the Jews away from Moses. Eventually, Stephen was arrested and put before the Jewish court.

Acts records the powerful speech Stephen gave at his trial. From beginning to end, it's obvious that his words were filled with the Spirit's power and inspiration (See: Acts 7:1-53; also, Luke 21:12-16). Sadly, the opposition wasn't even interested in listening to Stephen. In a fit of rage, they pulled him out of the city and stoned him to death (See: Acts 7:58). But notice the remarkable way he reacted during all of this.

> But he, <u>full of the Holy Spirit,</u> gazed into heaven and saw the glory of God, and Jesus standing at the right hand of God... And as they were stoning Stephen, he called out, "Lord Jesus, receive my spirit." ⁶⁰And falling to his knees he cried out with a loud voice, "<u>Lord, do not hold this sin against them.</u>" And when he had said this, he fell asleep.
>
> - Acts 7:55,59-60 (ESV)

Stephen's life was lived in the power of the Spirit. It was obvious to those who knew him (See: Acts 6:3-5,8,15; 7:55). Even in his death, we see the Spirit sustaining and empowering him. Simply put, Stephen was a man filled with the Holy Spirit.

This is the kind of life Jesus intends for all of us. Jesus followers are to be filled and empowered by God's Spirit to do God's work, God's way, in God's kingdom, just as Jesus did (See: Luke 4:1,14,18; Hebrews 9:14). In this lesson, we're going to study the Holy Spirit and gain an understanding about the essential function

He plays in the life of a Jesus follower. There are three ways we can describe our relationship with the Holy Spirit: fellowship with the Spirit,[91] walking in the Spirit[92] and ministering in the Spirit.[93] As we look at each, we will learn something foundational for our Christian life.

Fellowship with the Spirit

Most of us have heard that being a Christian means having a personal relationship with Jesus Christ. It's something we hear pastors talk about at the end of sermons. Growing up in church, I heard this my entire life. Early in my life, I vividly remember feeling especially close to God. Yet as I grew older, there were times when my relationship with God would seem to fade. Thankfully, it wouldn't be long before I'd feel the Spirit drawing me back to renew my relationship with Him. I'll share a story that happened more recently when God did just that. But for now, let's look at what the Bible says about how the Spirit helps us draw close to God.

As we saw back in lesson 13, Jesus promised his disciples that the Father would send a "Helper"—the Holy Spirit. It's time now to look more carefully at the role that Jesus said this "Helper" would play in our lives. Notice what Jesus said in the final chapters of the book of John,

> And I will ask the Father, and he will give you another Helper, to be with you forever, even the Spirit of truth, whom the world cannot receive, because it neither sees him nor knows him. You know him, for he dwells with you and will be in you.
>
> - John 14:16-17 (ESV)

Notice that Jesus called the Spirit "another Helper." This signals the primary role of the Spirit in our lives—the one who helps! It's through the power of the Spirit that we are able to have fellowship with God (See: Romans 8:26), minister to others (See: I Corinthians 2:4), and ultimately persevere through the difficulties and trials in life (See: Ephesians 3:16; Jude 1:20-21).

Jesus also called him the "Spirit of truth." Just as Jesus taught his disciples spiritual truths and protected them from error, so the Spirit will teach and guide us. Notice what Jesus said, "But the Helper, the Holy Spirit, whom the Father will send in my name, he will teach you all things and bring to your remembrance all that I have said to you." (John 14:26 ESV). A bit later Jesus said, "When the Spirit of truth comes, he will guide you into all the truth..." (John 16:12 ESV).

Biblical theologian Larry Helyer pointed out that the Spirit's teaching will be submitted to the Father and to the Son. He won't "speak on his own..." This means that the Spirit will not give new, private, ground-breaking teaching that was not revealed to us by Jesus.[94] Unfortunately, history is full of false teachers who've started new religions, leading multitudes astray, simply because they claimed to have "fresh revelation" from the Holy Spirit. Interestingly, there are several warnings in the New Testament against this very thing (See: II Corinthians 11:4; Galatians 1:6-9; I John 4:1-3).

---

91. Romans 8:16, 26; I Corinthians 12:3; 13:14; Philippians 2:1; I John 1:3
92. Romans 8:3-5; Galatians 5:16, 25
93. Romans 12:6-8; 15:19; I Corinthians 12:4-11; Ephesians 4:11
94 Helyer, Larry. The Witness of Jesus, Paul and John: An Exploration in Biblical Theology (Downers Grove, InterVarsity Press) 2008. p. 373

133

Finally, Jesus told his followers that the Spirit will "dwell in" them. This must have been a shocking promise for these Jewish disciples. They grew up hearing stories of God's Spirit falling on men and women. Once God's Spirit had fallen on them, these me and women did incredible things—think Samson. David or Elijah.[95] But here, Jesus was promising that God's Spirit wouldn't just fall on them but "dwell in" them, suggesting that there would be an even greater outpouring of God's power upon their lives!

This was certainly reasonable since they had witnessed the Spirit's power firsthand in Jesus' own life. They saw Jesus' baptism and watched the Holy Spirit descend upon him as a dove (See: Matthew 3:16; Mark 1:10: Luke 3:21-22; John 1:31-34). Obviously, they regularly witnessed him do the impossible as he healed the sick and even raised the dead. So for Jesus to tell them that the same Spirit who had dwelt in him would dwell in them was an incredible promise!

As we've seen in previous lessons, the disciples did experience moments when God had done the miraculous through them, but these experiences were only tastes of what was to come. What the disciples hadn't yet experienced while Jesus was still with them was the intimate relationship with God that Jesus had. That was going to change. After Jesus ascended to Heaven, the Holy Spirit came and these disciples experienced God in a whole new way.

At this point, you might be wondering, "But how do I enjoy this kind of special relationship with God today? If it's true that the Spirit dwells in us, how do I practically experience this special relationship?"

To answer this, let's look again to Jesus and see what it looked like in his life. If we follow how the gospel of Mark introduces Jesus, we can see how Jesus' special relationship with the Father and the Spirit worked. After his baptism and time of testing in the wilderness, Jesus began announcing the arrival of the Kingdom of God (See: Mark 1:9-14). He demonstrated this "arrival" with powerful displays of spiritual power and physical healings. With a simple word, Jesus could cast out demonic spirits and heal the sick. His power seemed limitless (See: Mark 1:21-33).

But there's something significant that Mark records immediately after all of Jesus' miraculous work,

> And rising very early in the morning, while it was still dark, he departed and went out to a desolate place, and there he prayed. And Simon and those who were with him searched for him, and they found him and said to him, "Everyone is looking for you." And he said to them, "Let us go on to the next towns, that I may preach there also, for that is why I came out." And he went throughout all Galilee, preaching in their synagogues and casting out demons.
>
> - Mark 1:35-39 (ESV)

We find Jesus praying, spending time alone with his Father. When his disciples finally found him, Jesus abruptly announced that it was time to go on to the next town despite people looking for him. It's obvious, Jesus had received guidance and direction for his ministry in prayer.

---

95. For a study on the Holy Spirit in the Old Testament see the following: Exodus 28:3; 31:3; 35:31; Numbers 11:26,29; 24:6; Judges 3:10; 6:34; 11:29; 14:6,19; 15:14; I Samuel 10:6; 11:6; 16:13-14; 19:20, 23; II Samuel 23:2.

We actually see this happen several more times during Jesus' life. For example, just before he selected his disciples, we read that Jesus, "went out to the mountain to pray..." (Luke 6:12 ESV). Another time, after hearing that John the Baptist was executed, Jesus dismissed everyone including his disciples and, "went up on the mountain to pray" (Mark 6:46 ESV).[96] Jesus' prayer life deeply connected him to his Father and kept the power of the Spirit flowing through his life. This should be our practice as well.

Take a close look at what Paul said to the Ephesian Christians,

> <u>I pray that from his glorious, unlimited resources he will empower you with inner strength through his Spirit</u>. Then Christ will make his home in your hearts as you trust in him. Your roots will grow down into God's love and keep you strong. And may you have the power to understand, as all God's people should, how wide, how long, how high, and how deep his love is. May you experience the love of Christ, though it is too great to understand fully. Then you will be made complete with all the fullness of life and power that comes from God.
>
> - Ephesians 3:16-19 (NLT)

Let's unpack this a bit. Paul prayed that these believers would experience something in their lives. Notice carefully, he asked that they might experience inner strength supplied by God's Spirit. He continued, "Then Christ will make his home in [their] hearts." Finally, that their "roots" would grow down into "God's love and keep [them] strong." These are colorful, vivid images that describe the type of fellowship that we are to enjoy with God! And notice that it is the Holy Spirit that makes this possible. It is the Spirit alone who supplies the power for us to enjoy this relationship with God.

Notice what Paul said in Romans, "So you have not received a spirit that makes you fearful slaves. Instead, you received God's Spirit when he adopted you as his own children. Now we call him, 'Abba, Father.' For his Spirit joins with our spirit to affirm that we are God's children" (Romans 7:15-16 ESV). It's the Spirit that frees us from the dread of condemnation. In fact, Paul made it clear that it's the Spirit who, "joins with our spirit and affirms that we are God's children."

Did you catch that? Paul said that we now can call God our "Abba" (See also: Galatians 4:6). This is amazing! It's the same term that Jesus used when he prayed in agony in the Garden of Gethsemane (See: Mark 14:36). This Aramaic word is roughly translated "Daddy" and would never have been used as a reference for God by Jews. God was far too high and holy for such a familiar term, but as we've seen, Jesus' love-relationship with God was very special. And now through the fellowship we enjoy because of the Holy Spirit, we too can call him "Abba-Father!"

---

96. Many more examples could be given. (See: Matthew 26:36; Mark 6:46; Mark 14:32; Luke 4:42; 5:16; 6:12; 23:39-40; John 6:15; 17:1-26).

A Personal Journey

Unfortunately, it's way too easy to slide away from true, intimate fellowship with the Spirit. I remember a time several years ago when this happened to me. Growing up, I had always set aside time each day to pray and read my Bible. This was my habit. But as is true with any relationship, things can grow stale. Thankfully, God pursued me!

The change started after I had a conversation with Cris Cockrell. He told me how God had been working in his life. I was his high school Bible teacher during his senior year, and we'd just gotten home from a mission trip to Guatemala. Cris had been at our school ever since his dad died when he was in middle school.

After our mission trip, God had stirred his heart to seek Him in a whole new way. So Cris, being an adventurous young man, thought the best place to connect with God was from the roof of his house. Of course, it was! (I think he just wanted an excuse to be on his roof. I mean how could his mom object, he was praying!)

Cris described the time he would just sit there praying and waiting quietly for God to speak to his heart. He told me that nothing happened at first, but he just stayed there and persisted in prayer. Eventually, he began experiencing a deep sense of love from God. Slowly the pain of losing his father was addressed on that rooftop. He told me that something "woke up" in him that spring. It was an incredible experience of "God-as-Father" or "Abba". For him, this was even more profound because of his loss. Amazingly, if you ask Cris about losing his dad now, he'll tell you that although it was awful, the joy of knowing God as Father has made everything worth it. Of course, Cris wouldn't have chosen to lose his dad so early in life, but as a result of his loss, he now lives with a deep confidence in his Heavenly Dad. (God always redeems our pain if we let Him.)

As I talked with Cris that year and saw the changes taking place in his life, I was moved. I had remembered that intimacy he was describing. I hadn't really run away from God but my fellowship with Him wasn't where it needed to be. So, I decided to change the way I prayed and connected with God. No, I didn't climb on my roof! But I did make some changes. I think that's the way it's supposed to be in a real relationship with a real God. Things need to change from time to time. It's true of my relationships with Michelle and my girls, and it's true of my relationship with God.

Walk in the Spirit

In the Genesis story, Adam and Eve "walked" with God. They enjoyed a healthy, pure relationship with God and each other. In other words, they lived in perfect love and obedience to God. But when they disobeyed God, they became "enslaved" to sin and selfishness. Their capacity for a sin-free relationship was destroyed. As representatives of the race, they passed on this damage to the rest of humankind. As the biblical story moves forward, we see God reach out in love to different men and women. However, in each story, sin rears its ugly head. Whether God was dealing with individuals or even entire nations, sin continually plagued the human race. Human history is really the tragic story of wanting to love God and each other freely and fully but not being able to do so. This is why the work of Jesus is so incredible.

He alone can restore our relationship with God and each other (See: Romans 6:6).

Notice how Paul explained it.

> By sending his own Son in the likeness of sinful flesh and for sin, he condemned sin in the flesh, [4]in order that the righteous requirement of the law might be fulfilled in us, <u>who walk not according to the flesh but according to the Spirit</u>. [5]For those who live according to the flesh set their minds on the things of the flesh, but those who live according to the Spirit set their minds on the things of the Spirit.

-Romans 8:3-5 (ESV)

Paul taught that Jesus broke sin's power over us. He did this by "condemning sin in the flesh." This means that Jesus entered human history as a man, but didn't fall to sin like the rest of humankind. Instead, he fulfilled the "righteous requirements of the law." He lived in perfect obedience to God. Now as disciples of Jesus, we've received the Holy Spirit and can "walk... according to the Spirit."

Biblical scholar Douglas Moo observed, "God not only provides in Christ the full completion of the law's demands for the believer, but he also sends the Spirit into the hearts of believers to empower a new obedience to his demands."[97] He explained that this passage isn't telling us that believers should walk in the Spirit, but that believers do walk in the Spirit. In other words, disciples of Jesus are those who "walk"[98] in the Spirit. Jesus' victory has released us from sin's authority and has placed us under another "authority"——the Spirit. We are to live "Spirit-controlled" lives.[99] This is what it means to "walk in the Spirit."

But here's the problem. I don't always feel like I'm living a "Spirit-controlled" life. I don't always "walk in the Spirit." In the New Testament, we have many references about how we're supposed to "walk" (live) as disciples of Jesus.[100] Yet we also know that Christians don't always live up to this. This is what has been called the "already-but-not-yet" tension. As Christians, we've "already" received the Spirit and are under His control, but we're "not yet" completely freed of sin's influence. Until Jesus returns, we must make a conscious effort to live out what we've been given in Christ. We must try to "be" what we "are."

I think it's like how you feel right after getting married. Up until your wedding day, you were single. Perhaps you were married later in life, and so for many years, you identified as single. But one day

---

97. Moo, Douglas. The Epistle to the Romans. New International Commentary on the New Testament, edited by Gordon Fee. Grand Rapids: Eerdmans Publishing, 1996. p.484.

98. In the New Testament, many times the word "walk" is used as a metaphor for how one lives. (John 8:4)

99. Paul goes on to say, that those who haven't received the Spirit are still under the control of the "flesh and so cannot "please God." (See: Romans 8:6-8). It's important to understand the term "flesh" correctly. This doesn't refer to our bodies (i.e. "flesh and blood). Rather, the term comes from the Greek word "Sarx" and in Paul's use means a realm dominated by sin. We are either under the realm or power of the flesh or the Spirit. Paul is arguing that Christ freed us from the realm of the flesh that was enslaved to sin. Now we're under the Spirit's control. Misunderstanding this can lead to the conclusion that Christianity looks poorly on "bodily" things. This was a teaching in some Greek philosophies but not Christianity. Instead, Christianity teaches that we should enjoy the good things (physical and spiritual) that God gives us. (See: Romans 14:20; I Corinthians 7:36; 10:25-31; Colossians 2:16-23; James 1:17)

100. For a New Testament study that looks at the many references of our "walk", see the following--Luke 1:6; John 6:66; 8:4; 11:9; 12:35; Acts 14:16; 21:21; Romans 4:12; 6:4; 8:4; 13:13; 14:15; II Corinthians 5:7; 10:2-3; 12:18; Galatians 5:16; 6:16; Ephesians 2:2,10; 4:10,17; 5:2,8,15; Philippians 3:17-18; Colossians 1:10; 2:6; 3:7; 4:5; I Thessalonians 2:11; 4:1,12; II Thessalonians 3:6,11; I John 1:6-7; 2:5,11; II John 1:4-6; III John 1:3; Jude 1:11.

everything changed. You're now married. Your life and identity has fundamentally shifted. Now, you must live that way! As Christians, we must live out our new reality. We're no longer under sin's power; we're in Christ. Now, we must live that way! This was exactly what Paul urged when he wrote, "If we live by the Spirit, let us also keep in step with the Spirit." (Galatians 5:25 ESV). We must make the conscious choice to live out what is true about us.

This idea shows up again in Paul's letter to the Romans,
When he [Jesus] died, he died once to break the power of sin. But now that he lives, he lives for the glory of God. So you also should consider yourselves to be dead to the power of sin and alive to God through Christ Jesus. Do not let sin control the way you live; do not give in to sinful desires. Do not let any part of your body become an instrument of evil to serve sin. Instead, give yourselves completely to God...

- Romans 6:10-13a (NLT)

But how do we do this?!? This is a critically important question. In my life, this has certainly been easier said than done! The battle with remaining sin in our lives is something that we must face. Scholar Robert Fung observed, "The work of the Spirit in the believer's life does not set the believer free from the warfare between flesh and Spirit."[101] We're in a battle and must consciously choose to walk in the Spirit.

Notice what Paul said about this,

> But I say, walk by the Spirit, and you will not gratify the desires of the flesh. For the desires of the flesh are against the Spirit, and the desires of the Spirit are against the flesh, for these are opposed to each other, to keep you from doing the things you want to do.

- Galatians 5:16-17 (ESV)

Robert Fung wrote, "To 'walk by the Spirit' means to be under the constant, moment-by-moment direction, control and guidance of the Spirit."[102] Here is the key truth: we must let the Spirit fight for us. When we choose to remain under the direction, control and guidance of the Holy Spirit, we will find the power of remaining sin weakening in our lives.

Let's go back to our marriage example. As a husband, I know that I am married. I know that this means that I am to remain faithfully committed to Michelle, my wife. My heart is hers... or at least it should be! (As I type this, my beautiful wife is sitting across from me working on her computer!). If this is what being married means, how do spouses stray? There may be lots of circumstances and scenarios, but it all boils down to some point when one or both in the marriage stopped "walking" in that marriage commitment. As any marriage counselor will tell you, there are healthy practices and rhythms that should be in every marriage that help stoke the fires of love and affection for each other. What you "sow" into your marriage, you eventually "reap."

---

101. Fung, Ronald Y. K., The Epistle to the Romans. New International Commentary on the New Testament, edited by Gordon Fee. (Grand Rapids: Eerdmans Publishing) 1988. p.252
102. ibid.

This is precisely what Paul meant when he said, "For the one who sows to his own flesh will from the flesh reap corruption, but the one who sows to the Spirit will from the Spirit reap eternal life." (Galatians 6:8 ESV). We must "sow" to the Spirit. This is how we unleash the power of the Spirit to defeat the strength of sin in our lives. Paul talked about the "fruit of the Spirit" (Galatians 5:22-23) right after he mentioned the "works of the flesh" (Galatians 5:19-21). Both the works of the flesh and the fruit of the Spirit are the result of the kind of "sowing" a person has been doing. If we regularly sow to the Spirit, God will produce the good fruits that are listed there. This is important. We don't produce this fruit, God does. As we saw in lesson 12, we need to use spiritual disciplines to create the conditions where God's Spirit can produce his good fruit.

In my own life, after God alerted me to the dryness that had slowly crept into my walk with him, I began going on regular prayer walks. I realized that I needed to make a more conscious effort each night in prayer. These walks have helped keep my mind focused. I have noticed a direct correlation between this "sowing" to the Spirit and my feelings of temptation. The more I sow in prayer, the less I feel tempted to sin. In fact, if I'm feeling especially tempted, I now see this as a warning that I need to start sowing to the Spirit more. I'm not saying we can "pray away" every temptation or struggle. But it's true, sowing to the Spirit unleashes His power to change and help us.

Ministering in the Spirit

Probably the most well-known and exciting thing about the Holy Spirit are the so-called "gifts of the Spirit." I've purposely put this aspect of the Holy Spirit at the end of the lesson because I believe that any manifestation of the Spirit in our life must flow from our fellowship with the Spirit and from our walk with the Spirit.

Notice what Paul said, "Pursue love, and earnestly desire the spiritual gifts, especially that you may prophesy" (I Corinthians 14:1 ESV). Paul wanted his churches to desire spiritual gifts. He knew that God's Spirit gave gifts to the people in the Church, "to equip the saints for the work of ministry, for building up the body of Christ..." (Ephesians 4:12 ESV). So as we discuss spiritual gifts, we must understand that these gifts are intended to operate within a church body. Spiritual gifts are always to be used to help and encourage others. But they're abused when we use them in ways that draw attention to ourselves or when we leverage them to gain prominence over others (See: I Corinthians 14:4-6; II Corinthians 11:5-21; III John 1:9). Spiritual gifts should point away from the gifted person,

be in the service of the other and ultimately glorify Christ. Let's look at an important passage that discusses spiritual gifts.

Paul wrote, "There are different kinds of spiritual gifts, but the same Spirit is the source of them all. 5There are different kinds of service, but we serve the same Lord. 6God works in different ways, but it is the same God who does the work in all of us" (I Corinthians 12:4-6 ESV). Here we clearly see that the Spirit is the source of the spiritual gifts. We see that the Spirit is God, "who does the work." This is why I said at the outset of this lesson that we must do God's work, God's way, empowered by His Spirit.

Paul continued,

> A spiritual gift is given to each of us so we can help each other. To one person the Spirit gives the ability to give wise advice; to another the same Spirit gives a message of special knowledge. The same Spirit gives great faith to another, and to someone else the one Spirit gives the gift of healing. He gives one person the power to perform miracles, and another the ability to prophesy. He gives someone else the ability to discern whether a message is from the Spirit of God or from another spirit. Still another person is given the ability to speak in unknown languages, while another is given the ability to interpret what is being said. ¹¹It is the one and only Spirit who distributes all these gifts. He alone decides which gift each person should have.
>
> — I Corinthians 12:7-11 (ESV)

Paul was explaining to this church how their spiritual gifts were to help each other. My purpose here isn't to look at each individual gift mentioned but instead to point out three things that I think are obvious from this passage.

First, it's clear that the gifts are divided up to many different people in the church body. This means that we need each other. No one person has all of the gifts. I think God intentionally does this so that we love and appreciate each other in our life. We'll discuss this a bit more in a later lesson on the church. [103]

Second, our gifts guide our responsibility to the church. If you notice, each of the gifts are intended so that the Spirit can do a work through that person. This is why taking a "Spiritual Gifts Test" is an important way for you to determine how God intends for you to serve in the church.

Third, it's the Spirit who, "alone decides which gift each person should have." This means that we shouldn't be envious or proud of the gifts we have or lack. It is a great relief to rest in God's control over our life. He's decided our gifts. I don't need to fret or worry about the areas where I'm not gifted. Instead, I need to assume that God will bring someone with a gift that I need into my life. [104]

Notice one more passage where Paul discussed these spiritual gifts.

> In his grace, God has given us different gifts for doing certain things well. So if God has given you the ability to prophesy, speak out with as much faith as God has given you. ⁷If your gift is serving others, serve them well. If you are a teacher, teach well. ⁸If your gift is to encourage others, be encouraging. If it is giving, give generously. If God has

---

103. Please check out the Spiritual Gifts Test at the end of this lesson.
104. It's true that Paul later tells this church to, "desire the higher gifts" (I Corinthians 12:31). This means that we can indeed pray for God to give us new gifts we don't currently have. We don't need to have a fatalistic view of our lives. We're told that, "we have not because we ask not." (James 4:2). However, here Paul is reminding the church that ultimately God decides what gifts we will have and so we can rest in His wise oversight. Sometimes, God withholds something from us so that we will remain dependent upon Him and others. (See: II Corinthians 12:8; Philippians 4:14-17)

given you leadership ability, take the responsibility seriously. And if you have a gift
for showing kindness to others, do it gladly.

— Romans 12:6-8 (NLT)

We've been given a great opportunity to participate in God's kingdom work. There is nothing more fulfilling and rewarding than to know that God has used you in the lives of others. When we are in our
"sweet spot" of ministry, the spiritual gifts that we've been given will enable us—through the Spirit—
to do what is humanly impossible (See: Colossians 1:29). In order to be mature disciples of Christ, we
need to minister to others. Leaning into our Spirit-given gifts is the only way to do that. As we'll see
in a future lesson, it's God's desire that every believer experiences the joy of ministering in the Spirit.

Here again, we see that God is the one who has done the "giving." Again, the gifts we've been given
provide direction for how we're supposed to serve in the church. But there is one new emphasis in this
passage. Paul stressed how we use our gifts. Being "gifted" isn't enough. We must learn to use our
gifts well. This may include developing our gifts with more education, enhancing the impact of our gifts
with more training and improving the use of our gifts with more experience. In other words, we play
a role in how effectively we use what God gives us. This is a profound truth. One day we'll give an
account to God for what we did with the gifts He's given us (See: Luke 12:48; 19:15; Romans 14:12; I
Corinthians 3:10-15; I Timothy 6:20).

Putting It All Together

As we conclude this lesson, I want to take a minute and talk about my own experience with the Holy
Spirit. I want to share how the principles in this lesson have played out in my life. As we've seen,
everything must flow from our "fellowship with the Spirit." It might be a surprise to you, but even
as a pastor and teacher, I've had to fight for fellowship with the Spirit. This means I must guard my
mornings (when I've determined to read the Bible each day). My nightly prayer walks are easy to skip
(and sometimes I do). One of the first things I pray as I leave my house is: "God help me pray. Give
me the desire to seek you."

We've got to be honest with God. He's not offended. I think the more raw and honest I am with God
the more He seems to listen. I can sense His presence when I press into prayer with fervency.

Second, my fellowship with the Spirit puts me in a place where I can "walk in the Spirit." This is the
moment-by-moment presence of mind that we need to have each day. As we go through our daily
activities, we're to pray unceasingly (See: I Thessalonians 5:17). We're to give thanks in everything (See:
I Thessalonians 5:18; Philippians 4:6). In a nutshell, we're to have our minds "set" on things above (See:
Colossians 3:5).

Finally, there are special moments in my life when I've experienced a powerful move of the Spirit.
Here, I can only share my personal experience. But I've had profound times when my fellowship with
the Spirit and walking in the Spirit empowered my spiritual gifts in a special way. It feels like my
spiritual gifts of teaching and preaching are electrified with God's power. More than anything, I sense
His presence carrying me along.

As we saw in the beginning of this lesson, Stephen was a man "filled" with the Holy Spirit. I believe this "filling" is something that every Christian should experience. Paul said just this, "And do not get drunk with wine, for that is debauchery, but be filled with the Spirit" (Ephesians 5:18 ESV). That's an imperative sentence. Paul isn't suggesting that we be filled with the Spirit; he's commanding it!

I believe the filling of the Holy Spirit is the inevitable outcome of someone who fellowships with the Spirit, walks in the Spirit, and presents their gifts in service to the Spirit. I think it's the sum total experience of our life in the Spirit. Yet, at times, I don't experience this. This is because I can also "grieve" (See Ephesians 4:30) and "quench" (I Thessalonians 4:19) the Spirit. Paul instructed his disciple Timothy to "...not neglect the gift you have, which was given you by prophecy when the council of elders laid their hands on you" (I Timothy 4:14 ESV). It seems clear that we can disrupt the "flow" of the Spirit into and through our lives. We can neglect our walk with Him. We can allow temptation and sin to take our eyes off of the Lord. And just like Peter walking on the water, we can start to sink (See: Matthew 14:30).

At the end of the day, our lives as believers should be lived as Paul lived his—in the power of the Spirit. As we finish this lesson, meditate on what Paul said in his letter to the Corinthians.

When I first came to you, dear brothers and sisters, I didn't use lofty words and impressive wisdom to tell you God's secret plan. ²For I decided that while I was with you I would forget everything except Jesus Christ, the one who was crucified. ³I came to you in weakness—timid and trembling. ⁴And my message and my preaching were very plain. Rather than using clever and persuasive speeches, I relied only on the power of the Holy Spirit. ⁵I did this so you would trust not in human wisdom but in the power of God.

- I Corinthians 2:1-5 (NLT)

MAY IT BE SO IN OUR LIVES!

THE SUMMARY:

Jesus said that he would send another helper, the Holy Spirit. This is exactly what Jesus did. Everyone who has surrendered their lives as Jesus' disciples receives the Holy Spirit into their life. He will guide and teach those who've said "yes!" He will help us understand truth from error. When God pursues us, the Holy Spirit helps us to respond. He helps us have a relationship with God. He helps us submit our wills to God and remain under His power. Finally, He helps us minister to others by giving us spiritual gifts. He fills us in order that we enact God's good will.

BIBLE STUDY

[Answer the following questions to enhance your learning.]

What are some of the characteristics of Stephen's life that point to him being "filled with the Spirit"?

How would you define "fellowship with the Spirit?" What practice in your life do you think helps you best connect with God?

Have you experienced "walking in the Spirit?" If so, describe what that was like? Did you feel under His power? If so, give a specific example.

What do you believe your spiritual gifts might be? Have you experienced God using you in a special way to help someone else?

Pray over what you've learned in this lesson. Write out a summarizing prayer below.

MEMORY VERSE:

"For the one who sows to his own flesh will from the flesh reap corruption, but the one who sows to the Spirit will from the Spirit reap eternal life."

- Galatians 6:8 (ESV)

FOR FURTHER RESOURCES ON THIS TOPIC:

Francis Chan, and Danae Yankoski. Forgotten God: reversing our tragic neglect of the Holy Spirit. Colorado Springs, CO: David C. Cook, 2015.

Charles H Kraft. I give you authority: practicing the authority Jesus gave us. Minneapolis, MN: Chosen, 2012.

Scot McKnight and Dave Ferguson. Open to the Spirit: God in Us, God with Us, God Transforming Us. New York: WaterBrook, 2018.

John R. W. Stott. Baptism and fullness: the work of the Holy Spirit today. Downers Grove, IL: InterVarsity Press, 2006.

For information on a spiritual gift test see: https://www.freeshapetest.com/

APPENDIX:

What about Speaking in Tongues?

There is controversy around some spiritual gifts. The debate is over whether or not the so-called "charismatic" gifts are still operational today and, if so, when they should be expressed. In the churches in which I grew up, we were taught that the "charismatic" gifts were limited to the time of the apostolic age when the church was first born. However, these spiritual gifts stopped by the end of the first century. This view is known as "cessationism."

One of the supporting texts used for cessationism is I Corinthians 13:8, "Love never ends. As for prophecies, they will pass away; as for tongues, they will cease; as for knowledge, it will pass away." I no longer hold this view. I am not convinced that Paul was ever suggesting that certain spiritual gifts would suddenly stop. Rather, if we look at the entire context of I Corinthians, it's clear that Paul assumed these spiritual gifts would continue until Jesus returns. This isn't the place for a full argument but I am convinced that our charismatic brothers and sisters are quite right to insist that all of the spiritual gifts are still in operation today. Many evangelical scholars agree on this point and the biblical support for cessationism is weak.

There remains disagreement over how these spiritual gifts should operate in a corporate church gathering. The intimate house-church setting that was common in the New Testament era had a different dynamic than our larger gatherings today. Some so-called "charismatic" churches believe the large Sunday worship gathering should be a place where all of the gifts of the Spirit are expressed. Other so-called "non-charismatic" churches either hold a cessationist view or believe some of the gifts of the Spirit are inappropriate in large Sunday morning church services. I personally believe that every believer should be encouraged to use the gifts they've been given. I believe more should be done in non-charismatic churches to allow those with gifts such as prophecy, tongues and healing to operate in the church. Perhaps smaller settings such as special worship gatherings or small home groups that closely approximate the first century church would be most appropriate.

For more on the appendix see:

Gregory A. Boyd and Paul R. Eddy. Across the Spectrum: Understanding Issues in Evangelical Theology. Grand Rapids: Baker Pub. Group, 2002. (Ch. 14; p.235-248)

Scot McKnight and Dave Ferguson. Open to the Spirit: God in Us, God with Us, God Transforming Us. New York: WaterBrook, 2018.

LESSON #17: Three Invisible Influences

There are three major influences that affect each of us as we try to follow Jesus. They are: early life experiences, our individual personality/temperament, and the larger American culture. Each of us look at the world through these lenses, and they usually affect us in subtle ways that are difficult to recognize. This lesson is a little longer than the other lessons in this book, so I was tempted to make this into three separate lessons. However, since they are all "influences" in our lives, I decided to keep them as one single unit. Since our purpose is to simply introduce important truths for our lives with Jesus, I've been as brief as possible. Many books have been written on each of these influences, so I've included book suggestions for each of them at the end of the lesson. Okay, enough said, let's get started!

Introduction

There is one particularly "cringe-worthy" moment in the gospel of Luke that will help introduce our topic.[105] It happened just as Jesus made the decision to make his way to Jerusalem for the final time. There, he predicted that he would be, "delivered into the hands of men" (Luke 9:44 ESV). The disciples didn't understand. They believed that he was Israel's true messiah who would conquer Rome and set up God's kingdom once and for all. As Jesus and his disciples began traveling south to Jerusalem, they needed to pass through Samaritan territory. The Samaritans were descendants of the 10 northern tribes of Israel who were conquered centuries earlier. So they shared a common ancestry with the Jews of Jesus' day but sadly a long-standing religious feud existed between them. The two groups hated each other and tried to avoid each other at all costs (See: John 4:7-26).

Jesus didn't play into Jewish prejudice and never avoided Samaritans. In fact, on many occasions, he made it clear that he was their messiah as well (See: John 4:26; Acts 1:8). So, as Jesus planned his trip to Jerusalem, he sent his disciples ahead to arrange lodging. But when they arrived in the Samaritan town, the residents were only willing to provide hospitality if Jesus was planning to stay with them. If Jesus was only passing through, he could find somewhere else to sleep!

Notice what happened when they come back with the unhappy news. "And when his disciples James and John saw it, they said, "Lord, do you want us to tell fire to come down from heaven and consume them?" (Luke 9:54 ESV).

Can you picture that? These Jewish boys were so offended at the Samaritan rejection, they basically decided

---

105. Perhaps the most common and intuitive reason people have for believing the gospels is the simple way the characters are presented. The men and women are just ordinary regular folk. There's no attempt to make heroes out of these future leaders. So whether we're reading about the embarrassing boasts of Peter or the repeated childish arguments the disciples had over who was greatest (See: Luke 9:46; 22:24), we have realistic, true-to-life, accounts of the early Jesus movement. Everything is recorded, even the ugly parts!

In addition to the literary reasons just mentioned, modern scholarship and archeology has shed more light on the culture and world of ancient Palestine. Unsurprisingly, these new discoveries further help corroborate the gospel accounts. Moreover, there have been great advancements in textual criticism in the past century, including the recovery of very ancient manuscripts. So we can say today, with more conviction than ever, that the gospels were written within the lifetime of the disciples of Jesus and that our modern Bibles accurately reflect what was written 2000 years ago. For some interesting books on this subject. See: Craig Evans. Jesus and His World: The Archaeological Evidence. (Louisville, KY. Westminister John Knox Press) 2012; Richard Bauckham Jesus and the Eyewitnesses: The Gospels as Eyewitness Testimony 2nd ed. (Grand Rapids, Eerdmans publishing) 2017.

it would be best to nuke them! Incredibly, after spending three years with Jesus, they still couldn't see how this attitude violated everything Jesus had taught them (See: Matthew 5:38-45; John 3:16-18). The look on Jesus' face must have been incredulous. It's too bad Luke didn't tell us exactly what Jesus said, instead the text simply says, "...he turned and rebuked them. 56And they went on to another village" (Luke 9:55-56 ESV).

This little story illustrates the profound truth of how "invisible influences" from our culture and upbringing continue to affect us even after we've started following Jesus. These influences are always running in the background of our lives, almost like an operating system in a computer. Since they've shaped our thinking our entire lives, it's difficult to examine their influence to see if it's good or bad. As Jesus followers, we must be aware of them in light of the gospel and the kingdom values we've been discussing in this book.

Influence #1 - Family Influence and Early Life Experiences

A few years back, my wife went back to college in pursuit of a degree in Marriage and Family Therapy. As she threw herself into her studies, she would share the insights she was learning from her school work. We both gained a new appreciation for how family background and early life experiences fundamentally shape us as persons. As I began reading on this topic, I realized that many of our emotional responses can be the result of our early family environments. And since none of us were raised in perfect homes, most of us have some emotional habits that we may not realize are unhealthy. Obviously, this widely varies depending on our upbringing, but you can bet this first "invisible influence" still holds some sway over your life today.

To me, one of the most helpful authors on this matter has been Peter Scazzero. In his book, Emotionally Healthy Spirituality he wrote, "Emotional health and spiritual maturity are inseparable. It is not possible to be spiritually mature while remaining emotionally immature."[106] Scazzero recounted the journey that led him to that conclusion as he described the struggle he had as a pastor in New York for over 30 years. He was continually discouraged at the lack of genuine, deep transformation in the people at his church.

As the lead pastor, he knew his job was to oversee the spiritual needs of his congregation and so he tried several different programs to encourage deeper, more permanent life-change. First, they tried church-wide small group Bible studies, thinking a more intimate community would change people. After that didn't work, he thought it was a "spiritual warfare" issue, so he taught his church to confront the enemy in Jesus' name. Still not satisfied, he thought if their church could only develop a deeper culture of worship, people would automatically experience deeper transformation. Finally, he moved the church to serve the poor—perhaps that would create the permanent change in their lives. Even after all of these good and important initiatives, Scazzero still didn't see the wide-spread, transformation he'd expected.

It wasn't until the stresses of ministry caused deep fractures in his own marriage, did Scazzero begin to see something he'd been blind to since he'd become a Christian as a teenager. He was emotionally unhealthy. His childhood experiences and family background had been playing a huge role in his life as an adult. He began to identify fears and insecurities connected to his childhood that continued to drive him

---

106. Scazzero, Peter. Emotional Healthy Spirituality. (Grand Rapids, Zondervan) 2006. p.17

as a husband, father and now, pastor. These painful insights caused him to slowly reexamine everything in his life, including how he approached church and discipleship.

He wrote, "It wasn't until the pain exposed how much was hiding under my surface of being a 'good Christian' that it hit me: whole layers of my emotional life had lain buried, untouched by God's transforming power."[107] Scazzero explained that, as Christians, we tend to ignore or bury negative emotions that we don't believe are "godly" rather than explore where they are coming from. He says that when we do this, we fail to allow God's Spirit to work on the root issues driving our lives. We think more Christian activities will magically heal past trauma or ingrained values learned from childhood.

My Journey

These insights, along with what my wife was learning in her coursework, alerted me to areas in my own life where I was emotionally unhealthy. I felt one of the areas I could address was the area of my anger. Most of the time, I could control it, but sometimes I would boil over in anger toward my family. I was tempted to justify this since it didn't happen that often, and so, I thought, it couldn't be "that bad." After all, doesn't everyone fly off the handle sometimes?[108] Still, I was troubled by my anger, and even when it didn't show on the outside, at times, I could still feel it internally. Why did some things bother me so much?

So I began paying close attention to the things that made me angry, anxious, or feel insecure. I learned that these were secondary emotions and that there was something at the root of them. I came to see that some of the triggers that caused anger or anxiety were actually rooted in my insecurities from childhood. I've always known as a Christian, I shouldn't be an angry or anxious person (See: Galatians 5:19-21; Ephesians 4:26, 31; James 1:19; 1 Peter 5:7), I was now trying to see where it was all coming from.

I was the firstborn in my family and had two very high-achieving parents. So naturally, hard work and staying busy were strong values in my family environment. This, combined with my particularly sensitive personality (which we'll discuss in the next section), caused me to believe that my value and self-worth were connected to my achievements and my capacity to stay busy. As a young man, this drove me to work hard in sports and school. Now later in my life, I often feel a restless drive to be the best teacher or preacher possible and to fill every moment with activity. So if I ever felt lazy or if I believed that I failed in some way, I would experience a surge of negative emotions and insecurities.

When I started paying close attention to these emotional responses, I made the connection that much of my anger and frustration was tied to times I felt I could have done better or was disrespected by others. For me, disrespect was a signal that I hadn't achieved a high enough "score" in the eyes of another person. Since I began to see how my anger was tied to feelings of disrespect and realized that I viewed disrespect as an assault on my self-worth, I came to see that my real issue wasn't anger but instead, what I fundamentally believed about myself. I was blind to the "invisible influence" that had distorted my thinking.

---

107. ibid. p.11
108. A recent Harvard study has shown that nearly 10% of men suffer at times with intermittent explosive disorder (IED). This disorder causes "wildly disproportionate aggression" and the person can become so angry that they're likely to damage property or threaten or injure others. https://www.menshealth.com/health/why-so-angry.

149

This journey toward emotional health, although painful at times, has been invaluable in my walk with Christ. And while I was very fortunate to grow up in a Christian home with believing parents who loved each other and their children deeply, I still wasn't able to avoid developing some bad habits and an unhealthy view of self-worth. So even if you were raised in a great home environment, you'll still need to evaluate the values and ideas that you've carried into your adult life. While I still have a long way to go on this journey, the integration of emotional health and spiritual maturity has already impacted my Christian life.

Finally, for those who've experienced abuse, divorce and other trauma in their formative years, the emotional impact is difficult to measure. Everybody is different. Some may seem to come through trauma better than others, but chances are you'll need help toward recovery. Regardless of who you are, these influences don't magically disappear when you begin following Jesus. There's no "extra points" in trying to do this by yourself. It's usually pride or fear of rejection that keeps us from reaching out for help. But we can't let that stop us. As Christians, we're commanded to be there for each other (See: Romans 12:15; 15:1; Galatians 6:2; Philippians 2:4). Depending on your life experiences, you may need Christian-based therapy or a recovery group such as Celebrate Recovery. And I think everyone could benefit from reading books on spiritual and emotional health.

Influence #2 - Personality and Temperament

I don't think I fully understood how different and unique human beings are until I had three kids of my own. Even though they are still young (currently in elementary school), it's been hilarious and fascinating to see the differences in each of them. Same home, same parents, same school, same church but radically different personalities! My oldest is a fun-loving, type "A" personality, who started a baking business at 9 years old complete with business cards. The younger two are twins (even more "sameness") but are as different as night and day. The older twin is a rule-following, perfectionist, who wants to know where the line is so that she can tell everyone (especially her younger sister) where it's located. The youngest is more laid-back and artistic but definitely more comfortable dancing on the line! (She recently smuggled a cheat sheet into her first-grade spelling test!)

It's undeniable that each of us have very different personalities and temperaments. As Jesus followers, it's important to understand that God doesn't want to change that part of you. If you've always been an extrovert, energized by people (like my firstborn), that shouldn't change after you begin following Jesus. If you enjoy quiet evenings at home and would rather have a good conversation than going to a party, that's simply the way God made you. We must understand God's transformation in our life enhances what He originally created in us. God doesn't destroy us; He restores us.

I've met many who think they must become a different person rather than accepting how God has made them. I've struggled with this myself. I tend to be more introverted and contemplative, but I can't tell you how many times I've felt guilty that I wasn't better at sharing my faith with strangers. I would see other Jesus-loving believers with outgoing personalities share their faith with ease, while I struggled to know how to get a conversation started! What's important to know is that both the introvert and the extrovert have strengths and weaknesses that need to be brought under the rule of King Jesus.

Strengths

Let's talk about our strengths first. Each of us have natural abilities. These talents and gifts can be physical, mental, emotional and (after you've become a Jesus follower) spiritual.[109] These strengths have carried us throughout our lives. Whether you've thought about it or not, you've probably depended on them your entire life. It makes perfect sense to leverage our natural aptitudes to our advantage. If you're in a career, it was most likely a strength, talent or special ability that got you your start. If you're married, there were personality strengths that first attracted you to your spouse and vice versa.

Strengths are gifts! However, as Jesus followers, we must learn to submit these strengths to him. Peterand Paul both had incredible gifts. Peter was a bold, strong leader that earned him the nickname "rocky" (See: Matthew 16:18). Paul was a tenacious and brilliant thinker, whom God used to plant many churches and write more of the New Testament than anyone else. However, our gifts can get us into trouble. It's easy to depend upon them rather than God. Listen to what Paul said,

> "...Even though I have received such wonderful revelations from God. So to keep me from becoming proud, I was given a thorn in my flesh, a messenger from Satan to torment me and keep me from becoming proud. 8Three different times I begged the Lord to take it away. 9Each time he said, "My grace is all you need. My power works best in weakness." So now I am glad to boast about my weaknesses, so that the power of Christ can work through me."
>
> - II Corinthians 12:7-9 (NLT)

It seems that some people in this church doubted if Paul was really as qualified as other Apostles. So he felt compelled to list some of the things that he had endured for the sake of the gospel (See: II Corinthians 11:16-33). In addition to the many hardships he suffered, Paul received incredible insights and revelations (See: Acts 9:1-22; 27:23; II Corinthians 12:1-6; Galatians 1:12). Luke recorded many miracles God did through Paul (See: Acts 14:9,19-20; 16:18, 25-26; 19:6; 20:10; 27:23; 28:3-6, 8).

Needless to say, there was a lot Paul could have boasted about. He worked harder than any other apostle, and it showed (See: I Corinthians 15:10)! It's obvious that he was extremely gifted, but take a close look at what he said God allowed into his life to keep him from pride. "So to keep me from becoming proud, I was given a thorn in my flesh..." (I Corinthians 12:7 NLT). We're not sure what this "thorn" was but it clearly slowed Paul down and reminded him of his weakness.

Unfortunately, it's very common that our strongest abilities become our greatest liabilities. The good gifts that God has given us can easily become sources of pride and self-dependence. It would be silly to boast about something we're not any good at. But sadly, it's all too common to leverage our strengths to position ourselves above others. Paul said that this thorn taught him to depend on Christ's power— his grace. You see, God's grace must support us. We must depend on him. It's got to be his power we lean on and his purpose we live for or else we become puffed up in pride and waste our lives in earthly, trivial, pursuits. As a Jesus follower, I must understand that sometimes God might allow pain or weakness in my life to keep me aware of my great need for Jesus. It's much better to live with a weakness that keeps me humble than to live in prideful strength that ultimately leads to a wasted life. And so we find in our weakness a strength supplied by Christ to do his will, his way.

---

109. For more about "Spiritual gifts" see lesson 16 on the Holy Spirit.

Weaknesses

So what about our weaknesses? There are two ways we usually talk about the weaknesses in our life: weaknesses of character and weaknesses of personality.[110] As I said earlier, following Jesus shouldn't fundamentally alter your personality or temperament. However, some personality traits are highly valued in some families, churches and in our larger culture. So, it's common to think that some other personality traits are fundamentally flawed. (Sometimes loud and outgoing kids are continually scolded, and other times slower-paced kids are always told they're lazy.) Remember, God doesn't "mass-produce" human beings. He's made us as individuals, and we shouldn't be forced into another person's mold.

In the course of my teaching career, I've witnessed the devastating results of when a child's natural personality traits weren't valued by parents or other adults in their lives. As parents and mentors, we should nurture the natural gifts and wiring of others. Our goal should be the same as God's—to see them flourish into the best version of themselves, not to become someone completely different!

However, weaknesses in character are things that Jesus will address in our life. In my observation, I think there are some personality types that may be more prone to certain character weaknesses than others. It's important to distinguish between a personality trait and a character weakness. The high-strung type "A" personality may be naturally aggressive (not necessarily a bad thing), but they can struggle with treating people appropriately. It's easy for this type of person to lack tact and to dominate others. While the slower-paced personality might be great at detail work, they can at times, lack appropriate drive or become overly perfectionistic and inflexible.

As I mentioned in the previous section, my sensitive personality naturally inclined me to unhealthy ideas of self-worth. As a Jesus follower, I needed to let what God says define who am (See: Romans 8:15; I John 3:15). For those who find it easy to dominate others, they must learn to take a step back and show God-honoring submission to others (See: Romans 12:9-16; Ephesians 5:21). The slower-paced people who struggle with being responsible, need to learn to work hard at their jobs (See: Ephesians 6:5-9; Colossians 3:18-24; I Thessalonians 5:14; II Thessalonians 3:8-10). The examples could go on. We all have areas for growth. But God is faithful. He will use people and experiences in our lives to refine our character and make us into better versions of ourselves (See: Romans 5:3-5; James 1:2-4; II Peter 1:3-8).

On the other hand, we must be willing to change and grow. We're good at justifying bad habits. We can easily excuse character weakness with phrases like: "That's just the way I am" or "That's just how I was raised!" But we shouldn't hide behind that! The great thing about being a Jesus follower is that he defines and refines who we are now. Our old identity and patterns are being transformed. He is remaking us in His image, which incidentally, will also be the best version of ourselves. That's what matters now.

One final word here: Learning about personalities and temperaments can help us understand one another better. As we learn that the traits we find annoying in others are simply the way their personality functions and are rooted in different reasons than we intuitively assign, we can learn to have more patience and grace with others. This also helps us understand why we "click" more easily with some people but find meshing with other people more difficult. These insights can help our marriages, parenting and work-relationships. We can also learn the best way to relate to others since each temperament tends to

110. I'd like to thank Pastor Mike Nay for reminding me of this difference.

have different emotional needs. I've listed some good resources below for more information on discovering your own temperament and learning about the four major personality types that have been identified.

Influence #3 - American Culture

As we consider this final influence, think again about the story that we looked at in the first section. From our point of view, the disciple's suggestion is crazy. Incinerate an entire town just because they wouldn't give Jesus a place to sleep!?! Yet this makes perfect sense if you're a first century Jewish boy with a nurtured hatred for Samaritans! This is exactly what cultural bias does to us. It blinds us to things that should be obvious.

Our culture is no different. Here's a quick observation. Since I've become an adult, our nation has grown more sensitive to the experience of minorities in our country. For example, gay marriage has been legalized. Transgender accommodations are now expected in public schools. Movements like "Black Lives Matter" have formed to spotlight current examples of black oppression in our land. And most recently, the "#metoo" movement has unmasked the ugly oppressive culture of sexual harassment and misconduct that exists in Hollywood and in Washington D.C.

While each of these issues are very different and debate continues to swirl around these topics, what isn't debatable is that in less than a generation, our mainstream culture has shifted. For better or worse, the cultural viewpoint on these issues has changed or is in the process of changing. What isn't tolerated today was winked at yesterday. However, the opposite is also true. Our grandparents couldn't imagine tolerating yesterday what's out in the open today. Sexual exhibitionism and graphic pornography are commonplace. There's open hostility toward our national leaders and even a growing disrespect for our country. To be sure, some of this existed in the past, but it wasn't mainstream. My point is simple. Every generation in every culture has values they prize and sins they tolerate.

This has always been a tension for Jesus followers. As the Church grew beyond the borders of Palestine and spread throughout the larger Greco-Roman world, it was clear that the values and practices of pagan Rome were at odds with the teachings of Jesus. So the early church leaders needed to make sure that the new Gentile converts to Christianity understood areas of their former life that needed to change. Notice what Paul wrote to people living in the wealthy city of Corinth,

> Don't you realize that those who do wrong will not inherit the Kingdom of God? Don't fool yourselves. Those who indulge in sexual sin, or who worship idols, or commit adultery, or are male prostitutes, or practice homosexuality, [10]or are thieves, or greedy people, or drunkards, or are abusive, or cheat people—none of these will inherit the Kingdom of God. [11]Some of you were once like that. But you were cleansed; you were made holy; you were made right with God by calling on the name of the Lord Jesus Christ and by the Spirit of our God.
>
> - I Corinthians 6:9-11 (ESV)

Even by today's permissive standards, pagan Rome was extremely immoral. The city of Corinth was the "sin-city" of the Roman Empire. The city's reputation for sexual license was so common, that a Greek poet coined the term "korinthiazesthai" ("to Corinthianize") which meant, "to fornicate." Corinth was a wealthy trading post with a large temple dedicated to the goddess Aphrodite situated on a high hill overlooking the city. The temple employed hundreds of cultic prostitutes which led "worshipers" into Aphrodite's temple each afternoon. The city's association with prostitution was so well known that if you called a lady a "Corinthian girl", you might just get slapped![111]

In reality, Corinth wasn't much different than the rest of the Empire. There were very few sexual re strictions for Roman men. Extramarital liaisons were commonplace. Homosexuality and pederasty was completely accepted (even encouraged) especially among the nobility. On the other hand, Roman women among the noble classes were very restricted. They were expected to remain sexually faithful to their husbands and lived under very strict cultural rules. To make matters worse, the majority of the population were either slaves or extremely poor. As you can imagine in such a culture, sexual exploitation was very common.[112]

So as the church entered this pagan world, intensive training was needed so that new disciples could learn what from their past was no longer acceptable for a Jesus follower. It must have been extremely challenging for new believers to follow Jesus' conservative teachings on sex and marriage (See Matthew5:31-32; 19:1-10). After all, Jesus' teachings on marriage and divorce even shocked his Jewish audience, how much more to the gentile pagans! So notice in the passage cited above, how Paul encouraged these former pagans from Corinth to disassociate themselves from their former life. He was fighting against a cultural blind spot that threatened their commitment to Jesus.

Sexual ethics is just one example. We can hardly imagine what the religious paganism of ancient Rome was really like. There was a literal pantheon of gods and goddesses each demanding patronage and worship. There were local deities that promised protection and prosperity to citizens of local towns. There were national gods that governed fertility, sea voyages, healing, war and just about everything else! There wasn't any place in life that wasn't intertwined with pagan worship—including buying food. Just about all available meat would have either been in the pagan temples themselves or in markets just outside. Eating the meat that had been offered to the gods was part of temple worship.

Imagine how difficult it must have been to be a Christian in that environment. Superstitions die hard. In fact, many former pagans felt they were being disloyal to Jesus if they ate this "idolized" meat (See: Romans 14:1-4; 20-23; 1 Corinthians 8:1-13; 10:14-31). This is why we see these kinds of cultural issues being addressed throughout the letters of the New Testament. Learning how to be a faithful citizen of God's kingdom while still living here on earth was a paramount concern for the early disciples. Thankfully, we aren't faced with these particular challenges today. But this raises an important question: What are the cultural "blind spots" we face today? What are the things that are so commonplace in our culture that we might not ever see them as threats to our allegiance to king Jesus? Obviously, there is a lot that could be written here, but our purpose in this book is to only introduce these ideas to you. Because of this, we'll limit ourselves to a brief discussion of two major areas.

111. Freedman, David N. The Anchor Yale Bible Dictionary. (New Haven, Conn. Yale University Press) 1992.
112. Westfall, Cynthia Long. Paul and Gender. (Grand Rapids. Baker Academic) 2016. p. 25-26, 192-193

First, our American culture is a consumer-based society. As I write this, today is Cyber-Monday. Analysts predict that more than 6.6 billion dollars will be spent today alone. We are consumers. Shopping is a national pastime and black Friday now starts on Thanksgiving Thursday—doors open at 6 PM. In a culture of consumers, just about everything becomes a commodity to be bought or sold. As customers, we are the center of our little universes. So, we naturally believe people and things exist to make our lives better. We live in the constant pursuit of comfort.

Advertisers don't help. They exist solely for the purpose of increasing our appetite for creature comforts with the promise that the new and improved gadget will make our lives easier. Old virtues such as contentment, patience and sabbath rest are sacrificed on the altar of consumerism. We falsely believe that we need more and more in order to enjoy the good life. Consequently, life is lived at a frantic pace because we think if we work a little more, if we squeeze a little harder, we can afford the next "must have" that just came out. And, if we can't afford it, no worries, credit cards can feed the beast of consumerism. All goes well until we finally find ourselves buried in debt—enslaved to our things and overworked trying to pay for it all!

Meanwhile, we can't even hear Jesus' words,

> "Don't store up treasures here on earth, where moths eat them and rust destroys them, and where thieves break in and steal. [20]Store your treasures in heaven, where moths and rust cannot destroy, and thieves do not break in and steal. [21]Wherever your treasure is, there the desires of your heart will also be."
>
> - Matthew 6:19-21 (NLT)

Frankly, our consumer-based culture is at odds with Christian discipleship. Many of us are just too busy to follow Jesus. Our treasure has stolen our heart, and we've ignored Jesus' warnings (See: Matthew 6:24-30). Our priorities are completely out of whack. We will touch on this in our lesson It Takes a Church to Raise a Christian.

Second, our obsession with personal happiness and the "American Dream" is a threat to our commitment to Jesus. Rugged individualism was a popular term coined in the depression era, and it encapsulates the American Spirit. We are a "pull-yourself-up-by-the-boot-straps", "can-do" kind of country. Because of this, we've risen to become the world's most powerful nation. Unlike our European cousins, we've always prided ourselves on not having American nobility. We believe the American dream and a right to personal happiness should be available to anyone with enough ingenuity and a willingness to work.

Today, this American Dream narrative is being challenged, as minority voices have pointed out that the playing field is far from even. Hopefully this is changing. However, no one seems to question if we've taken the whole concept of "pursuing happiness" a bit too far. So how can our commitment to the American Dream conflict with our commitment to Christ? Let's conclude our lesson by looking at two threats this cultural blind spot holds against discipleship.

First, pursuing the American dream and seeking first the kingdom of God is extremely difficult (Matthew

6:33 ESV). Our culture continually pushes us toward self-fulfillment. Obviously, the freedom to pursue a dream or a career can be a great blessing, but for the disciple of Jesus, these pursuits must remain secondary to God's kingdom. As we've seen, most people in the first century had no personal freedom. They wouldn't have struggled with a preoccupation of "bigger and better" and marking things off of their "bucket list."

In fact, notice what Paul said to the Christians at Corinth on this topic:

> Each of you should continue to live in whatever situation the Lord has placed you, and remain as you were when God first called you. This is my rule for all the churches... The important thing is to keep God's commandments. [20]Yes, each of you should remain as you were when God called you. [21]Are you a slave? Don't let that worry you—but if you get a chance to be free, take it. [22]And remember, if you were a slave when the Lord called you, you are now free in the Lord. And if you were free when the Lord called you, you are now a slave of Christ. [23]God paid a high price for you, so don't be enslaved by the world. [24]Each of you, dear brothers and sisters, should remain as you were when God first called you.

> - I Corinthians 7:17, 19-24 (ESV)

This runs completely against our cultural value. Paul was telling these Christians that their service in God's kingdom was far more important than improving their lives here on earth. It's true that Paul tells slaves to gain their freedom if possible. However, from the context, it's obvious this wasn't an overriding concern for him. For most of us, though, improving our lives in the here and now is all we can think about. Instead, Paul and the other apostles continually remind these ancient churches to keep their hearts and minds on building God's kingdom (See: I Corinthians 2:9; 6:3; II Corinthians 5:1-9; II Peter 1:10-16).

Finally, it's extremely difficult for Americans to surrender—to Jesus and to one another (See: Mark 8:34-38; Ephesians 5:21). We don't surrender; Americans don't submit. While the unalienable right to "pursue happiness" is enshrined in our founding documents, we forget the way of Jesus is a voluntary "death" (See: Romans 6:2-7; Galatians 2:20; Colossians 3:1-5). As a result, it almost seems un-American to completely surrender your life over to Jesus.

I'm afraid Jesus' warnings to the rich apply to us. "Truly, I say to you, only with difficulty will a rich person enter the kingdom of heaven. 24Again I tell you, it is easier for a camel to go through the eye of a needle than for a rich person to enter the kingdom of God" (Matthew 19:23-24 ESV). Our wealth, our pursuit of comfort and our belief that we have a basic right to be happy can stop us from living as faithful disciples of Jesus. These things aren't evil in themselves, but they can easily become cultural idols that control and enslave us. So, as American Christians, we must realize that these potential blind spots can be hindering our total obedience to Jesus.

We've only briefly looked at these three invisible influences. Many books have been written on each of these. It's my hope that this introduction gave you some insights and might spur you on to further study. Look for more resources below.

THE SUMMARY:

There are invisible influences that try to turn your "yes" into a "no." We must be aware of how our childhood, personality and American culture can negatively influence us as we try to follow Jesus. A wise disciple is aware of these influences and consciously confronts and reckons with their negative aspects.

BIBLE STUDY [Answer the following questions to enhance your learning.]

Which invisible influence do you believe has the greatest impact on you personally?

Reflect on your early childhood environment. How might the way you were raised impact your life as a Jesus follower?

As you consider your personality and temperament, what are some specific ways your natural inclinations can be helpful to you as a Jesus follower?

As you consider your personality and temperament, what are some specific ways your natural inclinations might be a hindrance to you as a Jesus follower?

What is the biggest way our American culture impacts you personally as a Jesus follower?

Pray over what you've learned in this lesson. Write out a summarizing prayer below.

MEMORY VERSE:

"Wherever your treasure is, there the desires of

your heart will also be."

-Matthew 7:21 (NLT)

FOR FURTHER RESOURCES ON THIS TOPIC:

INFLUENCE #1
John Baker. Life's Healing Choices: Freedom from Your Hurts, Hang-ups, and Habits. New York, Howard Books, 2007.

Peter Scazzero. Emotional Healthy Spirituality. Grand Rapids, Zondervan, 2006.

INFLUENCE #2
David Brenner. The Gift of Being Yourself. Dowers Grove, Ill. InterVarsity Press, 2015.

Florence Littauer. Personality Plus. Grand Rapids, Baker Books, 1992.

John Ortberg, The Me I Want to Be: Becoming God's Best Version of You. Grand Rapids, Zondervan, 2014.

INFLUENCE #3
Unchristian: What a New Generation Really Thinks about Christianity-- and Why It Matters. Grand Rapids, MI: Baker Book House, 2012.

David Kinnaman and Gabe Lyons. Good Faith: Being a Christian When Society Thinks You're Irrelevant and Extreme. Grand Rapids, MI: Baker Book House, 2016.

Nancy Pearcey. Love Thy Body: Answering Hard Questions about Life and Sexuality. Grand Rapids, MI: Baker Books, 2018.

Herbert Schlossberg. Idols for Destruction: The Conflict of Christian Faith and American Culture. Wheaton, Ill. Crossway,1990.

GOD'S PEOPLE: THE FAMILY

We started this book letting you know that saying "yes" to Jesus brought you into a family. Now it's time to talk about that family. Every family has an ethos or culture that distinguishes it from others, and the Christian family is no different. We are a spiritual family that God formed because He chose to rescue and redeem us. We're His, and He's ours! Jesus delivered us from the power of Satan, sin and death. Notice Jesus' piercing insight and powerful promise.

> If you abide in my word, you are truly my disciples, [32]and you will know the truth, and the truth will set you free..." Jesus answered them, "Truly, truly, I say to you, everyone who practices sin is a slave to sin....[36]So if the Son sets you free, you will be free indeed.
>
> - John 8:31-32, 34, 36 (ESV)

We're the family of the "freed ones!" In this section, we are going to discuss the church. First, we are going to talk about the "spiritual friendships" that should exist within the church. Jesus reached out in love to each of his disciples and showed them what friendship in his kingdom should look like. We're going to see that the early church enjoyed deep relationships with each other as they centered their lives on the kingdom of God and the mission that laid before them. Second, we will look at the role the church must play in growing up a new Christian. It's in the church that we should see how a Jesus follower lives. Finally, we're going to talk about how our commitment to a local church should look. There are powerful cultural forces that can weaken our connection to the community. Our view of the church and its role in our life must come from God's word.

LESSON #18: The Twin Sisters: Spiritual Friendships & Ministry

I'll never forget the first time I felt like God used me in His kingdom work. I was in high school, and a kid my age had just started going to our church with his family. Before long, this guy became a Christian, and we became best friends. It was at that same time that our church started a discipleship campaign. Older Christians were assigned to newer believers to meet regularly and go through a series of booklets about Christianity. Since I was raised in church, the pastors asked me to mentor Robin. Looking back, I don't think I was at all ready, but this experience was probably one of the biggest reasons why I am a pastor today. My weekly meetings with Robin radically changed my life. The questions he asked pushed me to find answers. Together, we learned how to pray, read our Bible and share our faith with others. It was a spiritual friendship that helped set my priorities in life. Today, he's a pastor in the Seattle area. Looking back now, there's no way either of us could have seen how this friendship would shape our futures.

As a result of that experience, I realized two things. First, there was nothing more exciting, more fulfilling and more important than joining God in His great kingdom work. Second, having friends like Robin made following Jesus so much easier! In this lesson, we're going to look at the importance of spiritual friendships and regular ministry to others. I can certainly say that in my Christian life, nothing has helped me grow more than these two things.

Twin #1 - Spiritual Friendships

It's no secret that friendships are extremely important to us. God designed us to need relationships, and for either good or bad, our friendships greatly influence us. We see the power of friendship throughout the Bible. In the Old Testament, famous friends include: Ruth and Naomi (See: Ruth 1-3), Jonathan and David (See: I Samuel 18-20), Elijah and Elisha, (See: I Kings 19-II Kings 2) and Daniel, Shadrach, Meshach and Abednego (See: Daniel 1-3). In the New Testament, friendship is everywhere. We see it first in the powerful friendship that Jesus developed with his disciples. Then as the church exploded after Jesus' resurrection, we see the great love and friendship that the early believers enjoyed with each other.

Let's look at Jesus first. Running counter to the tradition of the Jewish rabbis of that time, Jesus explicitly called his disciples "friends." He said,

> There is no greater love than to lay down one's life for one's friends. [14]You are my friends if you do what I command. I no longer call you slaves, be-cause a master doesn't confide in his slaves. Now you are my friends, since I have told you everything the Father told me.
>
> - John 15:13-15 (NLT)

It's clear Jesus was still their leader, but he lowered the power dynamic between them and invited them into authentic friendship. And if Jesus was willing to consider his disciples friends, how much more should we consider each other friends? Jesus, in fact, commands just that! "A new commandment I give to you, that you love one another: just as I have loved you, you also are to love one another. By this all people will know that you are my disciples, if you have love for one another" (John 13:34-35 ESV). This wasn't just a passing comment or a nice sentiment. Jesus intended that our love for each other be the thing that distinguishes his disciples from everybody else!

Turning to the rest of the New Testament, it's surprising how spiritual friendship runs in the background of nearly every book. There are so many places that we could see this, but I think the forgotten little letter to Philemon gives us a unique look at the spiritual friendships in the early church.

Paul wrote this letter late in life while in prison. Evidently, while there, he met a young runaway slave named Onesimus. It just so happened that Paul knew this young man's master, Philemon. Paul led Onesimus to a relationship with Jesus and decided he should send him back to Philemon with this letter in hand. First, notice how Paul addressed his friend, "Paul, a prisoner for Christ Jesus, and Timothy our brother, To Philemon our beloved fellow worker 2and Apphia our sister and Archippus our fellow soldier, and the church in your house" (Philemon 1:1-2 ESV).

Paul recognized him as a "beloved fellow worker." This type of language is used throughout the letters of the New Testament. It seems that the disciples regularly greeted each other as "fellow workers" or "fellow soldiers" or "co-laborers".[113]

---

113. I Corinthians 3:9; II Corinthians 8:22-23; Philippians 4:3; Colossians 1:7; 4:11; I Thessalonians 3:2; Philemon 1:24; I Peter 5:12-14

Paul then thanked Philemon for his "labor." He told him that news of his great generosity and love for other believers had reached him even in his prison cell. Then Paul dropped the bombshell. Onesimus, his runaway slave, had been with Paul there in prison (probably 1,300miles away!). We're not told how Paul met Onesimus, only that Paul had led the young slave to Christ. Now Paul was writing a letter on his behalf as he sent him back to his master.

Notice how Paul spoke of this runaway slave.

"I appeal to you for my child, Onesimus, whose father I became in my imprisonment. (Formerly he was useless to you, but now he is indeed useful to you and to me.) I am sending him back to you, sending my very heart" (Philemon 1:10-12 NLT). We can see the genuine love and concern Paul had for this runaway. Paul told Philemon that he wanted to keep Onesimus with him since he was a great help during his imprisonment, but he wasn't willing to do so without Philemon's permission. So he sent him back. But notice again how Paul saw the situation. "It seems you lost Onesimus for a little while so that you could have him back forever. 16He is no longer like a slave to you. He is more than a slave, for he is a beloved brother, especially to me. Now he will mean much more to you, both as a man and as a brother in the Lord" (Philemon 1:15-16 NLT).

Paul urged Philemon to consider Onesimus as a "brother." It's hard to overstate how counter-cultural this would have been in the Roman Empire. For a man of obvious wealth like Philemon to consider his runaway slave a brother was outrageous! Yet this was what Paul expected. In fact, Paul finished the letter hinting that Philemon would "do even more than I say" (v.21). Inside the church, the disciples of Jesus considered each other family——a family of workers who treated each other as equals regardless of their status in the larger culture. We'll discuss this powerful truth a bit more in our lesson on the church, but for now it's important to point out the expectations for love and care for each other that existed in the early church.

The great Christian novelist and apologist, C.S. Lewis commented on this fact of early Christianity. He believed that it was the remarkable love that existed within Christian fellowships that helped the early Church survive the hostility of the larger, dominant Roman culture.[114] He wrote, "The little pockets of early Christians survived because they cared exclusively for the love of 'the brethren' and stopped their ears to the opinion of the Pagan society all around them."[115]

Lewis's observation is spot on. He pointed out a powerful truth about humans——we naturally care about what others think, and other's thoughts and opinions influence us! That's why we must choose our friends so carefully. Later, he vividly described his own social life. "Alone among unsympathetic companions, I hold certain views and standards timidly, half ashamed to avow them and half doubtful if they can after all be right. Put me back among my Friends and in half an hour——in ten minutes——these same views and standards become once more indisputable. The opinion of this little circle, while I am in it, outweighs that of a thousand outsiders..."[116] The power of friendship is undeniable.

---

114. If Lewis was right about how the deep intimate relationships of the early church protected them from the larger Roman culture, this gives fresh insight into another purpose for Christ's "New Command." (John 13:34-35). In addition to wanting his disciples to follow his example in love, Jesus is giving the infant church the strong protection they need against Rome's staggering influence. This would have been particularly important in the Gentile churches when they would no longer have the ethnicity and culture of Judaism to bind them together.
115. Lewis, C. S. The four loves. (New York: HarperCollins) 1960. p.70
116. ibid.

But this cuts both ways. Paul put it bluntly and concisely, "bad company corrupts good character" (I Corinthians 15:33 NLT). The apostle knew the effect a good influence could have to reinforce one's faith, but on the other hand, he knew a bad influence could just as easily undermine that same faith. In fact, there are warnings throughout the New Testament about the kinds of people we shouldn't allow into our life.[117] In my experience, this balance is difficult. We want to have a positive influence on others but also know that there's things we should avoid as a Christian. How can we really influence non-Christians if we don't hang out with them? But on the other hand, how do we guard ourselves from being influenced away from Jesus? This leads us to the second part of this lesson: Ministry.

Twin #2 - Ministry

What's interesting about the relationships we see in the New Testament is the kind of language they used to talk about each other. We saw this a bit in Philemon. Words like fellow-worker, fellow-soldier, beloved brother, sister, son and mother appear in nearly every letter in the New Testament. It's not just that people in the early church considered each other family. They did. But joining a group of people and developing a sense of family isn't all that extraordinary. That was already happening within some groups in the ancient world and still happens today. Members of the armed forces regularly describe a brotherhood or sisterhood with those they serve alongside. Even some tight knit athletic teams develop a sense of family within their team.

This is certainly special. But the early church experienced something more. Their relationships were "mission-centered." In other words, the gospel wasn't simply something they preached to people who didn't know Jesus; it defined how they felt about each other. They certainly understood themselves as part of God's family. But theirs was a spiritual family on a spiritual mission fighting a spiritual battle. Their family had a special DNA. They shared a collective calling.

I think this is vital to the health of a disciple. Without a sense of mission and calling, our Christian life loses its vitality and strength. Without this, our friendships with other believers lack depth and purpose. To put it bluntly, we cease having "spiritual friendships." However, when we're in life-giving relationships with other believers who are centered on living the life of a disciple, we will find that these relationships strengthen our faith. And it's here that we see a tremendous truth to living a successful Christian life. We must do life together. This is how we can thrive in a world full of negative influences. When we live in healthy relationships with other believers, we have the strength to influence others. It's only then that we can befriend non-believers, love them just like Jesus did, and not be pulled away from our faith in Christ. This is because they're not who we're looking to for support and acceptance.

Lewis wrote about this as well. Notice his insight, "For we all wish to be judged by our peers, by the men 'after our own heart.' Only they really know our mind and only they judge it by standards we fully acknowledge. Theirs is the praise we really covet and the blame we really dread."[118] Becoming a Christian doesn't change the fact that we crave approval from our friends, but it changes the kinds of friends we look to for that approval. This is why spiritual friendships are so important.

---

117. See the following texts for warnings about evil influences corrupting one's walk with Jesus: Luke 17:1; I Corinthians 5:9-11; II Corinthians 6:14-17; Ephesians 5:5-12; II Thessalonians 3:6-15; I Timothy 5:11-16; I Peter 4:2-5
118.bid. (my emphasis)
119.He's going to kill me when he reads this! :)

It's interesting that Jesus sent his disciples out "two by two" (See: Luke 10:1). They might have covered more ground if they went alone, but Jesus knew the importance of spiritual friendships. We also see this in the trips recorded in the book of Acts. With few exceptions, we read of teams of people going together to preach the gospel to others (See Acts 1:14; 3:1; 13:2; 15:37-40; 19:22,28; 20:4).

I've said that spiritual friendships and ministry are twins because they go together. Let me share how this has been true in my life. My first memory of Eddie McGath happened in 1995. He and his wife came to Las Vegas to lead a week of special chapels for our Christian school. Back then, the school was very small and had limited resources. I had graduated a year earlier with five others and was off at college that first year. But since it was around Christmas, I had a chance to meet him.

The middle and high school buildings included a few old trailers on a gravel lot next to a Presbyterian church. Our chapels met inside the church, and there Eddie set up his "stage" and led chapel for our students. I remember thinking how dynamic and gifted he was! I never thought that we'd be friends or actually start a church together.

Each year, Eddie traveled back to preach for a week at our school. After I graduated college, I started teaching middle school history and Bible. Every winter, I'd hang out with Eddie during his annual visit. It was always so thrilling to see God use him in the lives of our students. Then while they were here serving in 2004, Eddie and Connie suffered a deep, personal loss. Our school community surrounded and loved them as they grieved. As other events developed, they felt the clear leading of God to move out here and start a church as part of the school ministry. If you ask him, Eddie would tell you that it was the faith and love of Sue Blakeley (my mom) and her staff that made moving out to the Las Vegas area so compelling. And so they moved.

There were four of us friends who started the Church at Lake Mead—Eddie, Mike, Jeremy and me, Brad. (As I think I mentioned in an earlier lesson, Eddie was quite a bit older than the rest of us, but we didn't let his age slow us down.) The four of us served together for nearly 7 years. Eventually, Mike and Jeremy moved to the East coast while Eddie and I continued serving at the church. But what I've found about true, genuine, spiritual friendships is that the relationship can transcend distance. You can remain close and connected to those brothers or sisters even when distance might end a typical friendship. Spiritual friendships are truly eternal.

Recently, God shocked us all when He made it clear to Mike and his family that they needed to move back and serve once again at the church. But that's a story for another time! All I can say is that ministry is unpredictable and exciting. The spiritual friendships I've enjoyed over the years have blessed and enriched me both as a person and Jesus follower. The community I've experienced was exactly what Jesus intended for his disciples. It's been a true joy to serve Jesus alongside my best friends!

Finding Good Friends

For some of us (myself included), developing new friendships in different social settings is difficult. I always laugh when I take my little girls to the park, and in less than 10 minutes, they introduce me to their new "best friend." If only it were still that easy! As we get older, I think friendship gets more difficult.

I've had lots of conversations with people who have admitted that they really don't have many friends. The reasons for this vary. A move to a new town, a new stage in life, even a new job with new stresses can all be reasons for failing friendships. Other times, things like divorce or losing a spouse can cause people to struggle socially. Most times, it's a combination of reasons. And of course, many times, new Christians discover their old friends aren't interested in Jesus (at least not right away) and so they can have difficulty finding friends committed to Christ.

As we finish this lesson, I'd like to give a few observations about how to practically develop good friendships.

First, as we discussed above, I think spiritual friends are commonly found when serving. This can be on a mission trip, in a church ministry, at a life group or in any other place where your focus is on God's mission. I believe   spiritual friendships easily form in that type of environment.

Second, I don't think friendships in general are found if you go out looking for them. True friendships are usually formed accidentally. In fact, there's nothing more smothering to friendship than trying to force it. You've got to just let it happen. Again, I think C.S. Lewis is helpful here. He wrote, "Friendship is born at that moment when one person says to another: 'What! You too? I thought I was the only one."[120] Friends are two people drawn together by common interest. This is why people who are looking for friends rarely find them. If you want friends, you need to pursue things that interest you. As you do this it won't be long before you'll bump into people with the same interests—all the ingredients necessary for friendship.

Third, we often don't consider the role our personal character and maturity play in friendships. It's just plain difficult to be friends with an immature, selfish person. Healthy friendships only happen when two people express genuine interest and care for the other. However, trauma in our past or poor upbringing can seriously hinder someone's ability to interact with others in a healthy way. Ministries like Celebrate Recovery and Christian counseling centers can effectively help people come to grips with their past and get to a place where they can care for others and experience healthy relationships.

Lastly, as a Christian, our relationships should always have an eternal dimension. Regardless of what drew you together in the first place (basketball or basket-weaving), as a Christian, Jesus should be a topic of regular conversation. For some of us, this might be awkward at first. We might not be used to bringing up spiritual conversations with our friends. But we've got to break through. This will be easier with friends who are already Christians, but regardless, we must determine to turn every relationship in our life into a spiritual relationship. With our Christian friends, we must take steps to center our friendship more firmly on Christ. With our non-believing friends, we must slowly, prayerfully, steer the relationship toward Christ. We will lose friends in the process, but we'll gain new ones too. Ultimately, the most important thing we can do for our friends is point them toward Jesus!

---

120. ibid. p. 64

THE SUMMARY:

As Christians, we're supposed to do life together. Jesus masterfully built spiritual friendships with his disciples and commanded them to love each other just as he had loved them. This should be the experience of every disciple of Jesus. However, deep spiritual friendships don't happen unless both people are centered on the gospel. This is why spiritual friendships and ministry are "twins." When we give ourselves fully to God's great kingdom work, He will knit our hearts together with other believers that have the same kingdom pursuit. The only way to fully experience the community described in the New Testament is to give yourself fully to God's kingdom and live out the life of a committed disciple within the community of believers.

BIBLE STUDY [Answer the following questions to enhance your learning.]

How would you describe the friends in your life? Are they "spiritual friendships?" What types of things (hobbies, common interests) draw you and your friends together?

Based on our study today, describe the relationships that existed in the early church?

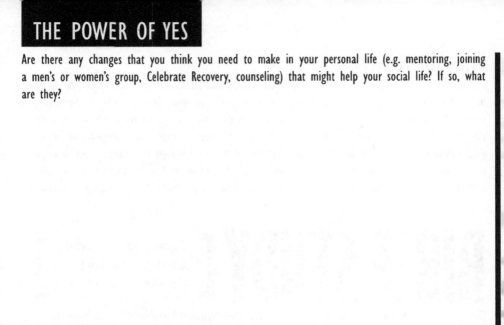

Are there any changes that you think you need to make in your personal life (e.g. mentoring, joining a men's or women's group, Celebrate Recovery, counseling) that might help your social life? If so, what are they?

Is there a ministry that you believe you might like to begin serving in?

Pray over what you've learned in this lesson. Write out a summarizing prayer below.

MEMORY VERSE:

"But if we walk in the light, as he is in the light, we have fellowship with one another, and the blood of Jesus his Son cleanses us from all sin."

- 1 John 1:7 (ESV)

FOR FURTHER RESOURCES ON THIS TOPIC:

Mindy Caliguire. Stir: spiritual transformation in relationships. Grand Rapids: Zondervan, 2013.

Henry Cloud and John Townsend. Boundaries: when to say yes, how to say no to take control of your life. Grand Rapids: Zondervan, 2017.

Henry Cloud and John Townsend. Safe people: how to find relationships that are good for you and avoid those that aren't. Grand Rapids: Zondervan, 2016.

C. S. Lewis. The Four Loves. New York: HarperOne, 1960.

LESSON #19: The Jesus Revolution

"I'm spiritual but not religious; I'm just not into organized religion." Sound familiar? Today, more and more people believe that they can have a connection to God outside of the church of Jesus.[121] In fact, nearly one-third of all college-age adults want nothing to do with religion.[122] Whether it's the public scandals of the Catholic church or the perceived (and actual) intolerance the Church has shown outsiders, the Church in America is seen more and more in a negative light.

Our society is changing in other ways too. Life is faster—more demanding. Some curses are mixed in with the blessings of technology. It's getting harder to disconnect from our jobs and responsibilities. This makes any free time on the weekends precious real estate. Everything is infinitely more complex as our nation grows more secular, more multicultural, more pluralistic and more divided. At the same time, church attendance is going down.

American Christians aren't immune to this cultural pull away from the Church. Today, we are less biblically literate and less connected to a church community even though we have far more resources and educational tools than our parents ever did. A generation ago, most Christian fellowships had several different services a week; today, many churches only expect regular attenders to show up just a few times a month.[123] In a nutshell, the Church of Jesus is losing its American cultural prominence.

Growing up, my parents took us to church every Sunday morning, Sunday night and then back to the midweek service on Wednesdays. Life seemed a lot less complicated back then. We didn't have Netflix, Facebook or Instagram enabling us to stream videos to our smartphones 24/7. We spent more time with actual, physical people (what a concept!). In addition to our connection to our church, our family life began to center around the work at Lake Mead Christian Academy. God used my mom, dad and a team of others to start the school in 1989. As that ministry grew, so did our connection with more and more Christians. As I consider the relationships and community that I enjoyed growing up, dozens of names come to mind, each contributing to my young life as a Jesus follower.

In this lesson, we're going to look at the incredible vision Jesus had for his followers when he launched his Church. We'll look at the role the Church is supposed to play in a believer's life and how his beautiful vision of diversity and unity can powerfully speak to our nation today. I believe there's nothing more revolutionary, more powerful and more important on this earth than the church of Jesus. It's a place where the lost are found, the sick are healed, the marginalized are accepted and races are unified. It's a sacred space, the intersection of heaven and earth—a place where we meet God and worship Him.

---

121. A recent poll indicated that 75% of Americans believe a person can live a pretty good and decent life without being a Christian. Cited in Kinnaman, David and Lyons, Gabe. Good faith: being a Christian when society thinks you're irrelevant and extreme. (Grand Rapids, MI: Baker Books) 2016. p.33

122. Kinnaman, David and Lyons, Gabe.. Good faith: being a Christian when society thinks you're irrelevant and extreme. (Grand Rapids, MI: Baker Books) 2016. p.12

123. researchers David Kinnaman and Gabe Lyons considered a "practicing Christian" someone who, "say their Christian faith is very important to their lives and attend church at least once a month." p.27. They found that just 30% of Americans are considered "practicing Christians" using that definition.

A Revolutionary Vision

You are the light of the world—like a city on a hilltop that cannot be hidden. No one lights a lamp and then puts it under a basket. Instead, a lamp is placed on a stand, where it gives light to everyone in the house. In the same way, let your good deeds shine out for all to see, so that everyone will praise your heavenly Father.

- Matthew 5:14-16 (NLT)

You have heard the law that says, 'Love your neighbor' and hate your enemy. But I say, love your enemies! Pray for those who persecute you! In that way, you will be acting as true children of your Father in heaven. For he gives his sunlight to both the evil and the good, and he sends rain on the just and the unjust alike.

- Matthew 5:44-45 (NLT)

It's dangerously easy to become over-familiar with the words of Jesus. Passages like the ones you just read are revolutionary. But because we've heard them so often, we don't realize how radical they are. As Jesus began teaching, it became increasingly clear to those who first heard him that he wasn't like other rabbis. His teaching was full of authority and passion. To the religious elite, it was heretical and subversive; to the broken and marginalized, it was life-giving and liberating. He was unlike any other.

And his students weren't typical either. They were ordinary people: fishermen and tax collectors, a few prostitutes and some religious Pharisees, wealthy women and influential men, despised sinners and at least one anti-Roman terrorist. They formed a unique community—a group of people with little in common. Jesus challenged nearly everything they had believed about God, the Law and people.

You could say they were on a journey. Their walk together was messy but transformative. Some days there were great steps forward with profound breakthroughs; other days, disastrous retreats back into old prejudices and hate. Yet, through it all, Jesus patiently led and loved. He gave them a vision for what life together in his kingdom would look like.

But the Jesus movement wasn't just shaped by what he taught. It was also shaped by how he lived, the way he loved, the people he included and, perhaps most importantly, those he defended. The life Jesus lived in front of them gave his disciples a visible display of his values and mission. Since this Jesus community eventually became the church, it's important that we look at the community he formed.

The gospels give many glimpses into the incredible, unique life that Christ and his disciples enjoyed together. We'll only take time to look at one—the story of Mary and Martha. Jesus and his disciples were traveling down to Jerusalem. While in the area, they were invited over for dinner at Martha's house. Let's read Luke's account.

THE POWER OF YES

As Jesus and the disciples continued on their way to Jerusalem, they came to a certain village where a woman named Martha welcomed him into her home. Her sister, Mary, sat at the Lord's feet, listening to what he taught. But Martha was distracted by the big dinner she was preparing. She came to Jesus and said, "Lord, doesn't it seem unfair to you that my sister just sits here while I do all the work? Tell her to come and help me. But the Lord said to her, "My dear Martha, you are worried and upset over all these details! [42]There is only one thing worth being concerned about. Mary has discovered it, and it will not be taken away from her.

- Luke 10:38-42 (NLT)

Jesus loved to eat! It seems every time we read a story in the gospels, he's at a dinner party—sometimes even inviting himself over (See: Matthew 9:10; Luke 7:36; 19:5). At one point, he was even accused of eating and drinking too much (See: Luke 7:34)! So there he was over at Martha's house. Scholars believe that the way Luke introduced her indicates that she was the "patron" or the homeowner. We can imagine it would have been a great honor to host Jesus and his disciples for dinner. So understandably, Martha was working hard to make sure the dinner was a success. In this culture, this was completely appropriate and expected. Inside the home, the women ruled. They were in charge of the domestic duties, and getting dinner together was definitely a woman's job (I said WAS. I'm not suggesting anything about how it should be today!).

Jesus was in the other room teaching. Presumably his disciples were gathered around him as he taught. Here we can see what the "Jesus community" must have looked like—good food, Jesus teaching and, perhaps, some of the sick, healed. But let's take note of why Luke recorded this particular dinner party. Notice who was sitting at the feet of Jesus. It was Mary, Martha's younger sister. A woman! When Martha complained to Jesus that Mary should join her in the kitchen, the original Greek indicates that Martha expected a positive answer to her request.[124] But instead Jesus surprised her. He defended Mary's right to sit at his feet. This violated two cultural customs. First, as just mentioned, women were supposed to perform the domestic duties. Mary should have been helping with dinner. Second, generally women weren't allowed to be taught by rabbis. But not only did Jesus teach Mary along with the other disciples, he defended her!

In fact, women played a large role in the Jesus movement. Luke tells us that some wealthy and influential women supported Jesus financially (See: Luke 8:1-3). On several occasions, Jesus publicly commended a woman's "great" faith (See: Matthew 15:28; Mark 5:34; Luke 7:50). Further, Jesus' teachings on divorce equalized the way men and women were treated (See: Matthew 5:31-32; 19:1-10). And on a related subject, Jesus rightly held men accountable for their lust (See: Matthew 5:27-30), instead of blaming women which was the standard cultural practice of that day. Finally, as we noted in lesson 6, it was the women, and not the male disciples, who first saw Jesus alive after his crucifixion and took the message of the resurrection to the others (See: Matthew 28:1-10; John 20:14-18).

After Jesus' ascension, the role that women played in the early church continued to be counter-cultural and shocking. In the early church, women held leadership roles (See: Romans 16:1-2, 7; Philippians 4:2-3);

[124] Bock, Darrell L. Luke: The NIV Application Commentary. (Grand Rapids, Zondervan) 1996. p. 30

the educated women taught others (See: Acts 18:24-27; Romans 16:3-4, 6, 12; Titus 2:3-4; James 3:1); and women prayed and prophesied in the churches as well (See: Acts 21:9; I Corinthians 11:5).125 It's true there were some restrictions placed on women in the churches (See: I Corinthians 14:34; I Timothy 2:11-14). However, many scholars suggest these restrictions were the exception rather than the rule in the early church.[125]

Regardless of the debate about the details, there's no question: the early church was an utterly unique social phenomena. There is simply no place in human history where we find slaves and freedmen, men and women, Jews and gentiles, wealthy landowners and working peasants sitting together and calling each other brother and sister. Paul captured this perfectly in his letter to the Galatians. He wrote,

> For you are all children of God through faith in Christ Jesus. And all who have been united with Christ in baptism have put on Christ, like putting on new clothes. There is no longer Jew or Gentile, slave or free, male and female. For you are all one in Christ Jesus.

> - Galatians 3:26-28 (NLT)

In Christ, the social divisions of the larger culture were erased. Outside the church, there was slavery, social segregation and two very different sets of rules for men and women. Inside the church, there was love, equality and unity. In other words, it was family. Listen to how Paul described this in his letter to Colossae,

> In this new life, it doesn't matter if you are a Jew or a Gentile, circumcised or uncircumcised, barbaric, uncivilized, slave, or free. Christ is all that matters, and he lives in all of us... Above all, clothe yourselves with love, which binds us all together in perfect harmony. And let the peace that comes from Christ rule in your hearts. For as members of one body you are called to live in peace. And always be thankful.

> - Colossians 3:11, 14-15 (NLT)

This was Jesus' revolutionary vision for humanity. His church was pointing the world to a glorious future where human divisions would forever be eliminated. In these texts, we can see Paul and the other church leaders following Jesus' example of love for all people (See also: James 2:1-10).

What a beautiful vision! Well, that's at least the way it's supposed to be. Sadly, the church has struggled to live up to that glorious vision of social equality and universal welcome. The "fellowship" (the Greek word is Koinonia) of the early church seems like a distant dream (See: Acts 2:42-47). Today, our churches are commonly segregated both racially and economically. In his book, a A Fellowship of Differents, biblical scholar Scot McKnight reports, "Fully 90 percent of American churches draw 90 percent of their people from one ethnic group, and only 8 percent of American churches can be called multiracial, multiethnic, or interracial."[126]
Sadly, certain types of people just don't feel welcome.

This is something we must work to change. McKnight explained why: "Everything I learned about the Christian life I learned from my church. I will make this a bigger principle: a local church determines

---

125. Scholars are divided over if these restrictions were in place because of specific abuses happening in the local churches (e.g. Corinth and Ephesus) or whether if the restrictions were rooted in God's role for men and women. There are two groups of thought on this topic of the role of women in the church: the Complementarian view and the Egalitarian view. I'll include some books on this topic at the end of this lesson.
126.. McKnight, Scot. Fellowship of Differents. (Grand Rapids: Zondervan) 2016. p. 20

what the Christian life looks like for the people in that church. Now I'll make it even bigger still: we all learn the Christian life from how our local church shapes us."[127] Essentially, McKnight is warning us. If we don't seek to have a biblical church which displays the beautiful revolutionary vision of Jesus, the Jesus

followers growing up in that church will have a distorted vision of Christianity! That hits home when I think of three specific little girls growing up in our church. As a dad, I desperately want them to have a clear and compelling vision of true Christianity!

A Hospital and a Health Club

Before we close this lesson, we need to look at one more important feature of Jesus' revolutionary vision. Not only should his church be a place of social diversity where Jesus followers worship in unity, it must also be a place where the spiritually sick are welcomed and healed. You could say, a church needs to be a "hospital" for those who don't know Jesus and a "health club" to strengthen those who do.

Hospitals are incredible things. As a pastor, I'm in hospitals a lot. I've noticed how quickly a knowledge-able, caring doctor or nurse can bring calm and assurance to a sick patient and a worried family. As Christians, we need to play this kind of spiritual role in the lives of others. Our churches should be a place of comfort and healing for the spiritually sick.

But sadly, church isn't always a safe place for non-believers. Many outsiders already feel uncomfortable even before they get to church. Many have assumptions of what "church people" are like. In fact, most of the people I talk to don't feel like they're "good" enough to come. And these fears seem confirmed if our church isn't friendly and welcoming. It's so easy to send a signal that they don't "belong."

This past year, we've been thinking about this as a church staff. We've all been wondering how we can lead our church to be a friendlier place especially to "outsiders." But no one on the staff was more troubled about this than Janessa. God had been gently challenging her to grow in love for others personally, and this new growth stirred her to think of ways to make our community more caring. She knew that sometimes we only had one chance to make a loving impression on someone who was hurting.

A few weeks later, in a staff meeting, she presented the "Your Hello Matters" slogan. It was a simple idea designed to remind everyone in our church that their "Hello" mattered! We're hoping that this slogan catches on and that everyone takes ownership in making our community a welcoming place for new people. The truth is most people expect church staff to be friendly—after all they're paid. However, when the entire community demonstrates genuine hospitality, it's a powerful witness to God's love. People won't listen to the life-changing gospel of Jesus until they experience God's love first in us.

Interestingly, the apostle Paul actually criticized the church at Corinth for their indifference toward "outsiders." He wrote, "If, therefore, the whole church comes together and all speak in tongues, and outsiders or unbelievers enter, will they not say that you are out of your minds" (1 Corinthians 14:23 ESV). Paul wanted to make sure the Corinthian believers thought about how a non-Christian would experience their worship service.

---

127. ibid. p. 11 (emphasis in the original)

As we mentioned in the beginning of this lesson, Jesus modeled this tender love for outsiders all of the time. From the way he treated the woman at the well in John 4 or how he interacted with Zacchaeus in Luke 19, Jesus showed us how to love the spiritually sick. He was the Great Physician who came to bring healing to us all.[128]

The fact is, when a hospital is functioning well, sick people receive life-giving care. When it doesn't, people die. While it would be crazy to think that a hospital would reject someone for being too sick, unfortunately, we've all heard stories of churches doing just this! This must change. It's true that not every hospital is equipped to handle every disease, and a single local church can't meet every challenge in our community. But everyone must feel the love and welcome of God's people. If we aren't equipped to meet someone's needs, we must care enough to connect them with a place that can. I am thankful for the Christian rehab centers, homeless shelters, food banks and safe houses that offer the specialized care that a typical church can't. While this doesn't remove our own responsibility to care for the poor or to help the addicted, it does give us a chance to provide the best care to those who are suffering in severe cases. After all, the Church is called to be the hands and feet of Jesus (See: Matthew 25:31-45). If we don't care for these, who will?

The church must also be a health club, a place where people are spiritually instructed and trained. This is the counterbalance to the point we just discussed. If a church is "all hospital and no health club," then we fail to challenge mature Christians in their walk with Jesus. The church is the gathering of the saints. It must be a place where God is worshiped biblically and without apology. If we are overly worried about what non-Christians think, we'll inevitably compromise what we teach or how we worship. Notice what Paul wrote to a young pastor, Timothy, about the work he was to do in Ephesus,

> "I solemnly urge you in the presence of God and Christ Jesus, who will someday judge the living and the dead when he comes to set up his Kingdom: [2]Preach the word of God. Be prepared, whether the time is favorable or not. Patiently correct, rebuke, and encourage your people with good teaching. [3]For a time is coming when people will no longer listen to sound and wholesome teaching. They will follow their own desires and will look for teachers who will tell them whatever their itching ears want to hear. [4]They will reject the truth and chase after myths. [5]But you should keep a clear mind in every situation. Don't be afraid of suffering for the Lord. Work at telling others the Good News, and fully carry out the ministry God has given you."

- 1 Timothy 4:13-16 (NLT)

---

128. Jesus has been called the "Great Physician." There are a few places where Jesus uses the image of a "physician" in a spiritual sense. When asked why Jesus spent so much time with tax collectors and sinners. He said, "Those who are well have no need of a physician, but those who are sick." (See: Matthew 9:12; Mark 2:17; Luke 5:31). This means that Jesus, the Great Physician, spent his time with those who needed him--the sick.

Faithful pastors must lead the church spiritually. They must guard the church from error and watch over the spiritual well-being of the congregation. As Paul said here, it's a serious ("solemn") task. Jesus will return, and he will judge us when he sets up his eternal kingdom! If the truth of God's word isn't taught correctly, then people will be led astray and away from Christ. This is actually one of the driving passions behind this book: we want to give everyone in our church a solid foundation for their Christian life.

In this way, pastors are like trainers in a health club or coaches on an athletic team. We've been given the job to train and shepherd God's people. The apostle James, an early Church leader, warned pastors and teachers specifically about this. Notice what he said, "Dear brothers and sisters, not many of you should become teachers in the church, for we who teach will be judged more strictly" (James 3:1 NLT)

This is important business. Leading a church, shepherding God's people, and teaching others God's word should be done with the utmost seriousness. Please pray for your pastors!

Wrap Up

We started this lesson looking at how many view the Church today. Sadly, more and more people see the church in a negative light. Non-believers see it as hypocritical and judgmental. Many Christians see it as optional. This is a sad state of affairs! In reality, the church that Jesus started has changed the world and continues to do so! In countries all over the world, Christians are those doing the most good. The Church is leading the charge to alleviate suffering, end hunger and promote human flourishing. Christians are currently fighting human trafficking and working to end modern slavery.

While it's a shame that so many in our country have a low view of the church. I do believe things are turning around for at least two reasons. First, the revolution Jesus started still appeals—now more than ever. The vision Jesus gave of genuine love for others and welcome to outsiders resonates deeply in our culture.

Second, the church in the U.S. is changing. Many Christians realize that it's a problem to be only known for what we're against and not known for what we're for. This is what is behind the "For Henderson" campaign. We're determined to let our city know that we're for them not against them. This is what Jesus told us to do. He said that we are to, "...let your light shine before others, so that they may see your good works and give glory to your Father who is in heaven" (Matthew 5:16 ESV). Simple acts of love and good will open people's eyes and soften people's hearts to the truth and grace found only in the gospel of Jesus!

THE SUMMARY: Jesus changed the world. This is a fact of human history. The movement he started was radical and revolutionary. Jesus upended entrenched customs that reinforced social divisions. He bravely fought prejudice and hate. He dared to love the "other." His movement was built on a glorious vision of who God was and who we could be. His death broke the power of sin, and his resurrection gave us the power to love each other as he did. The church that Jesus founded has been fighting injustice and alleviating suffering for 2000 years. We cannot lose sight of our mission to be a hospital to the spiritually sick and a health club to those who know Jesus. A healthy church reaches out in love to the non-believer and nurtures and challenges the maturing Christian. It's a beautiful human mosaic composed of rich and poor, black and white, women and men, strong and weak. This is the human revolution Jesus launched when he founded his Church!

BIBLE STUDY [Answer the following questions to enhance your learning.]

Have you talked with people that have a negative view of the church? If so, what do you think their negative views were rooted in? If that hasn't been your experience, how do the people you regularly interact with view the church today?

Had you ever considered the church as a unique and powerful social phenomena? What was most interesting to you about Jesus' "revolutionary vision?"

Hospital and Health Club: We usually gravitate toward one or the other. Which type of church do you find yourself drawn to: a "hospital church" (a church focused on outreach and the lost) or a "health club church" (a church focused on building Christians up in their walk with Jesus)?

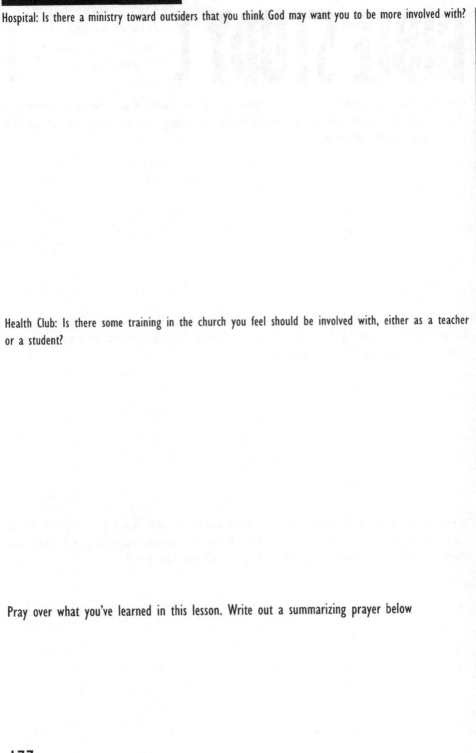

Hospital: Is there a ministry toward outsiders that you think God may want you to be more involved with?

Health Club: Is there some training in the church you feel should be involved with, either as a teacher or a student?

Pray over what you've learned in this lesson. Write out a summarizing prayer below

MEMORY VERSE:

"MEMORY VERSE:

"You are the light of the world. A city set on a hill cannot be hidden. Nor do people light a lamp and put it under a basket, but on a stand, and it gives light to all in the house. In the same way, let your light shine before others, so that they may see your good works and give glory to your Father who is in heaven."

-Matthew 5:14-16 (ESV)

FOR FURTHER RESOURCES ON THIS TOPIC:

Scot McKnight. Fellowship of Differents. Grand Rapids: Zondervan, 2016.

Walt Russell. Sustainable Church: Growing Ministry Around the Sheep Not Just the Shepherds. Grand Rapids: Zondervan, 2016.

LESSON #20: It Takes a Church to Raise a Christian

I'll never forget June 12, 2006. It was an awesome day. That was the day I became a dad! For Michelle and I, it was especially incredible. For us, it meant the end of the pain and uncertainty of infertility, and the beginning of a whole new chapter for us. Everything changed that day. As I held my little girl, the swirl of emotions was overwhelming. I couldn't believe this precious little life was in my hands. The weight and responsibility of this reality was almost more than I could bear. How in the world could I do this? What if I messed this up? It's been over twelve years since that day, and I still ask these questions sometimes. Each stage, each new faze, each first step, and each first day is new ground that keeps me on my knees praying!

God blessed us with two more girls. As I have held each of my daughters, I've often thought just how vulnerable and fragile tiny humans really are. Our culture prizes the healthy, strong and self-sufficient. But really, we all start out completely dependent upon others. The truth is this never changes. We need others, and we always will—we're born that way.

There's a parallel here with our spiritual family. Just as God planned for every human to be raised by a family, He's planned for every Christian to be raised by a church. In this lesson, we're gonna look at what the New Testament says about our relationship to a local church. We'll see what it means to be in a church and find that it is only in the context of a deep commitment to one another that we can really grow and develop as the disciples of Jesus that God wants us to be.

Marriage or Macy's

A few years back, Eddie asked me to do a series about the church and how our connection to our local congregation should look. As I prepared for that series, I thoroughly studied every place the New Testament talked directly about the church and the function it was supposed to play in a believer's life. I also looked at the more subtle and indirect passages that described the kind of relationships the early churches enjoyed. I noticed the emphasis was always on the collective church instead of the individual. And whenever individual members were discussed, they all were expected to play a role within the local church.

I also studied what Paul and others said about spiritual gifts. I saw that each member's individual gift was designed to function within the overall body of the church (See: Romans 12:3-8; I Corinthians 12:1-31). I realized that the idea of a Christian who wasn't connected to a local church would have been as unthinkable as a hand trying to work disconnected from a body. As I finished my study, it was obvious to me that a strong sense of God's kingdom and mission served to "glue" these ancient congregations together. I discovered that the relationships that the New Testament envisioned in the church were much richer and robust than what I'd seen in the churches that I'd grown up in.

Around this same time, I served on several mission trips overseas and met many Christians from other cultures. In places like the Philippines, India, Romania, Peru, Venezuela and Greece, I witnessed Christian communities. In some ways, they were like mine back home, but in other ways, they reminded me of what I was studying in the New Testament. The Christians in these countries were considerably poorer than the Christians where I lived. However, they seemed to enjoy a closer unity and love with each other than I experienced back home. I know that things aren't always as they seem when you're visiting only for a couple of weeks, but I couldn't help but notice their Christian community seemed much different.

I wondered about the difference. Why did my relationships in the American church fall so short of what I had read described in the book of Acts? Why was it so hard to imagine my church talking about each other in the same way that we see in the letters of the New Testament (See: Romans 16:1-23; II Timothy 4:9-22)? And why did I see this kind of community of believers in other countries?

As I reflected on this, two things came to mind. First, in these countries, evangelical Christianity was a minority, sometimes a persecuted minority. Second, I was seeing Christianity at work in a completely different culture. This allowed me to see what following Jesus looked like from another lens—a lens that didn't have my same cultural biases. This is an important insight. The culture we grow up in blinds us in some ways. To be sure, every culture has "blind spots," and I'm sure if I had stayed long enough, I would have noticed areas in those cultures that tend to affect Christians there negatively[129] But nonetheless, in these cultures, the emphasis on community and family let me see a little clearer what the individualism of my American culture had hidden from me.

So I gave a sermon entitled "Marriage or Macy's: what's your relationship to church?" I wanted to point out that we, as Americans, are culturally conditioned to approach most things as consumers. We emphasize individualism, and we often think and make decisions based on how things benefit us personally. Most of our decisions have a "what's-in-it-for-me" component driving them. And we've uncritically brought this mentality into the way we approach church.[130] We think of church as consumers—like a Macy's, instead of thinking of church as a commitment—like a marriage. I'm "loyal" to Macy's as long as they offer what I want. If they have a good sale, I'll shop there. But next week, if Target or Kohl's has a better sale, then I'll be shopping there.

There are several ways this consumer mindset affects our connection to a local church. First, we often start out on the wrong foot. For many of us, our initial decision about which church we should join is based on what it "offers" us. Does it have a good children's ministry? Do I like the worship? Do I like the pastor? (That one hurts!) Is it close enough to my house? Are the people friendly? The list could go on.

Of course, I'm not suggesting these aren't important things to consider when thinking about which church you should join. What I am pointing out is that we really don't see any of this in the New Testament. Instead, it seems the roles were reversed. When the disciples of Jesus met together, they expected to serve one another—to serve, not be served (See: Acts 6:1-7; Romans 15:1-2; I Corinthians 13; I John 3:16-19). Paul wrote, "For you have been called to live in freedom, my brothers and sisters. But don't use your freedom to satisfy your sinful nature. Instead, use your freedom to serve one another in love" (Galatians 5:13 NLT). Again, as we saw in the last lesson, Jesus-centered churches should function like hospitals and health clubs. We should offer programs to help people. However, if we're not careful, the foundation of our connection to our local church will be consumer-driven instead of commitment-driven.

Second, I think this "Macy's mentality" keeps some believers from deeply participating in the body life of the church. Again, since we're approaching church as consumers, we tend to only connect when it's.

---

129. For example, in many Latin cultures it's socially acceptable for a man to have a mistress. I can assume that the Church in those cultures may struggle with that cultural influence.

130. In the "extra credit" section of this book, I expand on how America culture has negatively influenced our discipleship to Jesus. There in the "third invisible influence, I discuss more of the cultural blind spots that keep us from obeying Jesus fully.

convenient or when we need something. For many of us, we attend a few weekly services a month and think that we're a part of the church. The New Testament paints a much different picture. I think the best way to show this is to look at several passages that discuss how believers were to treat one another. Read these verses and consider the type of commitment that would be required to truly do what they say

"Love each other with genuine affection, and take delight in honoring each other... When God's people are in need, be ready to help them. Always be eager to practice hospitality."   -Romans 12:9,13 (NLT)

"That there may be no division in the body, but that the members may have the same care for one another. If one member suffers, all suffer together; if one member is honored, all rejoice together."   - 1 Corinthians 12:25-26 (ESV)

"Bear one another's burdens, and so fulfill the law of Christ."
                                              -Galatians 6:2 (ESV)

"Always be humble and gentle. Be patient with each other, making allowance for each other's faults because of your love."
                                              - Ephesians 4:2 (NLT)

"Get rid of all bitterness, rage, anger, harsh words, and slander, as well as all types of evil behavior. [32]Instead, be kind to each other, tenderhearted, forgiving one another, just as God through Christ has forgiven you."
                                              - Ephesians 4:31-32 (NLT)

"And further, submit to one another out of reverence for Christ."
                                              -Ephesians 5:21 (NLT)

"Bearing with one another and, if one has a complaint against another, forgiving each other; as the Lord has forgiven you, so you also must forgive."
                                              -Colossians 3:13 (ESV)

"Therefore, confess your sins to one another and pray for one another..."
                                              - James 5:16a (ESV)

"Above all, keep loving one another earnestly, since love covers a multitude of sins. Show hospitality to one another without grumbling."
                                              - 1 Peter 4:8-9 (ESV)

The commands that we've just read all imply that we have a close relationship with the other Christians in our life. How can we truly love others if we keep them at a distance? Would we really confess our sins to someone we see a couple of times a month? Further, we'd probably never need to forgive people we barely know. This kind of thing only happens when we're deeply connected to each other. Yet, this is what the New Testament clearly says about our Christian relationships. Sadly, for many of us our church connections are shallow and weak. This is why we must commit to the community.

Third, a consumer doesn't take ownership. If I'm shopping at Macy's and there's a mess in the Men's department, I don't think, "I should clean that up; where are the hangers?" Instead, if it's convenient, I might let an employee know. But in a marriage, it's completely different. In fact, I wouldn't be married long if I just let my wife know every time the clothes in my closet were messed up. "Honey, my shirts are all on the ground again. Just wanted to let you know!" No. That wouldn't work. There's ownership in a marriage relationship. I'm committed. I don't expect to be served. I know better!

In a healthy church commitment, we're all "owners" of the mission. We have deep buy-in to the kingdom work that is being done through our local church. As I said earlier, the ancient churches were "glued" together by their commitment to the mission of proclaiming the gospel. There were "partners" (See: Philippians 1:5). So if the children's ministry needs help, guess what? That's all of our problem. If the church isn't friendly, we all need to fix that. Instead of asking, "What are they going to do about the music?!?" Ask: how can I help, and what can I do?

And here's the big point: I can't grow when I don't commit. There is a direct connection between an "all-in" commitment and dramatic growth. This is because commitment puts the protective walls necessary around my relationships so that intimacy can grow. Without commitment, intimacy simply can't happen. This is true in marriage. This is true in parenting. This is true in our spiritual relationships at church. And this is the biggest reason why the "Macy's mentality" has to go. Consumer Christians never experience the messy, beautiful, maddening, life-giving, painful, Spirit-enabled, Jesus-centered relationships that will help them grow into the disciple God desires them to be. Now let's look at the next way our local church connection helps us grow.

The Powerful Current of Community

I love the phrase, "Some things are more caught than taught." I love it because it's true. In fact, most of the things we learn in life are things we just "pick up" from those we are around. Everything from how we treat people to the kind of clothes we wear, even the people we're attracted to and careers we pursue come from other influential people in our lives. Parents know this. When a smart parent notices negative changes in their kid, they usually start asking questions about who they've been hanging with at school. They instinctively know new habits and values are "caught." This effect never stops. Adults feel it too. A new job or a move to a new city can put us around new people, and before long that new community begins influencing us.

This phenomenon shows up in church as well. As new believers develop connections with other brothers and sisters in the church community, they'll start to notice how these Christians live. They'll notice how they parent, how they treat their spouses. In fact, healthy church communities create a "current" of godliness that moves its members toward Jesus. The pastor might preach sermons about sacrifice or hospitality, but the lesson only "clicks" for us when we see someone in the church acting out that Christian virtue. It's not until I see Rick and Stephanie's relationship up close that I understand, "Husbands, love your wife, as Christ loved the church..." (Ephesians 5:25 ESV). We might hear a sermon on generosity and read Paul's words that we, "...should be rich in good works and generous to those in need, always being ready to share with others" (I Timothy 6:18 NLT). But, it's not until I see Jason or Chris or Todd or Sam or Wendy using their skills to help people that those verses come alive. In fact, it's my interaction with others in the church that makes me say, "Oh that's how you love your neighbor as yourself." Or, "So, that's what a man or woman who loves Jesus looks like." The church community should be full of living examples of people trying to live out the Jesus life.

Scot McKnight put it this way, "When God's people live in fellowship with one another, when they 'do life' together, the church embodies the gospel about King Jesus and people respond to the gospel about him."[131] What a powerful thought! When people in a church have close relationships with each other, the gospel comes alive and more people are drawn in. Obviously, no congregation does this perfectly and every church is full of people who still struggle with sin who sometimes don't live out their faith as they should (I'm certainly guilty). But it's still a family. A family of imperfect people who are striving to love each other. It's a community that draws near to Christ together and experiences his transforming presence among them. Notice this powerful passage from Hebrews.

> Let us hold tightly without wavering to the hope we affirm, for God can be trusted to keep his promise. Let us think of ways to motivate one another to acts of love and good works. And let us not neglect our meeting together, as some people do, but encourage one another, especially now that the day of his return is drawing near. - Hebrews 10:23-25 (NLT)

The writer of Hebrews explicitly stated that the church community should be a place where we, "encourage one another to acts of love and good works." Without the strong current of Christ's community, we won't have others to help us when things get difficult. We forget God's promises. We can get tempted to lose hope. Paul knew this well. He said, "Brothers and sisters, we urge you to warn those who are lazy. Encourage those who are timid. Take tender care of those who are weak. Be patient with everyone" (I Thessalonians 5:14 NLT). Paul is expecting the church community to play an important role in each other's lives.

Join a Life Group

So, how do we enjoy the type of community in our church we've been discussing in this lesson? The fact is most churches today are far larger than the ancient house churches of the New Testament. The churches of Peter and Paul were small persecuted congregations that formed underground networks within the major cities of the Roman Empire. Today, we enjoy religious freedom and have built large buildings to house our church family. This is why most churches have small life groups they encourage their attendees to join. In these life groups, the community and relationships that we read about in these ancient churches can take place in our modern life. In a life group, we can truly get to know each other. We can bear each other's burdens (See: Galatians 6:2) and help each other follow Jesus. In a life group, I lose the anonymity that

---

132. McKnight, Scot. Fellowship of Differents. (Grand Rapids: Zondervan) 2016. p.112

can happen in a large congregation and truly get connected with other believers. In that home setting, I am known and come to know others. That's why for most Christians, joining a life group is absolutely vital to their Christian growth.

THE SUMMARY:

It takes a church to raise a Christian. We are formed for a family. We need this community. The connections we make at a church grow us in ways that are sometimes difficult to fully appreciate. It's easy to underestimate the influence of godly men and women. But as we grow in a church, we "see" Christianity take shape in the lives of our brothers and sisters at church. As Scot McKnight explained, "A local church determines what the Christian life looks like for the people in that church." This is why we must work hard at building community. We must be "owners" and not consumers of the churches we attend. We must commit to make our local church the best we can. In our modern churches, a life group is perhaps the best way to live out the biblical expectations for church community.

BIBLE STUDY [Answer the following questions to enhance your learning.]

Have you approached a church from a "Macy's mindset?" If so, how has that affected your connection to the congregation?

Are there some other ways that you think our American culture hurts our connection to a local church?

Have you experienced the "current of community?" Are there some people in the church that you feel connected to or that you believe have helped influence your walk with Jesus in a positive way? If so, who are they and how have they influenced you?

MEMORY VERSE:

"Remember your leaders who taught you the word of God.

Think of all the good that has come from their lives, and

follow the example of their faith."

- Hebrews 13:7 (NLT)

LESSON: #21: Shepherds and Sheep

I don't know what this says about me, but if I ever come across a YouTube video about animals hunting or fighting, I can't resist watching. I hate to admit this, but one time I went on a 45-minute binge that included a lion hunt, a fascinating fight between a mongoose and a king cobra (go mongoose!), a python verses an alligator (somewhere in Florida I think), and then finished it off with a "conspiracy documentary" showing black and white pictures of 50 foot snakes and proof of other supposed-to-be-extinct super predators. Don't even get me started about that time I spent an hour researching if megalodon could still exist (hey, it's a big ocean out there!). Like I said, I don't know why, but I have this lurid fascination.

Even before YouTube was around, I remember reading about some alpha-predators in the Bible. As a teenager, I was fascinated as I read the book of Job's vivid descriptions of the Behemoth and mighty Leviathan (See: Job 40-41). I still don't think anyone knows for sure what those terrifying creatures were. I'm just glad I've never come across one! To connect my niche interest with today's lesson, the New Testament often describes the Christian life as a struggle or a war against a vicious predator. In fact, in several places we're described as "sheep" and Satan is depicted as a "lion" (or some other not so nice animal). Here's one example,

> Stay alert! Watch out for your great enemy, the devil. He prowls around like a roaring lion, looking for someone to devour. ⁹Stand firm against him, and be strong in your faith. Remember that your family of believers all over the world is going through the same kind of suffering you are.

> - I Peter 5:8-9 (NLT)

All throughout the New Testament, we are reminded that we are in a spiritual battle. There is a real enemy who "prowls" and seeks to devour Christians (See: Mark 4:15; Luke 22:31; Ephesians 4:26-27; 6:11-12; James 4:6-7; Revelation 2:10: 12:9-12; 20:2-10). Christ followers are constantly compared to animals that wouldn't make it as a school mascot. Can you imagine cheerleaders trying to come up with ways to get a crowd to cheer on the "mighty sheep?" Jesus also called us "doves"—not much better.

In other words, every time Jesus compares us to an animal, it's a prey animal! I didn't say "pray"—although after you read this lesson, I hope you do pray! I said, Jesus says WE ARE PREY! In this great cosmic battle, we're not the aggressor. We're the food. We're not all that strong. Really, we're pretty defenseless. In fact, none of us are any match for Satan (Read: Matthew 12:22-29; Mark 3:20-28; Luke 11:14-26). This is why we need Jesus. He alone is stronger than our enemy. He alone is our chief shepherd that protects his sheep from "wolves, thieves and robbers" (See: John 10:8,10,12). And Jesus gave clear instructions about how he planned to protect his sheep. So let's dive in.

As we saw in an earlier lesson, before Jesus ascended to Heaven, he had a powerful conversation with Peter. He told him to "feed my sheep" (See: John 21:15-17). Essentially, Jesus made him an "under-shepherd." Decades later this shepherd, Peter, wrote with seasoned experience to other "under-shepherds." And it's there in this passage we find three important things to consider about spiritual leadership and how good spiritual leaders protect us in this cosmic battle against evil.

> And now, a word to you who are elders in the churches. I, too, am an elder and a witness to the sufferings of Christ. And I, too, will share in his glory when he is revealed to the whole world. As a fellow elder, I appeal to you: Care for the flock that God has entrusted to you. Watch over it willingly, not grudging
>
> ly——not for what you will get out of it, but because you are eager to serve God. Don't lord it over the people assigned to your care, but lead them by your own good example. And when the Great Shepherd appears, you will receive a crown of never-ending glory and honor. In the same way, you who are younger must accept the authority of the elders. And all of you, dress yourselves in humility as you relate to one another, for "God opposes the proud but gives grace to the humble.
>
> - I Peter 1:1-5 (NLT)

First, Peter addressed the "elders" in this church. These congregations obviously had clearly defined leadership. In fact, spiritual leadership in the early church was immediately visible in the book of Acts. In the very first church in Jerusalem, the apostles themselves led (See Acts 2:42-27; 6:2-7). Years later, after many original apostles had gone, there were still elders making decisions about spiritual matters in Jerusalem (See Acts 15:6-19). We see this in other churches throughout the New Testament as well (See: I Timothy 5:17; Titus 1:5; James 5:14). Notice what Paul wrote, "Now these are the gifts Christ gave to the church: the apostles, the prophets, the evangelists, and the pastors and teachers. Their responsibility is to equip God's people to do his work and build up the church, the body of Christ" (Ephesians 4:11-12 NLT). It's clear: churches are to be led by spiritual elders, and this is for our own good!

Second, these leaders are to "care for the flock." Specifically, the elders are to "watch over" the sheep. Their spiritual oversight is mentioned in several other passages in the New Testament also (See: Acts 20:28; I Thessalonians 5:12-13; I Timothy 5:17; II Timothy 4:1-5; Titus 1:5; 2:1-8; 3:1-2). The writer of Hebrews said it plainly, "Obey your spiritual leaders, and do what they say. Their work is to watch over your souls, and they are accountable to God. Give them reason to do this with joy and not with sorrow. That would certainly not be for your benefit" (Hebrews 13:7 NLT).

This is actually a huge reason to be committed to a local church. We all need oversight. Even the shepherds! We're all flawed humans, susceptible to temptation and sin! Every Christian needs accountability. We all need people who shepherd and care for us and constantly teach us God's ways. The truth is while some of us take the role of shepherd, we're all sheep who can easily go astray (See: I Peter 2:25)! In fact, this is one of the most difficult parts of my calling. I've seen the slow destruction that happens to a person's faith (and life) when they drift away from the godly spiritual oversight that a church provides. I've seen this happen to pastors, and I've seen it happen to others. The danger is real.

Finally, Christ-like spiritual leaders are to be servant leaders. Jesus taught and modeled this (See: Luke 22:24-30; John 13:15-16). Peter had seen Jesus serve others when he was alive and leading them. Now

187

years later, Peter had learned this lesson and was instructing elders to be servant leaders. This is an important qualification for spiritual leaders. Sadly, we've all heard stories of people misusing their position of spiritual authority. This does great damage to people's lives. Spiritual leaders should be surrendered to Jesus and humbled by what Jesus has done for them. Godly pastors must model Christian maturity and love to those they lead.

As we reflect on what Peter taught in this passage, the plain truth is that God intends every believer to be connected to a local church and under spiritual authority.[133] We're not supposed to live rogue, autonomous lives. That's where the wolves and lions live. And while our American culture prizes personal freedom and individuality, we must give up that autonomy and submit to a faith family that's united under Christ's authority.

Four Crucial Commitments

As I said in lesson 20, we can't grow if we don't commit. As sheep, we're going to naturally drift away from important things that will help us grow and keep us spiritually safe. So let's finish our lesson by looking at four ways to stay connected to spiritual accountability within our church community.

First and foremost, we commit as a family to worship together. Human beings were created to worship. If our worship isn't directed toward God, we inevitably worship a substitute. The Bible calls this idolatry (See: Exodus 20:4; Matthew 4:10; Luke 4:8). Our local church directs our corporate worship to the one true God. For over 2,000 years, Christians have been worshiping together. A podcast or an on-line experience can't replicate the gathering of the saints together in worship. So we must commit to regular, corporate worship in person.

Second, we commit corporately to God's word. When the church family gathers and a pastor teaches God's word boldly and accurately, the church is instructed in the word of God. The faith is preached. The truth is proclaimed (See: I Timothy 4:1-16; Titus 2:1). And the community is called to action. It's in this setting, we gather and feast together on God's word. In our church gatherings, our spiritual lives are nourished. Here we commit to each other and corporately humble ourselves to God.

Third, we need to commit to our church family financially. As Jesus followers, we are to financially support our church's mission and the spiritual leaders that oversee that mission (See: I Corinthians 9:11-12; I Thessalonians 5:12-13; I Timothy 5:17-18). Most pastors and church leaders have dedicated their lives and education to shepherding the flock. Our financial support allows them to serve the church (See: Acts 6:2; I Peter 5:2-4). Jesus allowed people to support him during his ministry (See: Luke 8:3), and he instructed the disciples to allow people to support their ministry (See: Luke 9:3-4; 10:10:4-10; I Corinthians 9:13-14). Giving to our local church is an act of worship and should be done with a generous and cheerful heart (See: II Corinthians 9:7). Our financial commitment to our local church results in each of us having a share in supporting all the kingdom work happening in our community and abroad.[134]

---

133. This includes shepherds (I Timothy 5:19)! Every Christian needs spiritual accountability. We all need other that we submit to and allow to speak into our lives. Church leaders are not excluded. This is why healthy churches should have a plurality of leadership where everyone has someone they answer to. Most churches are led by an elder board or some formal board of spiritual leaders for exactly this purpose.

134. Here we've only briefly touched on giving and finances. The purpose of this book is to give a brief introduction to what is important for a Jesus follower. This topic deserves a lot more study and understanding. We recommend Dave Ramsay's Financial Peace University for more instruction on how a Christian should view their finances.

This brings us to our final point: We must commit to the unique mission of our church. The mission of our church plays out in two ways: locally and globally. Locally, each church has been strategically positioned by God to be a light in their local community (See: Matthew 5:16 Acts 1:8; Titus 1:5; Galatians 6:10). As a congregation seeks to love the people around them, God will give them opportunities to serve their city, in Jesus' name (See: Matthew 25:31-46). Pretty soon, the opportunities to help others in their community will guide the church in how to best present the gospel (e.g. homeless shelters; addiction treatment facilities or programs; single mother support ministries; Christian schools; Christian daycares; counseling centers, the list could go on). Essentially, the church should serve to meet the needs of their local community.

These ministries of mercy help to spiritually form the members of the congregation. When people connect to the mission of their local church, their gifts, experiences and passions are used to contribute to this mission. And here's where the magic happens. It's only then we find the joy of using our gifts within a local body (See: 1 Corinthians 12:4-32). And as more people connect, God gives more vision to the church. Soon, brand new ministries are started and the influence and reach of the church grows. Who knows, maybe God will use you to begin and lead the next ministry (See: Acts 13:1-3)!

This happens on a global scale as well. Most local churches have ministry partners in other nations. As disciples of Jesus, our vision for the gospel must go beyond our own local community to include a passion for all nations to hear of our savior's love. Paul was a passionate missionary. He expected the local churches to care about God's work in other places as well. He took financial support from many churches in the Mediterranean area to support those believers suffering in Jerusalem (See: Romans 15:25-26). We're a part of a spiritual family that is doing amazing work in all areas of the globe. As we mentioned at the beginning of this book, this has been the hallmark of the Christian faith for over two millennia. It's exciting. It's fulfilling. And it only gets started when you connect to the local church!

THE SUMMARY:

We're sheep and we need shepherds. Even shepherds need shepherds! Essentially, every Christian needs accountability. God has designed this to take place within a vital commitment to a local church. We can't thrive as a Jesus follower apart from the loving oversight of spiritual leaders in our life. Spiritual leaders are men and women called by God to oversee the spiritual life of others. These gifted Christians have a unique calling to help nurture the faith of others. Within the church, we find a place for corporate worship, biblical instruction and financial commitment to God's kingdom work. Within the community of the church, there's safety from the spiritual attacks of our enemy.

BIBLE STUDY [Answer the following questions to enhance your learning.]

Have you ever felt like you were under a spiritual attack? If so, how did you get through that struggle? After reading this lesson, how do you think a commitment to a church might help someone experiencing a spiritually difficult time?

Based on the lesson, explain why we need spiritual shepherds in our lives.

When you think of "spiritual authority" what types of images or emotions come to mind? How has your personal experience been with leaders in positions of spiritual authority? What are some things that you believe are important for churches to do to make sure spiritual authority is never abused?

Which of the "four crucial commitments" do you believe is most important? Were there any that you had not really considered before reading today's lesson?

Pray over what you've learned in this lesson. Write out a summarizing prayer below.

MEMORY VERSE:

"Bear one another's burdens, and so fulfill the law of Christ."

- Galatians 6:2 (ESV)

FOR FURTHER RESOURCES ON THIS TOPIC:

John Dickson. The Best Kept Secret of Christian Mission. Grand Rapids, MI: Zondervan, 2013.

James McDonald. Vertical Church: What every heart longs for. What every church can be. Colorado Springs, Co: David C Cook, 2015.

Scot McKnight. Fellowship of Differents. Grand Rapids: Zondervan, 2016.

LESSON: #22: Conclusion: The Power of "Yes!"

> Then he said to the crowd, "If any of you wants to be my follower, you must give up your own way, take up your cross daily, and follow me. [24]If you try to hang on to your life, you will lose it. But if you give up your life for my sake, you will save it.
>
> - Luke 9:23-24 (ESV)

What do you want from life? When it's all over, what do you hope will be your legacy? Let's take this a step further, if you changed nothing, how will you be remembered?

Jesus presents us with a choice. He offers us a totally new way of living. He has the power to transform us—to free us from sin and selfishness, to make us new. But this comes at a cost, for him and us. For Jesus, it cost him his life. For us, it also costs us our life but in a different way. It costs us a surrendered life. We give our lives to Jesus. Every. Day.

Paul explained it like this, "My old self has been crucified with Christ. It is no longer I who live, but Christ lives in me. So I live in this earthly body by trusting in the Son of God, who loved me and gave himself for me" (Galatians 2:20 NLT). Following Jesus means allowing him to live his life through us. It means offering our entire selves to him. This won't be easy. There are going to be setbacks, and temptations will never stop (See: Luke 17:1; James 1:12-16). There will be times we fall (See: I John 1:8-9). But God is faithful (See: Hebrews 13:5-6). He'll empower us to get back up and keep following Jesus. As we wrap up this book, I want to leave you with a powerful truth that I hope will help you in this journey with Christ. It's the power of "yes."

Maybe the best way to explain this idea is to look at one of the last parables Jesus ever taught. As Jesus often did, he used stories to help his disciples understand things about God, eternity and his kingdom. This time was no different. So as they were walking from Jericho to Jerusalem for what would be the final time, he turned to them and said,

> A nobleman was called away to a distant empire to be crowned king and then return. [13]Before he left, he called together ten of his servants and divided among them ten pounds of silver, saying, 'Invest this for me while I am gone.' [14]But his people hated him and sent a delegation after him to say, 'We do not want him to be our king.'
>
> - Luke 19:12-14 (NLT)

As the story continues, the nobleman returns victorious. Now, he is king. So he calls his servants together to see how they did while he was away. Three servants are spotlighted in the parable. The first two servants were faithful during the king's absence. As a result, they are given cities to rule in the new kingdom. So far so good. But when the third servant is brought forward the story takes a turn. He wasn't trustworthy. His heart had turned against the king. If you read the story carefully, this servant is similar to the wicked citizens who hated the king (See: Luke 19:20-23). Instead of working for the king, he lived for himself and had nothing to show for his life. As the parable ends, the unfaithful servant is removed from any share in his master's rule. His opportunity is lost! As far as the rebellious citizens who hated the king, they're executed. The king's rule is just and his judgment fair.

It's a sobering parable. But it powerfully describes the life of a Jesus follower. Jesus is the nobleman who leaves his servants behind to work with his resources. One day, he will return in power! But in the meantime, we're called to serve him. And just like in the parable, there is going to be opposition. The world rejects God's rule (See: Romans 1:18-23; 5:10). So we must serve the King in hostile and difficult circumstances. Don't be surprised. Jesus told us it would be this way (See: John 15:20). Our mission is to offer salvation and forgiveness to a lost and dying world. They are deceived and have set themselves against God as enemies, just as we were before we met Jesus (See: II Corinthians 4:14; Ephesians 4:17-24). They don't know the goodness and love of our God. But it's our job to proclaim the truth of the good news.

Give Jesus Your "Yes"

So, here is the crucial question, how do we live a life of faithfulness to Jesus? How do we avoid following the third servant's example? It starts by giving Jesus your absolute "yes." We need to understand there is incredible power in our "yes."

Let me explain. Each of us have a "yes" we either give or withhold. Most of us are conditioned to give ourselves our "yes." We tell ourselves "yes" all the time. It's natural. It makes sense. In fact, giving our "yes" to Jesus is unnatural. It goes against everything we know. But this is the life of a Jesus follower.

We give our "yes" to Jesus because he gave his "yes" to us. He said "yes" when he laid down his life. He said "yes" when he saw us in our sin and shame. He said "yes"—a thousand times "yes." And thankfully, each time we fail and stumble, he continues to say "yes!" to us. And so, we do too.

As we think back to the parable, each servant faced a moment when they had to decide what to do with their "yes." Each faced the same hostilities. Each had the same opportunity. And each had the same amount of money to manage. The only difference was what they did with their "yes." The first two servants gave their "yes" to the king. Since the king was absent, this took faith. I'm sure they wondered: "Will he really return?" "Is facing these hostilities worth it?" "Will these sacrifices really pay off?" They decided "yes!" They lived a life of "yes." And great was their reward. The unfaithful servant said "no." Or more accurately, he said "yes"... to himself. He said "yes" to his comfort. He said "yes" to his safety. He said "yes" to what was easy and in front of him. And if you notice, he allowed his view of the king to be influenced by the citizens of that country. Our choices have consequences.

What Has Your "Yes?" Notice what the apostle Paul wrote on this topic,

> Do not let sin control the way you live; do not give in to sinful desires. [13]Do not let any part of your body become an instrument of evil to serve sin. Instead, give yourselves completely to God, for you were dead, but now you have new life. So use your whole body as an instrument to do what is right for the glory of God.

> - Romans 6:12-13 (NLT)

Christ has given us a new life. We must now, "give ourselves completely to God." This is that absolute yes we've been talking about. Notice what Paul went on to say, Sin is no longer your master, for you no longer live under the requirements of the law. Instead, you live under the freedom of God's grace. [15]Well then, since God's grace has set us free from the law, does that mean we can go on sinning? Of course not! [16]Don't you realize that you become the slave of whatever you choose to obey? You can be a slave to sin, which leads to death, or you can choose to obey God, which leads to righteous living. [17]Thank God! Once you were slaves of sin, but now you wholeheartedly obey this teaching we have given you. [18]Now you are free from your slavery to sin, and you have become slaves to righteous living.

> -Romans 6:14-18 (NLT)

Here's the profound truth: Whatever has your "yes" controls the rest. Paul tells us that sin is no longer our master. We've been set free. But the biblical view of freedom isn't what we normally think it is. It isn't "the ability to do anything you want." Instead, God's freedom is "the ability to do what you should." Jesus has set us free from sin which had kept us from living as we should. Now, we can choose to give ourselves completely to God and allow his Spirit to control us. For Paul, we're either slaves of sin or slaves of righteousness. So whatever has our "yes" will control the rest.

And here is where it gets exciting. Saying "yes" to Jesus opens us to a life of eternal meaning and purpose. Our life doesn't end. Actually, it just now can finally begin. When we give Jesus our strong "yes," he empowers us to live an abundant new life (See: John 10:10)! It's when we give Jesus our "yes" that we can experience the power of his kingdom in us. This opens the door to his powerful presence in our life. He begins to live his life in us. It's as if there is an ocean of heavenly power and blessing that God wants to pour out on earth. But He's chosen to use us as conduits of this grace. Each of us has a "yes" that's like a valve either opened or closed to God and His purposes. When we fully give Jesus our "yes," our valve opens, and God's presence and grace can flow freely through us. In other words, Heaven meets Earth when we give God our yes.

"Yes" Transforms the Mess

Before we close, there's one more incredible thing we need to talk about. It's the transformative power of "yes." As a pastor, part of my calling is to help believers grow and mature in their walk with Jesus. It's why I've written this book. Over the years, I've walked with many people on their spiritual journey. Since most of my ministry has been with high school students, inevitably topics such as lust, sex, pornography, poor self-image and pride have come up. In our conversations, it's easy for young people to view

Christianity as the religion of "No." No sex, no lust, no porn, etc. This is just good marketing by Satan. He knows that if he can convince us that Christianity equals "no," we won't be able to last very long. We can only say "no" for so long until our will-power runs out. And for a lot of us, that's not very long.

This is where the power of "yes" is so important. As we just read, Christianity offers us freedom from sin. It's the freedom to say "yes." When our eyes are drawn away from Christ and toward what we can't or shouldn't do, we will struggle to say "no." But when we're living a "yes-life," Jesus empowers us. In fact, the stronger our "yes," the easier our "no" (See: James 1:21-25).

There are two ways I can approach my marriage vows. I can think about saying "no" to all of the women (real or imagined) in the world or I can strengthen my "yes" to Michelle. And it's when Michelle has my strong "yes" that it becomes easier to give everyone else my "no." As I continue to feed my "yes," I experience an inner transformation. What you feed grows. So if you feed your "yes," you will naturally want to say "no" to anything that threatens that "yes."

This transforming power of "yes" also works for those of us who have said "yes" to all the wrong things for way too long. Guilt, shame and regret are powerful discouragers. They can make us feel like we're unworthy of the life of blessing and grace God wants to give us. We might feel like we're too far gone to really be used by God. Again, this is just Satan's scheme. We can't change our past, but God can redeem it. When we walk in the power of "yes," new patterns begin to emerge. As God's power flows through us, He starts to transform us. You won't walk in victory until you begin to actively open yourself up to God. And Satan knows this. This is why he's so dead set on using shame and guilt to keep you from believing that God can use you to bless others. He'll convince you that your past has disqualified you. After all, why should anyone listen to you? But that's where he's wrong. It's not you that you're offering, it's Christ in you!

The simple fact is, as we continue to walk in a life of "yes," we will experience transformation. It's impossible for this not to happen. Grace always transforms us. And that's why: when we say "yes," it transforms the mess. We can't let Satan tell us what we're qualified to do Instead, we must listen to what God says. "Therefore, if anyone is in Christ, he is a new creation. The old has passed away; behold, the new has come" (II Corinthians 5:17 ESV). When we live in the power of the gospel and open ourselves up to the transforming power of "yes," we'll see old habits and patterns die away. As we continue to give God our strong "yes" each day, it won't be long until we will hardly be able to recognize ourselves.

Christianity isn't a religion or a philosophy; it's an active relationship with the living God. It's a dynamic walk through life where you grow in love and intimacy with your Creator because of the incredible sacrifice of Jesus Christ the Son of God. This book is just an introduction to that life. There's an exciting, transformative way of living waiting for those who are willing to surrender their lives to Love. And that's who God is; God is Love (See: I John 4:8)! I pray that this book has helped you onwards in that journey.

THE SUMMARY:

There's power in "yes." Each day we wake up with a "yes." We get to decide who or what will get our "yes" that day. Whatever gets our "yes" will ultimately determine the rest. As a Jesus follower, I must intentionally choose to give my "yes" to Jesus each day. One day, our King will return. One day, the same resurrection power that raised him from the grave will raise us up in victory. Until that day, I must steadfastly look forward toward his eternal kingdom and faithfully give him my "yes" until he returns or until my earthly life is over. May we all continue to walk in the power of his resurrection! It will be worth it all when we see Jesus!

BIBLE STUDY [Answer the following questions to enhance your learning.]

Take a minute to reflect on your life. If nothing changed, how would you be remembered? Are there any changes that you believe God wants you to make right now? If so, list them here.

In what area of your life is the most difficult for you to give Jesus your "yes"? Is it in your relationships? Work life? At school?

Reflect on what has your "yes" right now. Sometimes we give others our "yes." It's easy to try to please others and to try to win their approval. Take a minute and think about who or what gets your "yes" most often. What changes can you make to be sure that Jesus has your complete "yes?"

Have you experienced the transforming power of "yes?" Have you seen what happens when you devote yourself completely to God? If so, recount that experience here.

Take the "yes" challenge. Commit to give God your complete yes for the next 21 days. Consciously give God your "yes" each morning. Recommit at noon and then again at 5pm. Set alarms on your phone to remind yourself to give God your "yes." Journal this experience and discuss this with your mentor. I'm betting you experience tremendous spiritual transformation and breakthroughs during this challenge. My prayer is that you will give God your "yes" for the rest of your life. This is what it means to truly be his disciple (See: Matthew 7:13--14; 10:38; 16:34; Mark 8:34-38; Luke 9:23; 13:24).

MEMORY VERSE:

"I have been crucified with Christ. It is no longer I who live, but Christ who lives in me. And the life I now live in the flesh I live by faith in the Son of God, who loved me and gave himself for me."

- Galatians 2:20 (ESV)

Made in the USA
Las Vegas, NV
01 January 2025

15525439R00115